PRACTICAL USER INTERFACE DESIGN

PRACTICAL USER INTERFACE DESIGN
Making GUIs Work

Carl Zetie

McGRAW-HILL BOOK COMPANY

London · New York · St Louis · San Francisco · Auckland · Bogotá
Caracas · Lisbon · Madrid · Mexico · Milan · Montreal · New Delhi
Panama · Paris · San Juan · São Paulo · Singapore · Sydney · Tokyo · Toronto

Published by

McGRAW-HILL Book Company Europe

Shoppenhangers Road, Maidenhead, Berkshire, SL6 2QL, England

Telephone 01628 23432

Facsimile 01628 770224

British Library Cataloguing in Publication Data

Zetie, Carl
  Practical User Interface Design:Making
  GUIs Work
  I. Title
  005.43
  ISBN 0–07–709167–1

Library of Congress Cataloging-in-Publication Data

Zetie, Carl
  Practical user interface design : making GUIs work / Carl Zetie.
    p. cm.
  Includes bibliographical references,
  ISBN 0–07–709167–1 (pbk. : alk. paper)
  1. Graphical user interfaces (Computer systems) I. Title.
QA76.9.U83Z48 1995
005.1$'$2——dc20   95–34164
                                                     CIP

12345 CUP 98765

Typeset by Alden Multimedia, Northampton
Printed and bound in Great Britain at the University Press, Cambridge
Printed on permanent paper in compliance with ISO Standard 9706

Contents

Preface   vii

Acknowledgements   viii

Introduction   1
   The mythology of the graphical user interface   1
   Aspects of the user interface   4
   The scope of this book   13

Chapter 1   Fundamental principles   17
   Introduction   17
   Elements of design   20
   Just enough psychology   37
   Case study: Microsoft Word   49
   Stages of user interface design   50
   Character versus graphical user interfaces   55
   Summary   56

Chapter 2   Conceptual models   58
   Introduction   58
   Models and the user   60
   Expressions and transformations   68
   Case study   82
   Summary   85

Chapter 3   Taskflow   86
   Introduction   86
   Design principles   87
   Mechanisms for implementation   113
   Major classes of taskflow   120
   Summary   124

Chapter 4   Dialog design   126
   Introduction   126
   Dialog flow supports taskflow   127
   Dialogs and windows   136
   Summary   160

Chapter 5   Detailed design   **162**
  Introduction   162
  Controls   163
  Window layout and graphic design   184
  Application design   202
  Summary   206

Chapter 6   Errors and help   **207**
  Introduction   207
  Designing for error   208
  Mistakes and tolerance   221
  Help and documentation   229
  Summary   236

Appendix A   Choosing a design tool   **237**
  Evaluation criteria   238

Appendix B   The demonstration disk   **241**
  Installation   241
  Contents   241

References and further reading   **246**

Index   **248**

Preface

'The last thing one discovers in writing a book is what to put first'

Blaise Pascal

When most of us started out in the computing profession, the user interface was probably far from foremost in our reasons for wanting to be a computer professional. However, in recent years the importance of the interface has risen dramatically to the point where, in many applications, it dominates over all other considerations. With little experience and less training, we now find ourselves responsible for design issues that can make or break an application. With the ubiquity of windowed graphical interfaces, our users are comparing our designs with their word processors and spreadsheets and other best-selling desktop tools. They are not impressed.

I am a professional working in the mainstream of information technology, though I am old enough to remember when it was called data processing. I design, build, demonstrate and teach applications on ordinary platforms like Microsoft Windows and Unix. I deliver those applications to budgets and deadlines. My designs are used in their everyday work by ordinary people: secretaries, administrators, clerks, managers, senior executives, salespeople and financial advisers. My users can type, and mostly they can use a mouse. If you are in a similar situation, then this book is written for you.

When I first became interested in user interface design, I wanted a book that would explain the fundamentals of the discipline in a way that was relevant to commercial computing. There is, I discovered, plenty of material describing the exciting and exotic leading edge of user interface design, but little or nothing on the mainstream. It seems that many authors have simply taken the fundamentals for granted. This book is my attempt to fill that gap. It is not about the best, the most subtle, the most advanced techniques in user interface design. It is about the everyday, the practical, the get-your-job-done issues. It is intended as a book for the rest of us, ordinary computer professionals building for ordinary business users, equipped only with an enthusiasm to build extraordinary applications. If you are one of us, I hope you will find that this is the book you have been searching for.

Acknowledgements

Many of the ideas in this book were developed through a series of training courses, seminars, consultancy assignments and presentations that I have given over the past few years. These sessions were invaluable in helping me to refine this material, separating the wheat from the chaff. Many participants in those sessions raised thought-provoking questions and made valuable suggestions which I have incorporated into this book. These anonymous contributors are too numerous to thank individually, but I hope they will each recognize their own contributions.

I am deeply grateful to Dr Donald Norman, whose book *The Psychology of Everyday Things* (widely known as 'POET') was a catalyst that set me thinking in new ways about many issues, and enabled me to put a name to many others. Readers familiar with his work will recognize the considerable influence of 'POET' on Chapter 1, albeit set in a context specific to our needs. I hope readers will judge that I have done his work justice. Any shortcomings in that chapter are my own, not Dr Norman's.

Thanks are due to Lotus Development for providing a copy of Lotus Screencam, which was used to build the animated demonstrations on the accompanying diskette. Thanks are also due to Oracle Corporation for permission to reproduce screens and documentation from their Designer/2000 CASE product. Designer/2000 is a trademark of Oracle Corporation, and the documentation and other screens reproduced in the Lotus Screencam animation for Chapter 6 are copyright Oracle Corporation. All other trademarks are acknowledged.

I am indebted beyond measure to Mary Louise Ravese. It was her encouragement and support that persuaded me to stop complaining about the lack of a suitable book, and set about producing one. Her reviews, clarifications and suggestions eliminated many of my mistakes and oversights. Any remaining errors or omissions are, of course, my own.

Introduction

'The users took much longer than we anticipated to adapt to the intuitive user interface'

Microsoft Consulting project manager

The mythology of the graphical user interface

We have all been bombarded with propaganda, over the last few years, telling us that graphical user interfaces (GUIs) are easy to use, easy to learn, intuitive, productive, satisfying, attractive and generally A Good Thing. This is the mythology of the graphical user interface: that intuitive ease of use is something that you get for free when you build an application in a windowed environment. Certainly, the GUI environment offers the opportunity to present users with an interface that is dramatically more attractive and productive to use than traditional terminals; but this is by no means guaranteed, and it is certainly not free.

In fact, it is all too easy to build obscure, difficult, obstructive and downright ugly graphical user interfaces. There are many extremely poor user interfaces out there. Some are so poor, they are close to unusable. The briefest examination of applications, especially transaction processing applications, should dispel the myth of ease of use. In the face of the evidence, why then does this myth persist? I would suggest that there are at least two major aspects to the myth, each surviving in its own way.

Myth 1: User interface design is easy

One of the biggest obstacles to good design is the fact that user interface design looks deceptively easy. At first sight, anybody can paint a window layout, play with fonts and colours, and call it a graphical user interface. Desktop development tools have only magnified this problem. Just as 'macro' languages in desktop databases 'empowered' non-programmers to construct slow, cumbersome and inefficient code, so new graphical tools have 'enabled' people to build confusing, difficult and obstructive interfaces. 'Easy to buy' is *not* the same as 'easy to use'! In fact, user interface design is very hard: it is often more subtle than database design, and more complex than code design.

1

2 Practical user interface design

Part of this myth is that the consistency of all applications running under, for example, Microsoft Windows (MS-Windows) automatically makes them easy to use, without any effort from the designer. But where is this consistency? I find it very easy to change text fonts in the word processor that I use most of the time, but very hard to do the same in the word processor that I use occasionally. These are the number one and number two market leading word processors; it is unlikely that the difference is because one is dramatically easier to use than the other. Clearly there is no consistency between the 'change font' tasks in these two applications.

Consider an analogy — when starting work at a new company:

- Nearly everybody can get through the front door (although some doors seem to be designed to be difficult; what is going through the mind of a designer who puts a handle on a door you can't pull?).
- Experienced office workers will be able to use basic office tools such as the phone, the fax and the photocopier.
- Very few people will be able to submit an invoice or schedule a courier on their first day.

If we compare the situation of a user receiving a new application, we find:

- Nearly everybody can start the application, although some applications seem perversely difficult to get started.
- Experienced users of graphical user interfaces will know how menus, buttons and lists operate.
- Very few people will be able to carry out work tasks such as formatting a document or constructing a spreadsheet.

In fact, many applications, even so-called 'integrated suites', are only consistent at the lowest level of individual controls, and some software houses seem determined to undercut even that level of consistency. To get real work done requires familiarity at the level of tasks, not merely at the level of controls.

As in many aspects of the user interface, the Apple Macintosh is more successful at carrying consistency to a higher, more useful, level. But this is not free; it only comes about because Apple has made the effort to research and define these higher levels of consistency; because Mac developers care about (or have been educated about) their users, and in their turn invest the required effort to perpetuate those common approaches; and because the Mac marketplace refuses to accept poorly designed applications. This 'conspiracy of good design', which makes the Mac desktop a more attractive place to work, is one of the reasons that Apple, application developers and customers tend to refer to themselves collectively as the Apple community.

The myth of 'consistency for free' is so widespread that it is one of the greatest barriers to good design. It undercuts the need for good interface design by posing the question: 'Problem? What problem?'

Myth 2: User interface design is unimportant

Regrettably, many software designers and project designers underestimate the value of the user interface. This is partly because the effects of poor design can be hard to see and thus hard to quantify. It is rare that a designer has difficulty using his own application, and often the designer is remote from the real users. Unlike bad data design, which the designer can easily test for and correct, bad interface design is often only discovered when the application is implemented. By this time, the design team has moved on to the next project; they may never be aware, even if they care, how successful or unsuccessful their design was. As a result, user interface design becomes regarded as insignificant in the design process. It may even be delegated to the most junior member of the development team, in the belief that it does not affect the application's performance too much.

The peanut butter approach

Often, the user interface is not treated as an integral part of the design process and so is often left to the very latest stages of the project. I was asked to 'fire fight' on one consultancy project for which the user interface was so poor that the client was refusing to pay for any of the work, a perfect illustration of Alan Kay's famous remark that 'To the user, the interface is the application'. After examining the work, I contacted the project manager, who protested that the project budget 'still had three days set aside to sort out the user interface'. He seemed to believe that the user interface was like peanut butter: you could simply choose chunky or smooth according to taste, and spread it on the top of the almost-finished application.

It is distressingly common for user interface evaluation to be left to the very last stages of development, when it is too late to make substantial changes. Hix and Harston (1993) describe this approach colourfully as the 'priest with a parachute'. The 'human factors expert', who is of course an outsider, not a team member, lands in the middle of a project, blesses it and leaves. He is allowed to 'validate' the design and ask for minor corrections to 'violations' of the style guide, but if the design needs major changes, it is far too late for that. This approach almost guarantees confrontations between application designers on one side and the 'GUI police' or 'interfascists' on the other.

Poor design is an expensive mistake

As part of my research for one project, I conducted an interview with a flights specialist at a travel agency. She uses a very large and complex reservations system to book flights for customers. I asked her to walk me through the system; she replied: 'Well, I can only show you about a third of the functions. I just can't remember how to use the others.' Millions of dollars were spent developing this system; to all intents and purposes, two thirds of that budget were wasted implementing functions that even the most frequent and expert users cannot remember how to use. What would your development backlog look like if you knew which two thirds of your workload was a waste of effort?

4   Practical user interface design

One of the commonest excuses that I am offered for bad design is that 'Expert users will soon learn how to use it'. In fact, some user interface design is so poor that nobody ever becomes an expert user. If the user interface design is poor, important features do not get used. However innovative or creative your technical solutions might be, they will be wasted if you do not make them easily available to users. From a business point of view, if users cannot easily exploit the application's features, their productivity will suffer. If the application is extremely poor, it may even get shelved: a completely wasted effort.

Aspects of the user interface

One of the reasons that user interface design is so difficult is that it encompasses so many factors. Conversely, it is this multi-disciplinary nature that makes it so interesting and so challenging. It is also an area riddled with ambiguity and unanswered questions. Many of the factors that are important are subtle and well hidden; they may even be completely hidden in design, and only emerge in use. More often than not, good design or poor design is a consequence of the interplay between many complex factors, rather than the result of one single factor that can be identified and corrected. If you like the certainty of 'which loop runs fastest?' then user interface design is an area you should avoid. There are few rigorous measures of the 'best' user interface.

User interface design is also an area burdened with more than its share of clichés. 'User friendly', 'Easy to use', 'Intuitive': what do any of these terms *really* mean? It is hard enough to know what a 'user' is like, let alone whether the interface wants to be her friend. We will attempt to explore some of the make-up of 'ease of use' in Chapter 1 but the designer should be forewarned that, in the final analysis, many aspects of user interface design are, almost by definition, very subjective.

One very important consequence of this subjectivity is that the designer must be prepared frequently to concede to users. In many aspects, it is the user's point of view that counts; after all, the user is the one who has to use the application, so it is the user who should be the judge of whether something is 'easy' or 'intuitive'. The user interface designer must learn to be thick-skinned and not take criticism personally. If someone criticizes your code, and eliminates a bug or optimizes a loop, these are merely questions of fact, and at worst are a little embarrassing. If someone criticizes your user interface, on the other hand, it is very easy for that to be mistaken as criticism of your personal taste and judgement.

Having said that, we should bear in mind that there are important checks and balances to the rule that 'the user is king'. For example, a user may not be the best judge of whether an application that is initially easy to learn will be most comfortable and productive when she is more experienced. The user is not so much 'king' as 'president', and in a well-run democracy the desires of the president are balanced by the scrutiny of the judiciary and the rule of the legislature. It is our job as designers to play the roles of judge and lawmaker, proposing applications and evaluating their effect in practice.

Furthermore, there are cases where the user's satisfaction, comfort and so on are not the most important issue to the business that is paying. In other words, the commercial reality is that the user is not always the customer. For example, in raw data entry applications, the questions of accuracy and quantity may override all else. If good user interface design can be shown to *contribute* to these goals, then all well and good; but if not, we must occasionally accept that there are applications for which the primary needs lie outside the scope of user interface design, in just the same way as the major factor in the design of a racing car is not passenger comfort. Not every application is within the domain of user interface design.

Measuring the user interface

In the broadest sense, user interface design is about 'acceptability'. This sense can be very broad indeed, taking in cultural issues, workplace pressures, business engineering, ergonomics, physical and mental comfort, productivity and so on. Indeed, there is a significant literature and active discussion devoted to the question of what is and is not within the realm of the user interface designer. This book is intended to be an introduction to the issues of user interface design. It is also intended to be read by the mainstream designer, who typically does not have a lot of choice about, or influence over, those wider workplace issues. For these reasons, we shall confine ourselves to central and well-established issues of the user interface. The reader should be aware that there is a vast array of research untouched by this book.

From our point of view, user interface design is primarily concerned with two interrelated aspects of the whole application (or system). These are the *effectiveness* of the user; and the *satisfaction* of the user.

One major component of effectiveness is *productivity*. Productivity is related to speed of action, in the pure 'time and motion' sense, but also to speed of thought. As we shall discuss in a later chapter, the speed of execution of supposed 'shortcut' function keys may easily be swamped by the time taken to recall the required keystroke. Productivity must also be measured in terms of *accuracy*, both of data entry and of choice of the correct action. As well as pure cost and efficiency issues, productivity will usually have an influence on customer satisfaction. For example, a telephone service provider does not set a target for the speed of response to a directory enquiries call purely to 'churn' more responses from fewer operators, but also because the speed of response directly influences the waiting time of other callers.

Within effectiveness we must also consider ease of learning, for new users; ease of retention, for infrequent users; and ease of re-learning for users who take breaks or vacations. Overlooking these 'ramp up' costs can reduce dramatically the overall effectiveness of an application.

The user's *satisfaction* in her work may be influenced by many factors, including physical comfort, learning and personal growth, sense of achievement, cultural factors, workplace factors beyond our control and, of course, monetary reward. These factors may in turn be influenced by productivity, in the sense that the user may well be motivated directly or indirectly, or even remunerated, by high performance. Increased satisfaction in turn may lead to higher productivity, in a virtuous circle. The well-informed business will attach a substantial value to satisfied users, if only because of the savings involved in lower staff turnover, training costs and the lower productivity of new staff compared to experienced staff.

The user interface architect

In terms of the breadth of skill demanded of the user interface designer, the job is perhaps most comparable to that of an architect. The architect of a building must consider four related aspects of the design:

- *The appearance of the building*   The designer's brief might call for a traditional design that fits in well with other buildings, or a dramatically different design that stands out from its surroundings.
- *The functioning of the building*   An office block must take into account the flow of people in and out, security needs, the placement of service shafts and access points, the number and speed of lifts, the provision of lighting and air conditioning, and many other factors that contribute to the successful functioning of the design.
- *The engineering limitations of the construction materials*   A glass and steel tower can only be built so high before weight-bearing limits become crucial. Lifts can only go so fast. The realities of construction techniques inevitably limit the imagination of the architect.
- *The cost of construction*   An exciting and innovative design with light, airy offices and marble reception floors may be highly functional and extremely attractive, but few organizations will pay for its construction.

In exactly the same way, the user interface designer must consider:

- *The appearance of the application*   The designer's brief might call for a design that conforms to the standards for the platform in question, or a dramatically different design that stands out from its surroundings. In either case, users will immediately judge an application on its attractiveness.
- *The functioning of the application*   The application must be effective, efficient, and satisfying in use. These issues are addressed in considerable detail in the chapters that follow.
- *The engineering limitations of the construction materials*   Network bandwidth is a limited resource; the database can only process a certain number of transactions per second; the client machine has a finite screen resolution and speed

of response. Most business applications that use a graphical user interface are client/server, not pure client, and this sets important limits on the behaviour of the application.

- *The cost of construction*   An exciting and innovative design that exceeds all user expectations and redefines the boundaries of human–computer interaction would be a delight both to build and to use; but what the company needs is a solution to a business need, within budget, and finished to a deadline. In the business world, the value of better design must justify the cost of construction.

As is the case for the architect, these aspects of user interface design all interact with each other: the more innovative a design, the more expensive it is likely to be and the more it is likely to push the engineering limits of the underlying technology. This problem is perfectly illustrated by first generation videoconferencing technology, which purports to allow callers to see each other while conducting a telephone conversation. In practice, the picture may be refreshed as little as once or twice every second, producing such a jerky image that, as experiments have demonstrated, users prefer to look away from the screen once contact has been established. What is in principle an extremely attractive interface performs so poorly that it is ineffective.

If performance is poor, the sense of immediacy afforded by a well-designed graphical user interface is lost. Without a sense of immediacy, the illusion of direct manipulation breaks down. For example, a 'drag and drop' interface on an X terminal, although highly attractive to the user, may generate unacceptably large numbers of network packets, to the detriment of every other activity in the building. Similarly, if the database has been denormalized to improve the efficiency of on-line queries, users of data entry applications may find the performance intolerably slow.

The question 'How *well* does it work?', in principle an issue of implementation rather than of design, cannot be entirely separated from other issues under the broad umbrella of 'usability'. It should not be forgotten that adequate performance is an essential ingredient in the mix. To misquote Bismarck, interface design is the art of the possible.

Put the user first

Having said this, it cannot be overstated that designers of most business applications are far more in danger of sacrificing usability for the sake of performance or ease of implementation, than they are of specifying over-ambitious but underperformant designs. This naturally reflects our background as technical people working in an environment where the emphasis is on efficiency and performance.

The single most important purpose of this book is to enable the designer to see the world from the user's point of view; this involves gaining an appreciation of those factors that will affect the user's experience of the design. The whole of Chapter 1 is devoted to this topic, and the rest of the book is oriented to this goal.

Usability Testing

Usability is a complex concept that is extremely difficult to measure in any objective fashion: it is very hard to put numbers to ideas like 'ease of use'. Furthermore, usability is something that arises from the interaction of all of the components of the design; it is not something that can be readily decomposed. (In this aspect, usability is akin to program performance: a programmer can rarely point to one line of code and say 'here is the performance problem'; poor performance arises from the structure of an entire algorithm, not one line of it.)

The single most important contribution to measuring the user interface comes from representative user testing. Testing your assumptions against the reactions of real users is the only way genuinely to know whether assumptions are valid. Such testing is normally conducted by setting up monitored tests with selected groups of representative users. Well-designed tests are invaluable, but the designer should beware of certain dangers that can arise in poorly designed tests:

- *User testing must begin very early in the development cycle and continue throughout it*   Ideally, the conceptual model and every subsequent stage of design will be offered to users for comment. Paper sketches and discussions can be extremely valuable in establishing the users' mental model of their task. All too often, user testing consists solely of 'prototyping', in which users are invited to comment on the window layouts of an all-but-complete design. The resultant fiddling at the margins of the design is of little real value.
- *Tests must extend over a realistic period*   Tests that are too brief can favour ease of learning at the expense of ease of use. As the design becomes more concrete, extended testing is essential. Features that first appear helpful may later become obstructive. Such problems are difficult to extrapolate from tests lasting only a few hours.
- *Representative users must be carefully selected*   It is often difficult to identify the factors that contribute to different reactions that users have to a design. Sometimes age or social class may be relevant. Education, training and experience may be significant. Willing volunteers are almost by definition not typical! This can make it difficult for the designer to select truly representative users. A related problem is the constant need for fresh testers: the people who tested the first iteration of a design may be falsely productive through familiarity when testing the second iteration.
- *A selection of proposals should be offered*   When only one prototype is on offer, it may be accepted by default. In one project that I was called in to trouble-shoot, a customer was refusing to accept an application even though they had signed off a prototype of the user interface several months previously. The problem was that in the intervening months the users had gained significantly more experience with MS-Windows (which was new to them) and so had much higher expectations. When they had accepted the prototype, they had naively believed that the interface on offer was the best that could be done.

This is not an uncommon experience: users may accept whatever is offered because they believe that the choice is between the design being tested or nothing at all. The designer must make it clear to users that they are not merely being asked to approve the design on offer. This is a particular problem if testing is only conducted late in the cycle. Users are unlikely to suggest a radically better solution when faced with a near-complete prototype

One of the worst examples that I have encountered concerning false extrapolation from too-brief testing occurred with a system that was designed to replace a character terminal application. The application involved extensive searching of 'folders' to assemble the components of a 'case', apparently an ideal situation for a good graphical user interface. At the end of one day of training and use with the new prototype, test subjects were almost exactly as productive as with the highly familiar character terminal version. The designer assumed from this result that users would rapidly become even more productive with the graphical application and took the result as validation of his design. I would suggest that such a close match in performance between the new and old applications is an unlikely coincidence: perhaps the performance of the underlying database is limiting productivity; or possibly the users have hit some fundamental limit in the process itself, such as the concentration demanded by the task. The result clearly demanded an extended period of user testing to see whether productivity would level off or continue to rise.

Despite the difficulties outlined above, representative user testing remains the most vital tool in the designer's tool kit. Tognazzini (1992) and Hix and Hartson (1993) contain valuable advice on conducting and evaluating representative user tests.

Skills of the user interface team

One of the great challenges of user interface design is the range of skills that it demands from the designer. If, like many designers, your background is primarily technical, it can be extremely difficult to set aside that technical focus and concentrate on the interface from an entirely different viewpoint; in other words, to design what is best for the user, not most elegant for the designer, easiest for the implementor or fastest for the processor. For simplicity, we will divide the skills into three major sets: graphical design, cognitive and task engineering, and systems analysis. These are not rigid divisions, and certain skills cross all three groups; nor are these the only skills that might be found to be useful in user interface design.

Graphic design and visual appearance

To the user, the most immediately obvious aspect of any graphical user interface is its visual appearance. The appearance will determine the overall 'attractiveness' of the application. However, graphic design has an importance far beyond mere cosmetic appearance and icon painting. Choice of fonts and colours can have important ergonomic consequences; the clarity and readability of the interface depends strongly on visual choices. Poor design can ultimately lead to physical symptoms such as eyestrain, back pain and even repetitive strain injury (RSI). Colours and layout also have a strong role to play in communicating, helping the user to determine system state, associate related information, and generally navigate the application, and all of this has a significant impact on productivity.

Graphic design should in theory be left to a professional graphic designer; in reality, many budgets do not stretch to a dedicated graphic designer (or, to put it another way, the contribution of graphic design is not sufficiently well appreciated). In this book I have attempted to give enough guidance to prevent some of the worst errors in design that I often encounter from 'amateur' designers. The intention is to allow the reader to design an adequate user interface, involving 'safe' choices of graphical elements and layout. I hope that nobody, especially friends who are professional graphic designers, will take this as an endorsement of computer professionals doing a graphic design professional's job. It is merely a concession to the realities of development budgets.

If the application contains a significant graphical component, and makes extensive use of colours, fonts, icons, images and layout, the services of a professional graphic designer are essential. If the application is to make use of multimedia in any but the most trivial way, a specialist designer is vital.

Workplace issues and cognitive engineering

Once the user has got past the immediate 'look and feel' of the application he will encounter the 'usefulness'. This broad term includes issues such as determining how the application behaves, what it does, how easily it is learned and used, and how easily the user can carry out his business tasks.

Cognitive psychology can contribute high-level insights into memory, learning, perception and attention, which influence how people think and work. Such insights determine what kinds of design will play to the user's strengths, rather than burden his weaknesses. We need also to consider low-level issues including pure 'time and motion' ergonomics. Such an approach can have a dramatic impact on both satisfaction and productivity.

A broad approach to cognitive engineering (the practical application of cognitive psychology) takes in work environment factors, cultural factors, and in general, *human factors*. This discipline can revolutionize your design approach, if you let it: it is the driving force behind the move to 'user centred' rather than 'system centred' design. The latter approach begins with the question: 'What must the system do?'; the former begins with: 'What must the people do?'

In one sense this aspect of design is even more difficult than graphic design, which at least is directly visible to both designer and user. Cognitive issues are frequently intangible, hard to define, and hard to measure. Yet their impact is enormous. Professionals in this area are even harder to find than professionals in visual design.

Systems analysis

Lest we forget the significance of our own discipline, we should not overlook the contribution of 'classic' computing skills in the design. At the sharp end, it is computing skills that will determine what is or is not feasible, reasonable, or economic to implement.

When everybody else has finished dreaming of the ideal interface, commercial reality with its budgets and time scales and technical resource capabilities must have its say. The design team, informed from all directions, must decide which aspects of a design are worthwhile and an effective investment, and which aspects have a cost that is out of proportion to their value to the user. Some suggestions in the user interface design arena remind me of the suggestion that airliners should be fitted with parachutes in case all the engines fail simulta- neously. It sounds wonderful until you calculate the size of the parachute that would be required.

The sensitivity of the systems analyst or systems designer takes on added signifi- cance in the world of the graphical user interface. In the traditional 'host and terminal' character (or block) mode environment, the user interface is so limited in capability that many questions of user interface design are simply not worthy of attention: nothing can be done about them anyway. In the graphical environment, the designer must not merely be able to consider what tasks must be carried out by the user, but must also evaluate and compare the many different ways that these tasks might be carried out, as well as the interaction of his preferences with those of other team members. The systems professional needs to be open to the often intangible costs of technical decisions.

Who is responsible for the user interface?

At this point you may be wondering how any one person can combine all of these skills. In reality, of course, no one person can. Ideally, user interface design is carried out by a team of specialists, each of whom contributes a different exper- tise and a different point of view. In a perfect world, each team member also appreciates the domains of expertise of the others.

Analysis and design skills are comparatively easy to find in most organizations, though it is far from true that every systems analyst is a suitable choice for a user interface task analyst. The successful analyst requires a highly flexible approach and an ability to appreciate the contributions of other team members.

Many designers find it very difficult to make the transition to the graphical environment. Their designs resemble character mode applications with added artificial colour. The computer studies graduate who has taken a 'module' in 'user interfaces' should also be treated with a little caution. While many of these qualifications are very worthwhile, others teach nothing deeper than the difference between a check box and a radio button group; and still others are, in reality, courses on the implementation details of a particular window manager. If the team is to include such 'qualified' people, the project manager must probe beyond the paper qualification and uncover the actual course content.

Ideally, the design team will include, or even be led by, a human factors specialist. It is preferable, but not essential, that this person will have an appreciation of the technical implications of her decisions. Such combinations of skills are relatively rare, but one potential source of human factors skills should not be overlooked: useful skills can often be found among professional technical documentation specialists. They and other information specialists can play an important design role: many of them are skilled in understanding and explaining a user's work tasks. Indeed, many of them have qualifications in 'knowledge engineering' that go far beyond 'merely' writing the documentation after the fact of design. As well as an ability to explain, such people, both by inclination and by training, are able to take a user-centred view of the system, and present a technical requirement in a way that makes sense to a user, rather than to the designer. Documentors can also play an extremely important 'auditing' role: an application that is difficult to explain is certainly even more difficult to use.

Graphic design skills may be the hardest to come by within an existing organization; fortunately it is relatively easy to find freelance or agency graphic designers to work on a project-by-project design basis; and many colleges now provide specific qualifications in graphic design for information systems. This can be valuable, as a 'pure' graphic designer may be unaware of the way in which his suggestions for layout and colours interact with broader issues such as taskflow and perception.

The design team also needs to include a 'user advocate'. It is simply not realistic to put every disagreement within the team to real users, and test their responses. For this reason it is essential to have somebody whose role is to take the users' position, and argue their case. Sometimes this person will take competing prototypes away, evaluate them against each other, and report her findings back to the team. The user advocate is not the same thing as a 'user representative' in the testing cycle. A user representative should be a 'typical' user, skilled in the problem domain, who performs extensive tests defined beforehand by the designers. The user advocate is a full-time member of the design team, a creative contributor to the design team in her own right, not merely an evaluator of other people's proposals. She does not have to be typical of the user population; but she does have to be able to see the world from their point of view.

The scope of this book

What this book is about

User interface design is a complex, multi-faceted discipline. It is far from easy, and the much-vaunted ease of use of the graphical user interface is not something that the designer gets for free. Ease of use, clarity and productivity all have to be designed in from the top down, but the potential is there for the designer willing to look for it.

This book presents a systematic, top-down approach to understanding the fundamentals of user interface design. We begin with an examination of fundamental principles of industrial and domestic design, and examine their relevance to the idea of the user interface as a 'soft machine'. We then develop those principles through levels of increasing detail, moving from the most theoretical to the most practical, the most broad to the most detailed. The emphasis throughout is on the pragmatic, the tradeoffs to be made between the theoretical ideal and the implementation reality. The book is intended to be taken as a coherent whole, to be read in order, not as a collection of independent topics — no one chapter stands in isolation from the others.

Although the subject of this book is user interface (UI) design in general, we are specifically interested in the capabilities and challenges of the graphical user interface (GUI). Character and block mode terminals present a very different world with different challenges, which is beyond our scope. We are particularly concerned with specific issues of implementing GUI applications on mainstream windowing platforms such as Microsoft Windows (MS-Windows); Motif and other X-Windows based systems; and the Apple Macintosh (Mac).

The danger of writing about specific platforms is that one can rapidly be overtaken by events, even within the time taken to prepare and publish a manuscript. For the benefit of hypothetical future readers, I should explain that at the time of writing, MS-Windows 3.1 is the most widely installed platform, with Windows 95 about a year away from production release; Motif is on the cusp of being released from a research project under the academic control of MIT to become a purely commercial product; and Apple is rolling out System 7 to its users. NextStep is all but extinct, and the OS/2 Workplace Shell is finally enjoying limited and belated success.

Illustrative examples are taken mostly from Microsoft Windows based applications and, in order to find simple examples of particular principles, I have occasionally been obliged to draw on older releases of certain applications. I hope readers will not find this practice too unfair; the examples are intended only as illustrations, not as criticism of particular applications, versions or vendors. Although specific examples may become out of date, I hope that the principles illustrated remain valid.

14   Practical user interface design

What this book is not about

There are many issues in user interface design that are extremely important, but are simply beyond the scope of this book. Some we do not have room for, some are inappropriate for an introductory text, and others are quite simply well covered in existing works.

One major area that we do not cover in detail is the *process* of user interface design: how it is managed and implemented as part of the overall design process. This includes important topics such as prototyping, and measuring and testing the quality of a design. We also do not examine in great detail issues of systems analysis. Although we discuss the relationship between systems analysis and user interface design, the detailed techniques of task analysis and evaluation are not the purpose of this book. I have attempted to focus on the 'what' of user interface design, rather than the 'how' or 'why'.

There are many areas that are peripheral to the application itself that also deserve our attention, including documentation, online help, support and training. We shall touch upon these as they impact the user interface but each of them is a significant area of study, to do justice to which would require a book in its own right.

A note on terminology

Many different terms are used in discussing user interface design. One widely used term is 'usability', which can sometimes encompass other non-systems issues of the application, such as help and documentation, but it is often used to refer purely to the immediate user interface aspects of software systems. The term 'human factors' may also be used in a very broad sense, to include all of the above as well as culture, workplace, business workflow and many other non-systems issues.

In academic circles this area of study is usually known as human–computer interface (HCI). The equivalent older term, man–machine interface (MMI), is rarely encountered nowadays. In some parts of the world, the term computer–human interface (CHI) is found. HCI and CHI are completely interchangeable.

The question of the singular personal pronoun always presents a difficulty for authors. In my examples I have followed the emerging practice of using 'he' and 'she' more or less alternately. I have avoided the politically correct use of 'they' as a singular pronoun as many readers find it both clumsy and confusing . 'He' and 'she' are to be regarded as completely interchangeable throughout the examples and illustrative scenarios.

Whenever I refer to a designer, unless the situation makes the use more specific, the reader may take it that I am referring to any member of the design team, or indeed to the whole design team collectively. The designer may be analyst, technical designer, user interface architect, graphics designer or even implementor, depending on the context.

1 Fundamental principles

'When simple things need labels or instructions, the design has failed'

Dr Donald Norman *The Psychology of Everyday Things*

Introduction

This chapter is built on one simple idea: the fundamental principles of design that guide the designers of buildings, stereo hi-fis, camcorders and can-openers apply equally well to the designers of user interfaces. In this chapter we explore these basic principles, drawing analogies from tools in the everyday world, and derive a number of rules and guidelines that we can apply to the user interface.

In the words of Dr Norman quoted above lie two core concepts that pervade this book. First, simple things should not be difficult. The user should not be left staring helplessly at a blank screen, wondering how to begin. They should not waste their time wandering lost through menu upon menu, looking for a command that isn't even there; or staring at a control that behaves like nothing else they have ever used. Good design is compelling in its simplicity. Really good design is so compelling it disappears altogether.

People generally say 'I am going to wash some clothes'; they rarely say 'I am going to use the washing machine'. By contrast, people often say 'I am trying to program the video recorder'; they rarely say 'I am going to record a film'. The user interface of the washing machine has been made so simple to use that the machine disappears — not just from the language we use about it, but from our perception of the actual task to be performed. You may feel that it is foolish even to say that the machine has a user interface and yet you can program it to carry out a complex set of tasks with just a few simple control settings. The user interface of the video recorder is so overwhelmingly obtuse that not only do you not say 'I am going to record a film', as often as not you return home to find that you haven't recorded the film! Misprogramming the video recorder is a universal modern experience.

As a designer, you can feel delighted with your user interface if users say of your application, 'I am going to re-order some stock', not 'I am going to use the stock control system'. The greatest achievement that the user interface designer can aspire to is to make the computer disappear from the user's view. Realistically, we frequently do not have the time or resources to aim so high, but this is the ideal to which we aspire.

Figure 1.1 is a perfect example of how to make the simple complex. This message was produced because my printer had A4 paper and my document was set to American 'letter' size. Not only does the message bear no relation to the actual cause of the problem, the buttons available — Retry and Cancel — are apparently unconnected with the suggested action, 'resume the print queue'. Cancel what? The message, or the print job?

This is our most fundamental principle: simple tasks deserve a simple interface.

There is a second, more subtle, message in Dr Norman's words. Things that are not simple usually *do* need labels or instructions. Nobody expects to be able to drive a car without training. It is not reasonable to sit yourself down in the cockpit of a Boeing 747 and expect to be able to fly it, not even if you have flown a Piper Cub before. If your application is large and complex, it is unreasonable to present your users with an interface that resembles the bridge of the starship *Enterprise* and to expect them to be able to pilot it.

This is our second principle: complex tasks demand guidance and elucidation.

One cliché of user interface design that I often hear repeated goes 'If you don't know how to use it, it doesn't work'. In my opinion, this overstates the case: we do ourselves no favours as designers by setting ourselves such unrealistic expectations. One of the skills that you will need to acquire as a designer of interfaces that others will use is the judgement to tell the difference between the simple and the complex. The hardest part of this task is to put yourself in the place of the user.

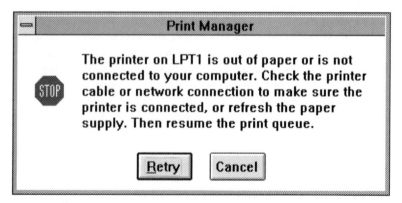

Figure 1.1. Print Manager: none of the above

The user's point of view

Consider a typical transaction processing application — almost any business application will do. It may be obvious to you that a transaction must be committed to the database before it is visible to another session; but to the average user, this is a baffling mystery. The record is changed on my terminal, but not on your terminal. Now move the poor user to a GUI environment, and give him two sessions on the same display: the data is changed in *this* window, but not in *that* window. A mystery wrapped in an enigma!

This ability to differentiate between the complex and the simple is a skill that you can really only acquire by learning from users. The more time you spend watching them work and listening to their questions, the more you will understand how our world, the world of systems and software, appears from the outside.

Behind every recommendation, every guideline, every principle that this book contains, you should assume the addition of the user interface designer's General Theory of Relativity: generally, everything should be considered relative to the user's point of view.

Beware of extremists

One note of caution: there are two kinds of user that you need to be wary of. The first is the technophile, the data processing 'wannabe'. Such people are easily recognized by the pile of glossy computer magazines on their desk, an unhealthy interest in the details of the implementation of the systems they use, and a tendency to treat computing as a religion of which you and they are the high priests. Technophiles are particularly dangerous as it is very tempting to be seduced by their enthusiasm and accept them as testers or user representatives. Beware! They are not representative of the majority of the users! They will encourage you to design in all kinds of 'power features', fast keys and shortcuts. Remember that our measure of excellence is that the computer disappears for the user. How happy will this person be if everybody can be a member of the priesthood, if there is no mystery, if anybody can use the system fluently?

The second danger group are the acute technophobes. Some years ago I wrote a very simple addition skills testing program for a teacher. I asked her to run through the test and tell me whether it was suitable for her seven-year-olds. As she struggled to understand the instructions, I began to wonder if I had, unconsciously, designed a horrendously difficult user interface. I was trying very hard to resist the temptation to lean over her shoulder and press keys for her. If she had so much trouble, how on earth would her pupils cope? Eventually she finished the test, and the screen announced, in letters five centimetres high, 'You have completed the test. Press the Return key to see your score.' The teacher stared at this screen for a full minute and more. Finally, unable to contain my frustration, I snapped at her, 'What are you waiting for?' She turned to me, apparently close to tears, and said, 'I don't know what to do next!'

There is nothing you can do for such people. They have a blind spot the size and shape of a computer screen. Given explicit written step-by-step instructions, they will follow them, regardless of the severest error messages announcing total failure or impending disaster. Nothing that happens on the screen is of the slightest relevance to them. No user interface can account for such people; they do not, in fact, interact with the application at all.

However, this should not be taken as an excuse to dismiss every user difficulty as technophobia: it remains the case that the vast majority of user problems are our fault, not theirs.

Avoid making special allowance for either of these groups. Remember that we are trying to design for the broad mass of users, the 80 per cent to 90 per cent who are competent but not expert. Trying to cope with the special needs of these two constituencies can become a bottomless sink for development resources, as ever-increasing effort is consumed in return for marginal gain.

The human–computer interface

The user interface is, by definition, the point at which human collides with computer. A good user interface designer needs to combine an understanding of both. The designer needs to be able to view the system from the user's point of view and simultaneously think of the user from the system's point of view. Remember, we are not designing an application to capture input, nor an application to display output; we are designing an *interaction* between the user and the application. To do this job effectively, we need to understand elements of design that enable effective use of tools, and the first half of this chapter is devoted to issues that affect how the system can best communicate with the user. Conversely, we also need to understand factors that influence how people work and learn. Although we have almost total control over the application, we have very little control over the users, so the second half of this chapter discusses issues that help the designer to exploit the strengths and avoid the weaknesses of most users.

Elements of design

Good and bad design is everywhere around you: in your office; in your home; in the way products are labelled in shops; in the maps and road signs and railway timetables you travel by; in the up, down and sideways arrows of airport signs; in the software you build and in the software you use. In many ways, a user interface is a kind of 'soft machine'. As designers we can form it at will to our needs, but in the final analysis it remains a device to be used by a person.

Everything that is designed to be used by people shares certain basic principles of design, and in this chapter we aim to uncover and make explicit those principles. Along the way we shall attempt to illustrate the relevance of these common principles to software systems, and in so doing acquire a common vocabulary of design.

One of the toughest obstacles to designing the user interface is the difficulty of expressing our ideas. If you are a data designer, you can show diagrams of your data model to another designer, and you can discuss them together in terms of normalization and cardinality and optionality. If you are a process designer, you can discuss completeness of data stores and balancing of flows. But if you are a user interface designer, you are almost entirely deaf and dumb. By the end of this chapter we shall have established a vocabulary that allows the user interface designer to criticize and discuss user interface design in the same way as the data or process modeller.

Much of the vocabulary that I adopt in this chapter is adapted from the work of Dr Donald Norman, a leading researcher in this and related fields, and I strongly recommend his book (Norman, 1988) as an excellent popular introduction to the importance of design. In fact, you may well find it useful to read that work before progressing to Chapter 2 of this book.

A vocabulary of design

We often talk vaguely about user friendliness and an intuitive interface, as if we all agreed what these terms meant. What *precisely* does it mean for an interface to be hard or easy to use? What makes it memorable or forgettable? What contributes to ease of learning? What makes the difference between an interface that is obvious and one that is obscure? What are the *elements* of good and bad design? Without a common design vocabulary, it is impossible for us systematically and consistently to identify the strengths, weaknesses, successes and failures of a proposed design. And if we cannot identify strengths and successes, it is a matter of mere chance as to whether we can repeat them.

Visibility

Think about the telephone in your office or on your desk. (If you are at your desk, take a look at it now.) Look at the checklist below. Check every facility that is available on your phone and *that you can use without referring to the user manual.*

- Redial the last number called
- Transfer a call to another extension
- Retrieve a transferred call if the other extension is engaged or does not answer
- Pick up another ringing phone in your group
- Pick up any other ringing phone

- Set up a three-way conversation
- Call back an engaged line when free
- Store and recall frequently dialled numbers
- Use the button labelled 'R'

In my experience, most people score between one third and one half. If you scored more than that, you probably have a 'crib sheet' taped to the phone. One of my favourites is the function to pick up another ringing phone: according to the user manual of my phone, I can pick up any phone I can hear if I 'dial *13 then the extension number of the ringing phone'. There is, as you will have noticed, a flaw in this. How do I know the extension number of the ringing phone? I suppose I can walk around to it and take a look, then walk back to my own phone so that I can pick it up.

Someone expended a lot of effort designing and building that sophisticated phone system. Your company probably spent a lot of time evaluating it and a lot of money installing it. Yet most people use barely a third of its capabilities. Some people say, 'Oh, my phone can't do those things'. Actually, it probably can, but you would never know by looking. Does this remind you of any applications you know — or even of any you have written?

This is the first basic characteristic of user interface usability: *visibility*. Visibility is a description of how easily and directly the user can see *what* can be done and *how* to do it. Figure 1.2 shows an example from Lotus Ami Pro, a well-known word processor.

The first time I saw this, I was totally baffled. I wanted to set the line spacing to 1.25 lines (which I can do easily in the other word processor I use regularly, Microsoft Word). After a while I started experimenting (because I am a curious person) and pressed the button labelled 'in.'. Remarkably, its label changed to 'cm.', a somewhat unexpected thing for a button to do. Excited, I pressed it again and again, and the label became 'pt.', then 'pica', then back to 'in.'. Well, I thought, I must have missed 'lines', so I went through again, more slowly and

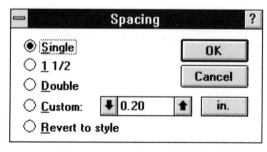

Figure 1.2. Set the spacing to 1.25 lines

carefully. Still no 'lines'. In some confusion now, I turned to the online help. I read it through, and eventually came to the reluctant conclusion that it could not be done. The only custom measure not available was the one that corresponded most directly to what I wanted to do. I had wasted around 20 minutes looking for a facility that was not even there.

I am sure that you can immediately propose a better design. The choice of measure could be a radio button group, or a pop-down list. If the designer had chosen one of these methods, rather than indulging himself in this cheap visual trick of changing the label, not only would I have known immediately what choices were available, I would have known how to choose between them. This is a small but perfectly formed example of poor visibility in the design of a control.

However, poor visibility is not limited to the design of individual controls. Figure 1.3 shows an example, also from Ami Pro, of a window whose design exhibits poor visibility. None of the critically important options that discriminate the search are displayed on the first window. As a result, every time I use this dialog box I have to open the second window, 'Options...' (Fig. 1.4), to verify that I am searching for exactly the match I want.

Notice also the 'Exact attributes' check box. This also tells me whether I need to check the options in a third window, reached by closing this window and clicking the 'Attributes...' button in the previous window. When I return to the Find and Replace window, none of the choices that I have made are visible. Although having three windows is inconvenient, that would not be such a great problem if the lack of visibility did not force the user to navigate to all three windows to verify the options and attributes in effect.

Figure 1.5 shows the equivalent dialog from Microsoft Word Version 2.0. In this design I can see at a glance exactly what I am searching for: the word 'figure', by

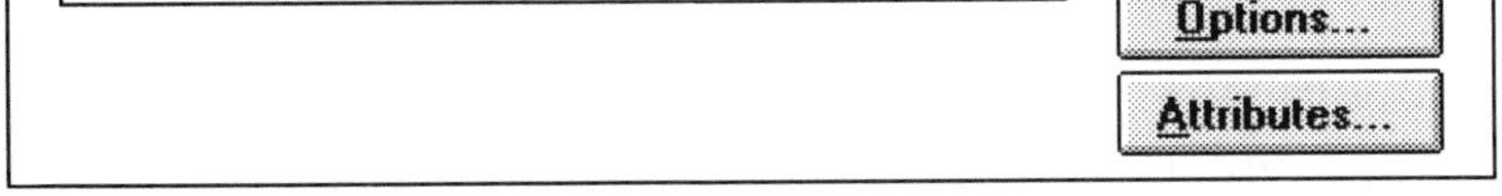

Figure 1.3. Is Ami Pro's search case sensitive?

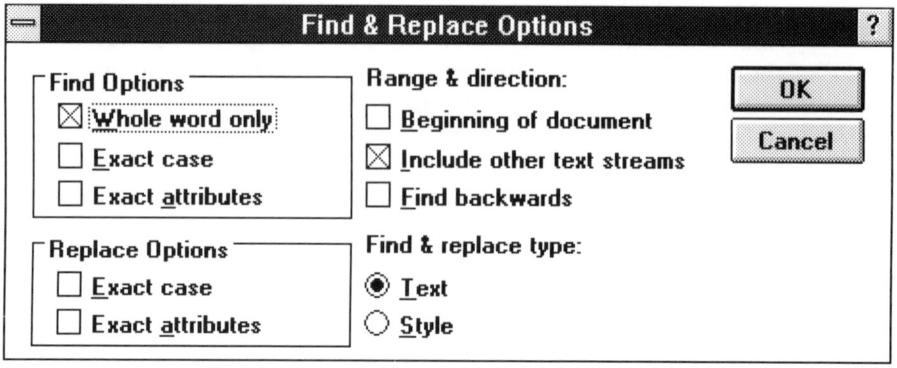

Figure 1.4. Ami Pro's hidden options

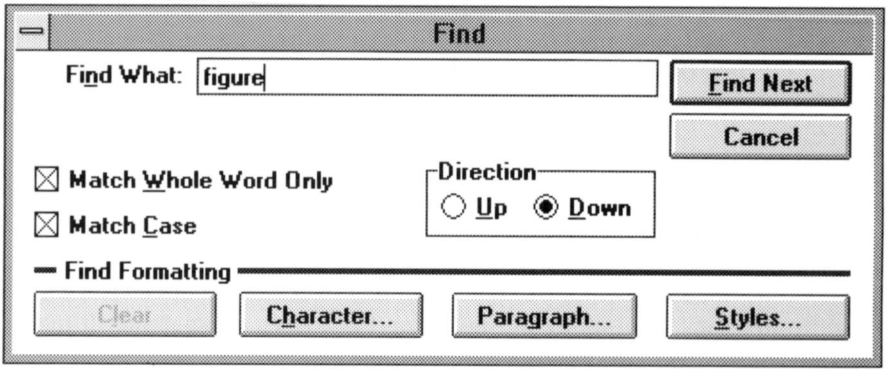

Figure 1.5. Is Microsoft Word's search case sensitive?

itself (not 'figures' or 'figured') in upper or lower case. If I want to add particular format characteristics to the search, a rarely used but useful function, it is obvious how I do that (or at least, where I start!).

This example illustrates how poor visibility directly impacts the effectiveness of the application. Cautious users may never even discover the richness of the search criteria available in Ami Pro. Good visibility is the key to encouraging your users to discover and utilize all of the functionality that you have so painstakingly provided.

Feedback

Consider your telephone again. Which of the following can you determine *by direct examination* or some other equally simple method?

- The number being dialled (with back up if you misdial)

- The number held for 'last number redial'
- If a 'call back when free' is pending
- If the phone is redirected, and if so, to what number
- Stored short-dial numbers and their codes

How can you reliably redirect your phone if you cannot see where you redirected it to? If you answered 'yes' to the question above, you are probably among the small minority who are blessed with a phone with a display. This small addition would transform the usability of the phones with which the majority of us struggle along.

My favourite office game is telephone tennis; you can play it with any telephone equipped with 'call back when free'. The rules are simple. You try to call someone but his line is engaged, so you enter the code for 'call back when free'. In fact he has put his phone on 'do not disturb', so it stays engaged all day. Finally, at four in the afternoon, by which time you have forgotten that you ever wanted to speak to him, he switches off 'do not disturb'. Immediately both of your phones ring. You pick yours up and say 'Hello?' He picks up his phone and says 'Hello?' 'Yes?' you say, 'Who is this?'...

This illustrates the second basic characteristic of user interface usability: *feedback*. Feedback is a measure of how easily and quickly you can determine the results of your actions. Good feedback operates at every level of the user interface:

- When you click on a button, it depresses.
- When you select text, it becomes highlighted.
- The title bar of the word processor tells you the name of the document you are editing.
- When text is on the clipboard, the 'Paste' command is enabled; when there is nothing on the clipboard, it is disabled.
- While a long-running operation is taking place, such as saving a file, the cursor changes to an hourglass.

The example in Fig. 1.6 comes from Microsoft Word again. As you alter options, the sample paragraph previews how the actual text will appear. You are provided with immediate feedback as you adjust each setting; you don't have to wait until you click OK and return to the real text. A similar example, illustrated by font selection, can be found on the accompanying disk.

This example illustrates the key attributes of feedback. Good feedback operates at the appropriate level. It shows you not merely what you did, but the *effect* of what you did. That effect is expressed at a level of abstraction that is meaningful to the user. This is demonstrated by the difference between old-style text processors, which showed you with embedded codes where formatting, for example bold text, began and ended, and word processors, which embolden the actual text

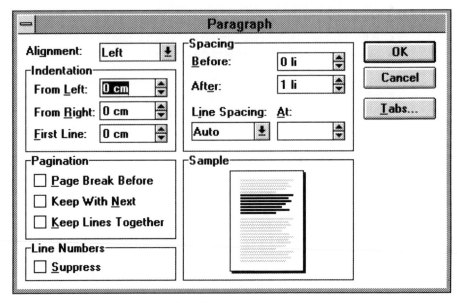

Figure 1.6. How the paragraph will look

affected. Good feedback reduces the size of the loop between action and evaluation of the action; it makes the interaction more direct. We develop this idea again later in this chapter when we discuss the burden of interpretation.

You will often hear glib talk of 'what you see is what you get' (WYSIWYG) as one of the advantages of a graphical user interface. The example above goes one better: it is 'what you see is what you are going to get'. In many cases, WYSIWYG simply means that what you see on the screen in your word processor or spread-sheet is what you will get on paper. But is this necessarily an advantage? Some-times it is more convenient to work with your text or cells *without* seeing what you get. For example, if you are constructing a large spreadsheet, you may not care to see the page headers, titles, and footers as they fall in your data until the construction is complete. Conversely, you may want to see column and row numbers and the cell grid as you work, but not when you print. WYSIWYG is not a cure for all user interface ills, and needs to be considered carefully. Feedback needs to be presented:

- In the right place
- At the right time
- At the right level

An example of appropriate implementation of this idea is the 'Page' view facility available in most word processors. In 'Page' view, the user can see the effects of margin settings, running headers and footers, footnotes and so on. However, this mode can be inconvenient for text editing, especially in older implementations: if you are editing a paragraph at the bottom of a page, you may find yourself frequently distracted by the word processor moving the paragraph back and forth between the bottom of one page and the top of another. In 'Normal' view, by contrast, the word processor acts like an 'infinite scroll' that the user can type into, regardless of page breaks. On the other hand, headers and footers are not visible. This choice of views allows the user to switch at will between a view in which it is easier to focus on entering data, but which is less of a literal presentation of the final document, and a view in which it is easier to focus on adjusting the final visual appearance. (Some very modern word processors manage to reconcile both requirements in one view, but few spreadsheets or other tools do so yet). When we say that WYSIWYG is desirable, what we actually mean is that the interface should exhibit good feedback and high visibility. It is important to remember that WYSIWYG is just one, albeit important, aspect of feedback.

In the business applications that we are typically building, we can divide feedback loosely into four different classes:

- Context information, such as which file you are editing, or which user you are logged on as
- System state, such as editing mode or clipboard paste availability
- Conversational response to actions, such as confirming saves (commits)
- Immediate response that guides individual keystrokes and mouse clicks, such as button depression, popping down a menu, or changing the cursor shape

These forms of feedback differ in many ways, but they all serve the same essential function: they remind you what you are doing or what you have done. In so doing they reduce the burden on the memory and concentration of the user.

Mappings

When I drove my new car for the first time, some of the controls were immediately easy to use; others required experimentation or reference to the manual. Some of the functions of the radio remain a mystery to this day. As an example of good design, the electric door mirrors are adjusted by a flat, rectangular pad about five centimetres wide. If you press on the left edge of the pad, the mirror tilts inward; press on the top of the pad and the mirror tilts upward. In fact, the control behaves exactly as if you were pressing on the mirror, rather than on the pad. Using the control maps precisely to the effect desired. This is an excellent example of a good *mapping*.

By contrast, to adjust the height of the seat there is a mechanical control, a handle that winds one way for up, the other for down. The only way to discover which way is which, is to try it. There is no obvious correspondence between turning the handle clockwise or anticlockwise, and the seat moving up or down. This is a very poor mapping.

Mapping is a description of the correspondence between the *function desired* and the *action required* to achieve it. Good mappings are perceived by the user as concrete, natural and direct. Poor mappings are perceived as abstract, indirect or arbitrary.

Consider the programmer's task of designing a dialog box for a Windows application. One of the most tedious parts of this task is setting the tab sequence of controls in dialog box. In various tools that I have used, I have seen three basic methods implemented:

- *Method 1: Each item (field, button, check box, etc.) in the dialog box has a property sheet*   One of the properties is the tab sequence number. To change the tab sequence of a control, the user must count all the controls, determine where she wants the particular control to fall in the sequence, open the property sheet, type the sequence number, and close and save the property sheet. She must then figure out how this has changed the sequence numbers of all the other controls on the dialog. For example, if she moves control number four to position eight, numbers five, six, seven and the previous number eight are all implicitly and silently renumbered. This is a very poor mapping: the correspondence between action and effect is indirect, requiring the user to deduce the effect.
- *Method 2: The names of the items in the dialog box are presented in a list, in order of the tab sequence*   To change the position of an item, she picks it up and drags it to its new position. This is a better mapping, but still is moderately indirect. The user needs to picture in her mind the physical positions of the controls on the window layout (or refer to another window showing the actual screen layout) in order to determine the desired tab sequence, although once she has chosen a sequence, it is comparatively easy to set.
- *Method 3: An image of the dialog box is presented*   The user clicks on each control in the order of the desired tab sequence. The numbers show her continuously the current tab sequence. This provides a very direct mapping from the action to the desired result. An example is shown in Fig. 1.7.

Incidentally, it is no coincidence that the mapping that is most difficult to describe corresponds to the method that is the most difficult to use.

Mappings will always suffer if there are fewer controls than there are functions. If you have sat through a sales presentation recently, you will have noticed an increasing fashion for 'software slide shows'. In the past, presenters prepared their material in Lotus Freelance or Microsoft Powerpoint, for example, then printed it onto transparencies, often losing the colours in the process; or had it made up, by a slow and expensive process, into 35 mm slides. Nowadays it is commonplace to show the presentation directly on the screen of a personal computer, and use some form of projection such as a tablet that sits on the overhead projector, a projection system or a very large screen monitor, to display the presentation to the audience.

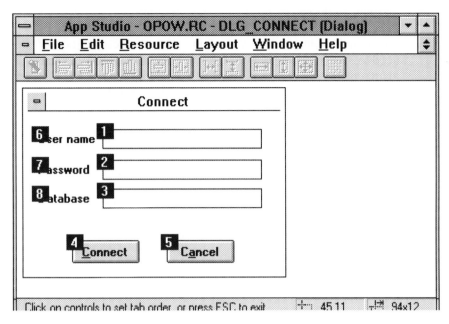

Figure 1.7. Microsoft Application Studio: a direct mapping of the tab sequence

To advance the slideshow, the presenter clicks the left mouse button. To move back one slide, he clicks the right mouse button. If he clicks *and holds* the left button, then moves the mouse, he draws a line on the slide. Inevitably, this overloading of the mouse buttons leads to disaster. In a presentation that I attended recently, a sales manager was presenting to a roomful of his colleagues. Against his better judgement, he was persuaded to present this way rather than use transparencies. Nervously, this first-time presenter started up the presentation, then clicked *firmly* on the left button to make sure it was pressed. A small line appeared on his slide. The presenter clicked again; another line appeared. Eventually, he turned in desperation to the audience and asked, 'Does anybody know how to move to the next slide?' I suspect it will be a very long time before he can be persuaded to use this particular feature again.

Recall the telephone example from earlier. One of the reasons that functions such as Call Forward are hard to remember is that (on most telephones) they are effected by arbitrary key sequences, such as '*14'. In choosing mappings, the telephone designer is hindered by two restrictions. First, there are not enough buttons for all the functions; second, each button must serve different functions depending on the configuration ordered by the purchaser. Basic economics mean it is not feasible to produce different keypads for different customers. The result is that functions are mapped to abstract actions.

As software designers, no such engineering limits apply. We are painting pixels, not cutting holes in plastic sheets, and we can change the labels on buttons and texts in fields without limit. We might expect the designer of user interfaces to be freed to implement the best design that he can imagine, without the limitations of 'hard' engineering. Paradoxically, in practice it seems that the lack of constraints in the world of software merely increases the scope for error.

Cues and Affordances

Another of the key characteristics of good design is the way that it *cues* the user. A well-designed control or window utilizes the user's existing knowledge to hint at the way that it is used. For example, as users of windowed applications we have all learnt to expect a button to perform an action when pressed. We call this the *affordance* of a button. Conversely, when we are looking for an action we will look at menus and buttons. A drop-down list hints to the user that a number of choices or options are available. When we are looking for a choice or selection, we look for lists, check boxes and radio button groups. Mappings and cues are closely related aspects of the interface.

If a control has an obvious usage, we say that it has strong affordance. The commonest low-level error that I encounter in user interfaces is poor choice of controls or, in other words, weak affordance. Recall the Ami Pro example from earlier: using a button whose label changes to implement a set of choices is a poor cue. The affordance of a button is not to cycle through changes, but to perform an action.

Figure 1.8 shows the Print Document dialog from Microsoft Word Version 2.0. Consider the option 'Print to File'. Is this an action? If so, why is it not a button? Or is it an option, like 'Collate Copies' alongside it? If so, what does it mean when checked? Print to file as well as to the printer, or instead of the printer? It is also possible to 'print' to the screen. In Microsoft Word, this is a separate menu command, called 'Print Preview'. In Microsoft Excel, on the other hand, 'Print Preview' is an option in the Print Dialog (Fig. 1.9). So is 'Print Preview' an option or a command?

Both of these Microsoft applications could be simplified by a better mapping with more appropriate cues. The choice could be three pushbuttons, as prototyped in Fig. 1.10. Of course, this is by no means the only possible self-consistent choice. If the destination were a choice between three radio buttons ('To File', 'To Screen Preview' and 'To Printer') it would clearly be an exclusive choice that determines the destination of the output. A third possibility would be to put 'To File' and 'To Printer' as equal choices, with 'Preview before printing' as an option that applies equally to both print destinations. How then to choose between these possibilities? The answer, unsurprisingly, is to ask the users. It is very easy to prototype all of these designs, and to conduct simple usability testing to find out which one makes most sense to most users.

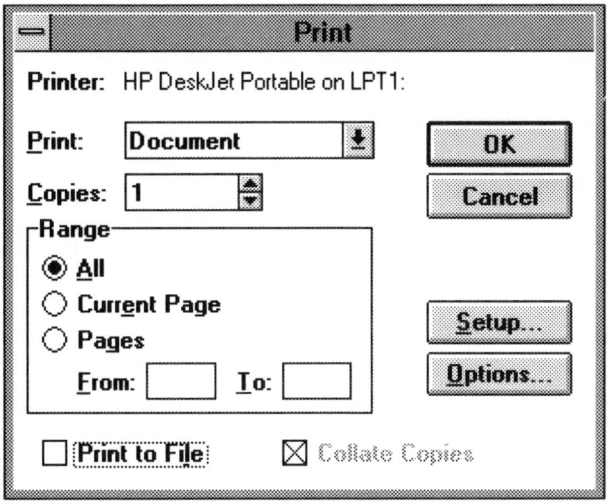

Figure 1.8. Microsoft Word Print dialog

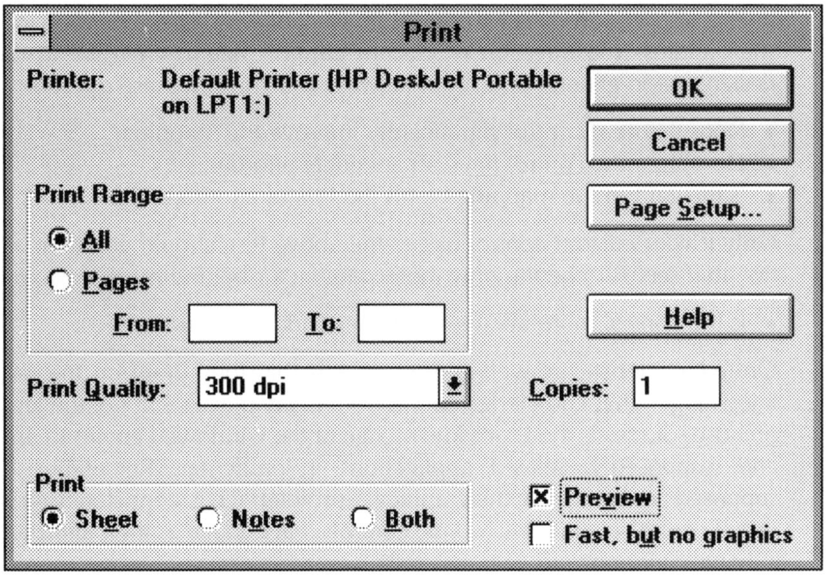

Figure 1.9. Microsoft Excel Print dialog

Some designers seem obsessed with creating new controls or inventing new behaviour for existing controls. (Lotus's applications are especially guilty here.) Indeed, some GUI design tools seem to go out of their way to encourage such behaviour. A new control will nearly always give a weaker cue than a familiar

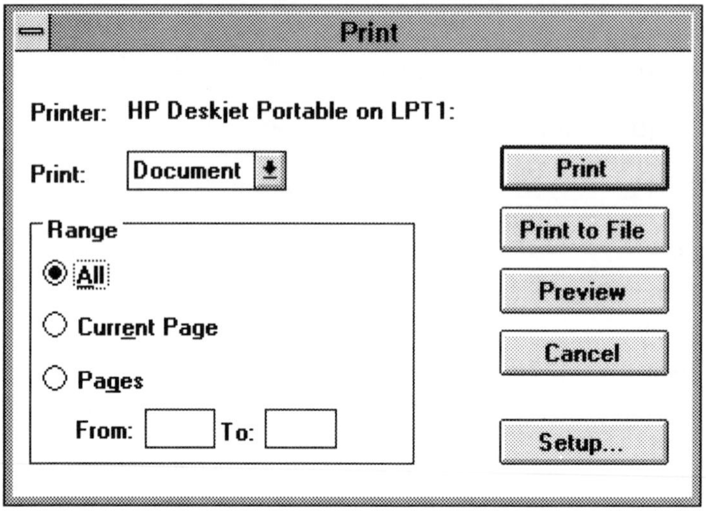

Figure 1.10. Prototype unified Print dialog with consistent cues

one; and using an existing control in a novel way gives contradictory cues. We shall address the question of custom controls again when we discuss detailed design, but in general you should always ask yourself these questions:

• Does the new control significantly improve the mapping?
• Does the new control have an adequate affordance?
• Is the gain in the mapping worth the loss of affordance?

Only if your custom control passes the above test, should you then ask the question that seems to be the only motivating factor behind many custom controls:

• Is the control more attractive than a standard control?

One characteristic of well-chosen cues is that they draw on the user's existing knowledge. That knowledge comes from many places, but not the least important of those sources is the user's knowledge of the windowed environment in general, and (supposedly) related applications in particular. Remember, one of the supposed advantages of the graphical user interface is consistency, and consistent use of controls — in other words, controls that behave as their affordance suggests — pays dividends.

The burden of interpretation

Visibility, feedback, mappings and affordance are not totally disjoint components of a design: for example, a good mapping begins with the right affordance, and involves high visibility and good feedback. The example in Fig. 1.8 is not only a poor mapping, it also has poor visibility — the opposite of 'Print to File' is not visible.

In practice most design errors involve a combination of poor visibility, feedback, mappings and affordance. These elements are the basic ingredients in the recipe. When these ingredients combine, they produce higher-order errors of design. Another way of thinking of these higher-order, combinatorial errors is in the way they hinder the user's understanding.

We can think of an application and its user as being, in some respects, a single 'system'; together they process information to achieve some business task. Without a user, the computer is purposeless. Without the computer, the user cannot perform her job. It is useful to consider the information in that system in three levels: representation, presentation and interpretation. At the lowest level, there is a *representation* of information; typically in a transaction processing application, information will be represented in a database. At the next level we have a *presentation* of that information by one or more applications. Again, in a typical application, presentation will be through screens and reports. Finally there is *utilization* of that information by a user. Between each of these levels there is a requirement for interpretation: the data is rarely presented on the screen in exactly the form it is stored, and the meaning to the business is rarely directly present to the user. The effort required to transform between each of these levels is a burden of interpretation.

Where is the burden of interpretation?

As an example, consider an order processing application. The database will store information in a particular representation, such as a record of the order received, a shipping record, a billing record and so on. This is presented in a consolidated form that shows the order details along with the order date, the shipping date, the billing date and the invoice date. The user may then utilize this, interpreting the dates presented to understand that a particular invoice is overdue for payment. Your first reaction to this may be to ask, why can't the *application* provide that interpretation? Instead of simply presenting dates, why can't it indicate that the invoice is overdue for payment? The answer of course is that it can, but unfortunately few applications do; and that is precisely the point of the question at the head of this section.

If the presentation of the data is very close to the representation, a large burden is placed on the user to interpret the data before it can be utilized. On the other hand, the application may take on the burden, presenting information to the user in a form very close to the utilization required by the user. Consider your own designs: is the burden of interpretation placed on the user or on the application?

In its simplest case, reducing the burden means using the user's vocabulary, rather than the system's. In many cases the user may have several different vocabularies; it is then the role of the designer to choose the one that is most appropriate to the circumstances. Another way of looking at this is to ask ourselves, what is the question that the user is posing to the system? In the example above, presenting information about invoices in the system in terms of whether they are overdue or not may be appropriate in certain circumstances, such as deciding whether to send out a reminder or final demand, or take other action. In other circumstances, such as forecasting cash flow, the actual dates themselves may be more useful. In other words, we can see that the user has two 'vocabularies', or viewpoints, depending on circumstances: one for collecting payment, the other for forecasting cash flow. The lesson here is that it is very easy to propose the rule, 'use the user's vocabulary', but it is far harder to determine which of the user's many vocabularies to use.

We can recognize burdens of interpretation as occurring on both input and output. The example above illustrates a requirement for the user to evaluate the information presented; in other words, an output gap. Equally, we can imagine situations where users have to interpret the actions they want to carry out into functions available in the system. These functions may be more or less close to the actions required. When there is a poor correspondence between user actions and system functions, the result is an input gap. Let us examine each of these possibilities more closely.

Input gaps

In a well-designed system, the functions provided by the system correspond closely to the actions intended by the user. All too often, however, the functions correspond to the internal behaviour or states of the system. As a result, the user is obliged to decompose a single real-world task into several system tasks. This kind of gap is exhibited by many transaction processing applications. The user is presented with a set of screens that correspond to editing the underlying database tables. To carry out a business task, the user must determine which tables to edit, and compose the business task from a number of system functions.

For example, in an order processing application, the designer will typically think in terms of master records (order headers) and detail records (order line items). The user, on the other hand, just thinks in terms of orders. The result is that, for example, the designer may oblige the user always to enter a header before he is allowed to enter line items, whereas the user may want to work the other way around. The user is obliged to decompose his single task into the designer's two tables. Perhaps the worst example of this gap is Mail Merge in most word processors. Microsoft Word Version 2.0's online help lists 14 distinct steps in the overview alone!

Consider the File Manager tool provided with Microsoft Windows 3.1 (one of the most highly criticized tools in the product). One of the most confusing actions within File Manager is moving and copying files:

- To *move* a file from one directory to another, click on the file and drag it to the destination.

- To *copy* a file from one directory to another, click and drag while holding the Control key down.
- If the file is moved from one *disk* to another with click and drag, it is actually copied.

So the user must first know whether the source and destination are on the same drive, before he can know what the copy command is — with Control if the drive is the same, without Control if the drives are different. File Manager fails to hide from the user a detail of the file system implementation that is totally irrelevant to the user's conception of the task to be performed.

Another example comes from the world of consumer electronics (just to show that software designers are not the only ones who make mistakes!). Both the stereo in my car and in my home have auto-reverse cassette players. Both have electronic control panels with buttons labelled '≪' and '≫'. In my car, '≪' always means Rewind, '≫' means fast forward. At home, on the other hand, '≪' means advance the tape to the left, '≫' means advance to the right. Before you can determine which control is fast forward and which is rewind, you have to figure out which way the tape is running! It is hard to fault the design in terms of visibility or mappings — it is perfectly clear what the controls are, and what they do. The fault is in the fact that what the controls do does not correspond to what the user wants to do.

The car stereo has another attractive feature that reduces the input gap. As you drive around the country, the frequency that a national radio station broadcasts on changes as you move out of range of one transmitter and into another. (For technical reasons, adjacent transmitters may not broadcast on the same frequency.) With older car radios, you had to re-tune the radio for best reception. With a modern radio, you can tune to a particular *station* rather than a frequency. The radio then re-tunes itself automatically to the strongest signal as you move around. In design terms, the interface of the radio is expressed in the terminology of the user and in terms of the tasks (needs) of the user.

Output gaps

The other side of this coin is the output gap. As well as the simple example above of how data is presented, we can widen the definition to include how easily the user can determine the state of the system. The 'state' in this context has a very broad meaning. It includes such things as whether there are changes outstanding (an edited file is unsaved or changed records are uncommitted), or whether the user is holding locks, or if the application is in 'query' mode or 'data entry' mode. The gap between the visible state of a system and the meaning of that state is an output gap.

In a well-designed system, the system presents information about its state and the results of actions in terms that match those required by the user, rather than in terms of the underlying system. As a result the user is not obliged to interpret the visible system state to determine whether the intended action succeeded or not. For example, the radio mentioned above displays the name of the selected station, rather than the frequency.

One GUI construction tool that I have worked with generates applications that regularly produce messages such as 'Transaction committed. Seven records posted'. In terms of feedback, this is hard to fault — it is perfectly true, and completely accurate; unfortunately it is totally meaningless to the user. One experienced analyst, the first time he saw this, read the message carefully, then turned to me and asked, 'Is that right?' Good question: how many records *should* have been posted? Unless you know how many tables the application is supposed to update in response to your action, the feedback is useless. A message such as 'Work saved', although presenting less information would have been more relevant, and in consequence more useful.

In between these two examples lies the kind of output that may be meaningful to some users but not to others. Some television weather forecasts present weather maps that show fronts, air pressure highs and lows, anticyclones and other elements of weather systems that are meaningful to a meteorologist. Other weather presentations show 'icons' representing clouds, rain, snow, wind and sun. In other words, the latter map is presented in terms that are meaningful to the average viewer, whereas the former map has to be interpreted by an expert before its implications can be understood. As in so many areas, only good knowledge of the users will determine the appropriate degree of interpretation or abstraction.

Summary

The elements that we have defined here and have illustrated by examples from both within and without the software world, will reappear throughout this book. They are principles that apply at each level and in every facet of design.

There are instances where these rules can be deliberately broken. One particularly interesting area is in the world of games. The famous computer game 'Adventure' is deliberately almost completely void of visibility and cues. This is part of the challenge. It is instructive to note that while this game is much played by technical people like ourselves, its attraction is almost wholly lost on the people who are generally the users of our applications. Chess-playing readers may like to consider the idea that part of the challenge of chess stems from the fact that the game is constructed deliberately to break many of these rules. For example, there is a huge burden of interpretation placed on the player: the gap between the visible positions of the pieces and the interpreted state of the game may be huge. It may be suggested that part of the art of commercial game design consists in breaking the rules of good design (in our sense) just enough to be challenging to your target buyers, but not so much as to overwhelm them.

Just enough psychology

It is not the purpose of this book to dwell on the finer points of perceptual theory or cognitive science. On the other hand, certain results from the world of psychology are so fundamental to the way that people work and learn that it would be foolish to ignore them. If we are aware of these principles, we can attempt to avoid many errors of design that reduce users' satisfaction and productivity. Without wanting to bury ourselves in conflicting theories of psychology, thought and learning, some well-established and widely accepted results will be of significance to us. Three areas are of particular relevance to the user interface designer: memory, learning and working styles.

The workings of memory will affect how easy users find applications to use. If we can align our applications with our understanding of memory, users will find that they are asked to remember less; and the things that they are asked to remember are more easily retrieved.

It is widely accepted that human memory has multiple levels of storage, though exactly how many levels is still a subject of debate. Most models of memory accept that there is an apparent mechanism of short-term memory, which works in ways that are very different from the way that 'learned' or 'memorized' infor-mation is processed in long-term memory. We will therefore examine short-term and long-term memory separately.

Learning is closely related to memory, but for the purposes of this book it is useful to draw a distinction between the way that users memorize *information* and they way they build, improve, discard and replace *concepts*, beliefs or models of the system with which they are working. Learning will strongly influence how quickly users reach a level of competence with an application, and also how high a level of competence they will reach.

Working styles will strongly affect the kind of application that users are most comfortable using. An application that one user finds too rigid, another may find lacks structure. Comfort in turn will influence the productivity of the user, as well as the strength of the motivation both to use and to learn the application.

Short-term memory

As we noted above, memory works on several levels, one of which is short-term memory (STM). This is also known as working memory in some models of memory, but I shall avoid that term as it is used with quite different meaning in other models. Short-term memory is used to hold information that we are working with but which is discardable once we have used it. If you like computer analogies, you can think of short-term memory as acting like the registers of a processor, whereas long-term memory is more like RAM or core, if you prefer the older term. It is inadvisable to push the computer analogy too far, though, as we risk straying into one of the most controversial areas of cognitive psychology!

Duration

Short-term memory really does have a very short duration, perhaps as little as 15 to 30 seconds when unaided. Retention in short-term memory can be extended through 'rehearsal' — for example, repeating a telephone number to yourself out loud until you can dial it. Rehearsal is akin to a juggler spinning plates: give the plate a spin every few seconds and it will stay up. It is also reminiscent of the mercury loop memories of early computers. Short-term memory also seems to be strongly 'acoustic' in nature. For example, things that can be recited with a rhythm or phrases that are alliterative are retained more easily.

In addition, short-term memory is very easily disrupted by external stimuli, as you will know if anybody has ever asked you what you are doing when you are in the middle of totalling a column of figures.

Capacity and chunking

There is a well-established principle that most people can retain seven (plus or minus two) 'bits' of information in short-term memory. Interestingly, it does not seem to matter too much how complex the 'bits' are. For example, most people can remember seven randomly chosen letters, or seven unrelated words, or the names of seven popular songs. In other words, we can increase the amount of information held in short-term memory by 'chunking' items together into more significant semantic units.

Studies have shown that one of the differences between novice and expert chess players is in the way that they picture the board. The novice thinks in terms of 'my bishop on that square and his rook on that one' — one chunk for each piece position. The expert thinks 'my bishop dominating the long diagonal, and his rook supporting his pawn structure' — one chunk for complex structures and interactions of pieces. This is one of the mechanisms that allows chess players to analyse positions to remarkable depths.

Experiments demonstrate that expert players are much better at reconstructing from memory chess positions briefly seen, but no better than novices at reconstructing random arrangements of the pieces. It takes considerable study as well as natural skill for a chess player to learn to chunk chess structures effectively. If we want our applications to be easier than chess, we have a responsibility to chunk efficiently the information that we present to the user.

Of particular relevance to us as designers is the fact that short-term memory is used to hold and resolve short-term goals. For example, if the goal is 'save the file', you hold this goal while you find and execute the save command. The user of any application (or anybody else carrying out a mental task) is continually building short lists of goals in short-term memory and resolving them. One of the key differences between a simple task (print a file) and a complex task (perform a mail merge) is whether the goal and all of the steps can be held in short-term memory.

Lessons for the designer

As we noted above, the capacity of short-term memory can be increased by chunking. Imagine a task consisting of nine steps. If the nine steps are distinct, few people will be able to hold the entire process in short-term memory. It must therefore be committed to and recalled from long-term memory, leading to a dramatic fall in productivity: every time the user recalls the goal, he forgets one of the steps. On the other hand, if you present the task to the user as three major tasks, each with three minor steps, the user is asked to retain only six chunks at a time (the three major steps and the minor steps of the major step in progress). Each major step facilitates the recall of the component minor steps. This strongly suggests that the application designer should structure complex tasks into sets of simpler tasks on behalf of the user. (Interestingly, well-designed sales presentations are structured in exactly this way: three or four major agenda items, each with three or four minor items under them. It is tempting to hypothesize a relationship with the capacity of short-term memory. Hypothetically, the audience could retain the overall agenda plus the current set of minor points in short-term memory, provided they are reminded sufficiently often.) Where the complexity of a task exceeds the capacity of short-term memory, the designer should consider ways of providing explicit, visible reminders and prompts to the user.

Because chunks are so easily lost from short-term memory, we should also design our applications to avoid unnecessarily breaking the user's attention. A very common mistake is to allow a subtask to become so complex that the user loses the thread of the main task.

Long-term memory

The workings of short-term memory are relatively easy for psychologists to test, and theories about its working are comparatively well established (though by no means universal; for example, there is some uncertainty about the way in which chunks are lost from short-term memory). In contrast, the structure and organization of long-term memory is far less well understood. Is long-term memory a single-level, homogeneous store or a multi-level store of different kinds of memory? Are memories literal images or some form of encoding? How are memories connected to each other? How are memories acquired, recalled and lost? Although there are many questions, some principles are broadly accepted.

Duration and capacity

The capacity of long-term memory seems to be, for all practical purposes, unlimited. There are cases of people who appear to be able to recall in photographic detail everything that has ever happened to them, right down to the emotions they felt at the time. However, this does not mean that we can oblige our users to commit large amounts of information to memory to use our applications! For most people, learning and recall of information require repetition and effort.

Although chunks can come and go from short-term memory at bewildering speed, it seems that a lot more effort is required to get an organized idea (as opposed to a sensory impression) into long-term memory. Correspondingly, more effort is required to recall chunks from long-term memory. Furthermore, memories in long-term memory seem to fade with time if they are not used. Opinion is divided over whether the memories are completely lost or merely become difficult to access.

Recognition and recall

One of the complexities of long-term memory is the problem of multi-level retrieval. Different ways of retrieving information appear to have radically different difficulties. Although these distinctions are not hard and fast, it is useful to distinguish between at least two levels. (This is a great simplification compared to accepted psychological models, some of which distinguish many forms of retrieval, but will suffice for our purposes.)

Recognition, the simpler of these levels, is a form of prompted retrieval. That prompting may come from the social context, environment, or immediate history of the task you are working on. Recognition occurs when we are asked to choose between a small number of possible answers, as in a multiple choice test. For example, if you were to be asked 'Which is the capital of Hungary: Prague, Budapest or Warsaw?', recognition would be at work. Recognition is strongly constrained by context. For example you may have experienced the embarrassment of meeting somebody you know well in one context, such as a business acquaintance, and failing to recognize them in another context, such as at a sports club.

Recognition is all about relying on just enough information: in a test of recognition we only need to be able to distinguish between the possibilities. As a result, recognition is easily fooled by near misses. For example, if 'Budapest' is replaced by 'Bucharest' in the question above, many people will mistakenly pick 'Bucharest'.

Recall is a kind of brute force access to memory. If we were to be asked for the capital of Hungary without being offered any choices, we would rely on recall. Sometimes recall appears to work by a kind of internal trial and error recognition. We ask ourselves, 'Is it X? Is it Y? Is it Z?' until finding an answer that we recognize. We have all experienced the sensation of knowing that we know something, without being able to recall the thing itself. When given the answer, we immediately recognize it as being correct. Recall can be aided by suggestion: the first line of a poem, for example, can unlock recall of the remainder. In general, knowing how something starts, whether it is a story, a poem, dance steps or a sequence of actions, greatly facilitates recall. In other words, memories appear to have 'entry points'. Sometimes it is only possible to recall something by finding an appropriate entry point and following it to the required memory. For example, if you were asked how many days in the month of August, you might well use an aide-memoire such as the rhymes that school children are taught. Thus you would recall the number of days in all the months from January to July, before arriving at August. This can hardly be described as an optimal search strategy, but it is a common phenomenon in recall mechanisms.

Unlike recognition which relies on 'just enough' discrimination, recall relies on all the information. To put it another way, recognition involves distinguishing the answer only from the other choices on offer; recall involves distinguishing the answer from everything else you know! Few people would disagree that recall is harder than recognition. Ask any student whether they would prefer to face a multiple choice or an essay test.

Lessons for the designer

When we exhaust the limits of short-term memory and have to resort to long-term memory mechanisms (as we shall inevitably and frequently have to do), we should promote recognition over recall wherever possible. For example, command line interfaces (command interpreters) rely almost entirely on recall. In the different command interpreters that I use on a regular basis, the text editor might be invoked as 'edit', 'e', 'vi' or 'edlin'. It is an effort of pure recall to remember the edit command in any given environment. One of the benefits of visibility, which we discussed earlier, is to promote recognition: when all commands or functions are visible, they are more likely to be recognized. When commands or functions are invisible, we must rely on recall (or in practice, crib-sheets taped to the side of the monitor or keyboard!).

Visibility alone, however, is not sufficient to support recognition. For example, suppose you are working in a Unix shell that provides commands such as 'grep', 'em', 'vi' and 'awk'. For the average user, making the commands visible would not be much of an improvement! Promoting recognition also demands choosing appropriate mappings and cues, and expressing functionality in the user's terminology.

There are many mechanisms to promote recognition; pop-down menus and pushbuttons are obvious choices. Well-organized menus are especially powerful. If the menu names and items are well chosen, the user will be able quickly to locate and identify the required command. Unfortunately, there are many menu systems that are a windowed equivalent of the Unix shell. One Microsoft Windows application that I use regularly includes menu items with names such as 'Impl', 'Db Des', and 'Ue'. And this is an application released in the 1990s!

Effective use of recognition also demands that different functions are easily discriminated; otherwise the interface demands an act of recall to separate them. For example, one application that I have used has a 'Control' menu, which includes the items 'Accept' and 'Apply'. One of these saves any changes and closes the window; the other saves without closing. Which is which? Unintentionally closing the window, and having to reopen it, makes this application extremely frustrating to use. Another application has menu items 'Print setup' and 'Page setup'. Remembering which parameters are set under which item is impossible. You simply have to hunt under both any time you want to adjust the settings.

Learning and internal models

If models of memory are relevant to how people use applications in an immediate, interactive sense and also in a short-term, goal-oriented sense, we also need to consider learning, which will affect how people use applications over the longterm. Learning will determine how quickly users become productive, how much of the capabilities of the system they learn to use, and how much they will retain when they are away from the application (for example, on vacation).

Although models of learning are even more complex and controversial than models of memory, two principles emerge that are of importance to us. First of all, intelligent people tend to learn not by rote but by developing internal models of the world. Second, people tend to learn as little as they can get away with; and as a corollary, having once learnt something, they are reluctant to give up that knowledge in favour of a better model.

The models that people build may be more or less accurate, and they manifest themselves in a number of ways depending on their sophistication and level of abstraction. For example, in solving the kind of number puzzles found in socalled intelligence tests, you may begin by tackling each problem independently, transferring only numerical skills from problem to problem. After some practice, you may begin to recognize that all such puzzles are drawn from a relatively small number of question classes, each of which can be tackled with a particular strategy. For example, one class of problems may involve number series such as 1, 5, 9, 13..., where the difference between each number is a constant. A second, more complex class might include the series 1, 5, 10, 16..., where the difference between each number is itself increased by a constant. Once you begin to recognize these problem classes, you have a transferable 'meta-skill': each problem can be solved by first discovering which class it belongs to, and then solving the particular instance of this class.

Theories and superstitions

This is just one kind of abstraction: the important point being that, in general, people tend to tackle many kinds of problems by looking for patterns, then abstracting rules that describe those patterns. (For these purposes, we can think of learning to use the application as being akin to solving a series of problems.) Having deduced a rule, the user then uses that rule, consciously or unconsciously, to make predictions about the behaviour of the application, and bases future behaviour on expectations deduced from those rules. These beliefs, if they are well founded, are like scientific theories about the application. This tendency to build models is so strong that users will often see patterns where none exist, and deduce incorrect rules from those patterns. I call these incorrect or partially correct beliefs 'superstitions', and once acquired they are very hard to dislodge.

Some superstitions are, to those of us of a technical background, completely irrational. For example, one user that I met was convinced that saving her work to her local disk was causing her network connection to be dropped. In fact, the network connection was thoroughly unreliable and dropped all the time. It was only the fact that the 'Save' command coincidentally tested the network connection and reported its failure that misled the user to form this superstition.

Other superstitions are more understandable. One application design tool that I use always prompts the user if she is about to do something that will discard work, such as closing a tool without saving any changes that have been made. There is just one exception: if she hits the 'Escape' key while in the window layout editor, the layout editor closes without prompting or saving. There is no warning of this. It is clear to my mind who is at fault here, and it is not the user!

For a third example let us return to the Unix shell. Beginners may start by learning simple commands such as 'cp' (copy a file), 'mv' (move or rename a file) and 'rm' (remove a file), from which they might infer the simple rule, 'command names are formed from the first two consonants of the command'. Next they learn 'vi', so the rule must be modified to allow for exceptions, although the two-letter rule still seems to hold. Then they learn commands like 'sort', 'grep' and 'cut'. Reluctantly they are forced to accept that there are no rules: some commands are sensible abbreviations, some are obscure abbreviations, some are the full name of the command, and some are apparently random syllables. They simply have to memorize the names of the commands. (In fairness, there are significant rules of structure embedded in the Unix system, but they are to be found in the realm of the system programmer, not in the levels most immediately visible to the user. Perhaps this is why it is often said that Unix is a far more attractive system for the technician than it is for the ordinary user.)

Hill climbing

Most users (but by no means all) will learn as little as they can get away with to use a system successfully. There are exceptions, of course: some users are highly motivated to become as proficient as they can with a tool or application, perhaps because they have great curiosity about the tools they are given to use, or for reasons of peer recognition. But these users are generally in a minority. For most users, once they have learned enough to survive, it takes strong motivation to persuade them to go further. Partly this is because of natural human laziness, but more often it is because of the way we design systems. In order to progress to a deeper level of understanding and a higher level of productivity, the user will have to give up what they have already learned.

In general people will not be consciously aware that they are pursuing this strategy; typically they will experience only a reluctance to give up their existing ideas. They will often resist or ignore new information or skills, presenting all kinds of plausible rationalizations for their behaviour, until the pressure to change is irresistible.

I like to compare this strategy to hill climbing. Users begin in a valley, with no knowledge of the application. With time and effort, they gain some understanding and knowledge of the system. They have climbed a foothill, and they have a reasonable view over the slopes below them. Now typically this low hill that the user has climbed involves building a simple internal model that is adequate for their understanding so far. In order to move to a higher hill they have to be prepared first to descend from the low peak they are on; in other words they have to discard the simple model in favour of a truer model.

I encountered this phenomenon many times when I used to teach the Unix environment. Course participants came from a variety of backgrounds, usually with a knowledge of some other operating system. During the first two days of the course, when we were presenting simple commands and basic skills, the participants would construct some internal model of the Unix shell, in terms of the environment they already knew. For example, MS-DOS users would assume that the shell was similar to the command interpreter they were familiar with. On the third day of the course, we would begin to use advanced features of the shell. In order to fully understand what was happening, and so to exploit the system most effectively, participants now had to be willing to discard the model they had built so far and replace it with a more accurate one; otherwise they would never come to terms with subtleties of the Unix shell, such as the way that file name 'wildcards' are expanded. Most people, being from a technical background and motivated to learn, made the transition without great difficulty. Others tried to mould the new material into their existing model, which of course was not a successful strategy. They struggled through the remainder of the course with an increasingly cumbersome and baroque internal model.

Lessons for the designer

Given that users are keen to learn rules and internalize models, the second-worst thing you can do is offer them systems where there are no rules to be found. The very worst you can do is to delude them into forming incomplete or incorrect rules. Ideally, a good designer will first conceive of a 'scientific universe' for the users, a system in which consistent, reliable rules are to be found. Second, the designer will construct the system in such a way that the users can easily discover the laws of the system, or even make the laws manifest from the outset.

As an example, consider the Apple Macintosh desktop. Very quickly, the user of a Mac forms the rule that a document is discarded by dropping it in the waste-basket. Soon afterwards the user discovers that a document can be printed by dropping it on the printer. In fact this method generalizes across the system. By contrast the Microsoft Windows user learns that some documents can be printed by dropping them on the Print Manager icon, but not all, as shown in Fig. 1.11. Documents cannot be deleted at all from the desktop, as the user discovers: the user must find another tool, such as File Manager or a DOS session. Where are the rules?

Rules such as those in the Mac's desktop do not occur by accident. They are designed into the core of the application or system. If the designer does not have a clear and explicit concept of the unifying rules of the system presented to the user, then we should not be surprised if the user cannot discover a coherent model. This idea of unifying rules is the subject of Chapter 2.

Since we also know that users are reluctant to discard the models that they have built, we should think very carefully about the popular suggestion of having a novice mode and an expert mode in our applications, one easy to learn but limited in scope, the other more difficult but more powerful. This is not to say that novice modes (or 'training wheels' as they are sometimes called) are not of value. Online coaches or tutors that guide the user through complex tasks, more prompting and verification, 'balloon' help, and other online aids are all extremely worthwhile. The danger to avoid is that of raising a barrier that makes the transi-

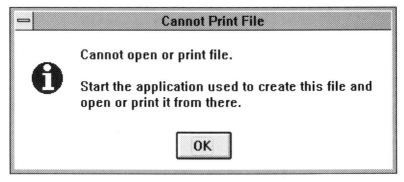

Figure 1.11. The associated application does not support 'drag and drop' printing

tion from novice to expert more difficult than it would be if there were only a single mode of expression. If learning the powerful expert mode means unlearning the simpler novice mode — if the two modes express themselves in quite different ways — many users will never get beyond the novice mode. Instead we should design our applications so that users can begin with a simple set of core skills. Within those skills, the key concepts, a true model of the system, are already embodied. Additional skills are then gained by learning independent sets of skills that build on and reinforce, rather than undermine, the original model.

Consider, for example, a flight booking system, designed to enable a travel agent to locate a flight that best matches the customer's requirements. The core skill in this application is to list flights matching certain criteria such as departure and destination airports, date and time of travel, and possibly cost. In a well-designed system, the user will learn that the model they are working with is based around the idea of 'flight segments': each leg of a journey is a segment. Initially the user will only know how to request and book single-segment journeys, and the idea of a segment may seem like a needless complication, since a segment is the same as a flight. However, as she progresses in experience she can move naturally to the skills required to plan multi-segment flights, taking account of minimum transfer times at different airports, incorporating stopovers into the customer's itinerary, and so on. The model that the user began with is extended, rather than discarded. On the other hand, if we allow the user to begin with a simpler concept that a flight is an indivisible whole, ignoring segments as an unnecessary complication, the user will later have to unlearn what she knows and relearn the concept of segments. Better to design our applications so that users can learn a true model in the first place.

Working styles

One of the greatest difficulties in designing for the user is the inevitable question, which user? Users come in all shapes, sizes, educational backgrounds, levels of motivation and temperaments, and it is a rare blessing to be given a homogeneous population to design for. It is also a rare extravagance to be allowed to design more than one user interface (or equally, an adaptable user interface) for the different user constituencies. Often the best we can do is to try to design for the majority; the concept of working styles is intended to help us to generalize about what will work well for the majority of the users in a given situation, and to try to minimize the impact on users who do not fit the stereotypes.

The needs of minorities will often be one of the most complex issues that the user interface designer has to deal with. This can be especially difficult if a particular minority is disproportionately influential. For example, the buying decision may be made by a cadre of managers whose skills and needs are quite different from the 'knowledge workers' who will most often use the application. Alternatively, you may be faced with an evaluation process that involves user representatives of far higher technical sophistication than the clerical workers who will be the ultimate users; the evaluators may be looking for complex functionality that is no real benefit to target community.

Personality types

The Jungian model of personality types attempts to describe personality using four pairs of opposites, discussed below. The model is best known through a kind of psychological profiling known as a Myers-Briggs test. The significance of the model for us as user interface designers is that it casts a lot of light on people's preferred styles of communication and working, and hence the style of application that they will find most productive. Equally importantly, it illustrates ways in which people who are attracted to computing differ from the 'average' person, which can help us to understand why users do not necessarily find our applications as intuitive as we do.

The four pairs of attributes are:

- *Extrovert/introvert* This has little to do with the everyday meanings of these words. An introvert is somebody whose natural focus of attention is inward; an extrovert is naturally focused outwards. Extroverts tend to be more natural communicators, because they enjoy external stimuli. This is not to say that introverts do not communicate well, only that it does not come as easily to them. Also, introverts may be unaware of when they are *not* communicating well.
- *Sensory/intuitive* Sensory people are attuned to the immediate impressions of their senses. They are practical and observant, and highly oriented to the concrete rather than the abstract. Intuitive people are more attuned to their internal world. They are creative and imaginative, and respond well to metaphors and patterns.
- *Thinking/feeling* Thinking people have explicit reasons for their actions, feeling people act more on overall impression. This is not to say that thinkers necessarily have better reasons, but they are definitely better at expressing them verbally. Most importantly, thinkers and feelers have a hard time making each other understand their reasons for doing something.
- *Perception/judgement* Judging people like to get the point, as soon as they feel that they have enough information. Perceiving people prefer to gather more information and postpone any decision. Judging types like to come to a conclusion as soon as possible, tending towards hard and fast choices. Perceiving types may never come to a conclusion at all!

The most important point to understand about this kind of test is that the comparisons are not judgemental. Although some of the words carry prejudices in everyday speech, in the test they are intended purely to be descriptive. It is also important to realize that the categories are not designed to be balanced; the test tells you how you stand compared to a particular point of reference, not some mythical 'average' of the population. The personality type is analogous to asking whether a person lives north or south of Edinburgh: it is patently meaningless to ask whether north or south is 'better'; it is equally obvious that the majority of people in Britain live south of that point.

Two of these categorizations are of particular interest to us. Studies have shown that around 75 per cent of the population as a whole are extrovert rather than introvert. In the computer industry, we see a quite different picture. Among programmers, a 1984 study (Sitton and Chmelir, 1984) found the population to be split 50–50 between extroverts and introverts; among Apple engineers, a good place to look for a high proportion of people concerned with the user interface, according to Tognazinni (1992), the split is 60–40 in favour of extroverts.

If we look at the sensory/intuitive comparison, the figures are even more interesting. In the population, 75 per cent are sensory rather than intuitive; among programmers it is again 50–50; and 75 per cent of Apple engineers are intuitive!

Lessons for the designer

As the figures above indicate, the average computer professional is quite different from the average user. We are more likely to be introvert than they are, and hugely more likely to be intuitive. In consequence our users will, in general, prefer user interfaces that are concrete (sensory rather than intuitive), with a lot of visibility, whereas we designers will not feel so uncomfortable using an application that relies on invisible, abstract models. As intuitive, introverted people we are quite happy to internalize our own models whereas our users want us to present a model explicitly to them. Users, on the other hand, may prefer well-defined paths through applications, rather than being asked to 'deduce' those paths. What we regard as flexibility, they may find to be vagueness and lack of direction. I have often heard debates about an aspect of a design where the implementor asks, 'Why can't we leave this free for the user to choose?' Broadly speaking, users may be far less enthusiastic about being 'left to choose' than we would be. They might be far more comfortable with a single, well-defined, professionally chosen path than the 'freedom' of multiple possibilities. Users do not necessarily see an application as a way of expressing their creativity!

Personality types are a way of generalizing about our expectations of the broad needs of different classes of users. I cannot emphasize too strongly that whenever we generalize, there will be exceptions! We have only considered the splits for the population as a whole so far. In our position as user interface designers, we also need to recognize that working styles are very strongly determined by the job or role demanded of the user, as well as the user's own personality. That is, we can think of a job itself as having a particular 'personality type', in other words the kind of personality best suited to that job. Few people have the luxury of being permitted to work purely in a style that conforms to their personality type.

I would strongly recommend to any designer:

- *Take a Myers-Briggs test yourself* (If you work in a medium-sized or large company, your Personnel or Human Resources department may be able to help.) This will help you understand your own preferred style of working, as well as helping you to understand how users differ from many of us.
- *When designing, try to understand the 'personality type' of the user or of the user's job* Try to imagine this person's style of working as you design. This will help you to understand the kind of presentation and interaction that is called for.
- *Try to team up with a colleague whose personality is complementary to yours* This person can be a valuable asset in helping you to understand how the other three quarters of the population think.

When users are evaluating your prototypes, if they find your ideas and presentation difficult to understand, avoid treating this as personal criticism. Ask yourself whether this is because you have designed an interface that is suitable for your personality type, but not for theirs.

Personality types and their impact on usability form an immense subject, and we have only scratched the surface of the subject in this section. Interested readers may wish to pursue Chapter 15 in Tognazzini (1992) and Chapter 8 in Thimbleby (1990). The former discusses in detail the differences between designers and users, and how we can make allowance for them in the design process. The latter draws some very interesting conclusions about users' working styles, which has important implications for the applications we eventually produce.

Case study: Microsoft Word

Microsoft Word Version 6.0 has undergone a considerable revision from the previous version (which was called, confusingly, Version 2.0). Many of the changes are very effective but others have not worked so well. We can usefully consider some of these changes and try to analyse their successes and failures in terms of the above terminology (Table 1.1 overleaf).

Overall, Microsoft Word Version 6.0 has gone a long way towards improving visibility and making the interface more concrete, but is still not perfect. Between Version 6.0 and the previous version, there are a number of changes in appearance that significantly improve the visibility and feedback, but some of the mappings remain clumsy. My impression on comparing the two is that Microsoft has attempted to respond to feedback from existing users, but in places might have done better to re-examine the fundamental assumptions.

If you have access to two implementations of a single application, either from different suppliers, or different releases of a single product, it is a worthwhile exercise at this point to practise your understanding of the material presented in this chapter by comparing and criticizing the two versions in the terminology presented, as I have done for Microsoft Word in Table 1.1.

Feature	Version 2.0	Version 6.0	Remarks
Create and format a table	Borders, shading, and title formatting are specified individually (many steps)	Standard templates allow commonly used formatting to be applied in a single step	Much reduced input gap
Create a cross-reference	Insert a bookmark at the target of the cross-reference. Later insert a field that references the bookmark	Insert a reference field, and at the same time select the item to be referenced	Two separate tasks have become one. The implementation is marred by an overly complex dialog (poor mappings)
See where you are on the page	The status bar at the bottom (Figure 1.12) of the screen shows position, e.g. 'At 5.9 cm'	Rulers at side and top (Figure 1.13) show both position and margin settings	Much improved visibility at the cost of some screen space
Change page layout and margin settings	Type measurements into dialog, or go to Print Preview	The side and top rulers can be manipulated directly	Reduced input gap, immediate feedback, direct mapping
Copy formatting	Obscure combination of key clicks and mouse selection. Subtle distinction between paragraph format and character format	'Pick and Drop' metaphor for copying formatting using new toolbar icon	An abstract, invisible, arbitrarily mapped action has become concrete and visible

Table 1.1

Stages of user interface design

When a programmer builds a large application, she does not plunge directly into coding without first structuring the code, identifying key algorithms and defining

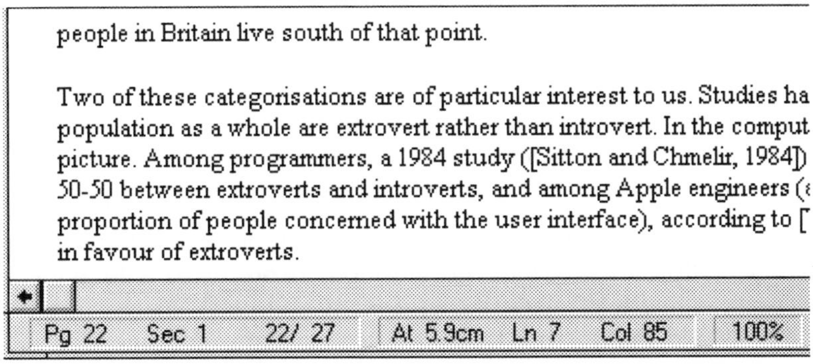

people in Britain live south of that point.
Two of these categorisations are of particular interest to us. Studies ha
population as a whole are extrovert rather than introvert. In the comput
picture. Among programmers, a 1984 study ([Sitton and Chmelir, 1984])
50-50 between extroverts and introverts, and among Apple engineers (
proportion of people concerned with the user interface), according to [
in favour of extroverts.
Pg 22 Sec 1 22/ 27 At 5.9cm Ln 7 Col 85 100%

Figure 1.12. Page position in Microsoft Word Version 2.0

Chapter 1
Fundamental Principles
"When simple things need labels or instructions, the desi
Psychology of Everyday Things'.

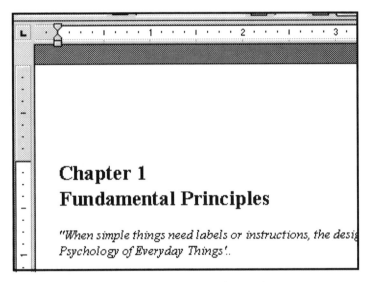

Figure 1.13. Page position in Microsoft Word Version 6.0

major data structures. Nor does a data modeller, faced with a complex database design, set down a complete model in a single uninterrupted burst of inspiration. A data modeller may well break down the design process into a number of stages:

- Select a data representation, identifying major entities
- Define table design and table relationships
- Complete column details
- Define column constraints and defaults

Of course, these steps are not completely distinct: late in the design process, the modeller may still be breaking out lookup tables or merging code tables, but the process still provides a useful framework to the designer. Analogously, we can propose a process for the user interface designer:

- Select a conceptual model, identifying taskflow
- Identify major windows and dialog flow
- Define fields and detailed window layout
- Define field constraints and defaults

These stages represent of course only a small portion of the total design effort. To be fully effective they need to be incorporated into an encompassing design method that relates the user interface to task analysis, prototyping, user analysis and many other tasks. These stages are only intended to outline the breakdown of the user interface, not to define the entire design process! This framework also defines the outline of the remainder of this book. Before embarking on that detailed discussion, I offer here a brief definition of each of these stages.

The conceptual model

A conceptual model characterizes the application. The model provides a framework, a set of consistent guidelines, within which the user discovers and learns rules. Rather than leaving the user completely free and unaided to form his or her own model, a good designer will explicitly choose a model and attempt to make that model manifest, or at least easily discoverable.

Let us consider simple text editors, which essentially fall into two classes: line editors, such as 'edlin' under DOS or 'ed' under Unix; and full-screen editors, such as 'edit' from DOS or 'Notepad' from Microsoft Windows. Table 1.2 compares these two styles of working in terms of the user's model, and the actions that are available to the user.

	Line editor	Screen editor
User model	A document consists of a sequence of lines	A document consists of a body of text
Editing actions	Insert, delete, join and break lines	Type. The editor wraps lines as necessary
Positioning actions	Specify line number. List text to verify position	Point and click with a mouse, or manoeuvre with arrow keys
Move blocks of text	Entire lines may be moved. Lines must be broken and joined manually	Choose arbitrary selections of text. Cut (or copy) and paste to new location

Table 1.2

When I use this example in seminars I occasionally hear objections to the effect that line editors are an archaic relic of old technology, a hangover from the days of 300 and 1200 baud dumb terminals linked to remote mainframes — these days, nobody would dream of writing a line editor. Unfortunately, this is not so! It was only relatively recently that DOS's line mode 'edlin' was replaced by the full screen 'edit'. Yet there has never been a technological excuse for a line mode editor on a PC. Poor design is more often due to lack of imagination than lack of technology.

I frequently see brand new Windows applications accessing relational databases that present the user with the fields 'Address Line 1', 'Address Line 2', 'Address Line 3' and so on. Windows is perfectly capable of presenting a multi-line edit box and the database can readily store the whole address as a single column. Yet the application obliges the user to split the address arbitrarily into separate lines. In fact, we are still writing brand new line editors and inflicting them on our users! In terms of the burden of interpretation, a line editor is closer to the representation of that data whereas a screen editor is closer to the utilization. This is a perfect illustration of the significance of choosing the right presentation. It is important to understand that the input and output gaps that arise in a line editor are not directly attributable to a poor choice of functions or commands. The commands chosen are about the best you can do once you have accepted this poor model.

Good design begins with a good choice of model. The overall structure and much of the detail of the design will often follow easily and naturally from a well-chosen model. A wrong choice of model, on the other hand, will cripple the design from the outset. Getting the model right is the single most important decision that the user interface designer must make, and the next chapter is devoted entirely to this subject.

Workflow and taskflow

Workflow is a characteristic of a business task; it describes the sequence of actions performed by a user or users to complete a business task. For example, in processing a stock delivery, the sequence might consist of:

- Identify the delivery (supplier, order number, etc.)
- Compare the delivery note with the original order
- Compare the actual delivery with the delivery note
- Accept (fully or partially) the delivery into the warehouse
- Enter the delivery details into the stock control system

By extension, we apply the term *taskflow* to an application. In this case, the term describes the sequences of actions supported by the application. Example taskflows from a typical word processor include:

- Check the spelling
- Check the grammar

- Perform a mail merge
- Save a copy of the document under another name
- Create a bulleted, indented list
- Convert text into tabular format

Notice, by the way, that I am using the word 'supported' in its (almost extinct) normal English sense. By 'supported' I mean that the application *helps* the user to carry out the task (as opposed to the computer industry's common usage where 'supported' generally means anything that is possible, regardless of how manual or difficult the task may be!).

Notice also that we are not using the term *workflow* in the way that it is sometimes used in the software industry; rather we are using it in the way it is used in the world of management consultancy or business re-engineering, where the term refers to the way a task is passed from person to person around an organization. (In the software industry, the corresponding area of study is *workgroup computing* or sometimes *workflow computing*.) Workgroup computing is a large subject in its own right; it will influence not only the user interface of individual applications, but also the way in which the whole system is subdivided into applications. It is possible to consider the requirements and implications of workgroup computing as a kind of conceptual super-model for your system.

Dialogs and dialog flow

A *dialog* is a subset of an application's windows consisting of a collection of connected windows that allow the user to carry out an action. *Dialog flow* is the related aspect of user interface design that describes the modality and possible paths through a dialog. Dialog flow, including issues such as modality, is one of the key characteristics that determine how users will 'feel' about your application: whether they find it too strict or too free, too difficult to learn or too restrictive in its capabilities.

Some of the dialog flows in a word processor include:

- Save as. . .
- Print/Print setup
- Insert a table
- Format the page setup (Fig. 1.14)

The relationship between dialog flows and the tasks that they implement is a subtle one, and will be discussed in detail in Chapters 3 and 4.

Detailed design

Detailed design is apparently the easiest part of the process. This is the stage at which detailed screen layouts, including field sizes, positions and prompts, are

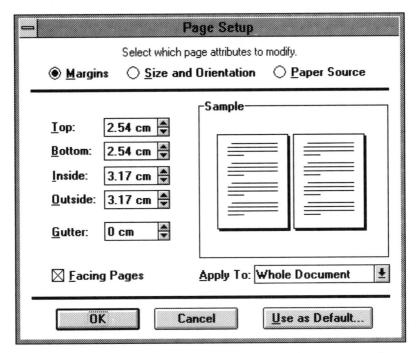

Figure 1.14. One window from the Page Setup dialog in Microsoft Word 2.0

defined. Specific choices of controls are confirmed. There are two major dangers in this stage. First, to many designers it seems that detailed design is all that there is to user interface design. One need only examine the contents of a typical design style guide to see where most of the attention has been focused: field sizes, window colours, and whether or not windows will have scroll bars. As we have tried to demonstrate above, detailed design is only one, albeit important, aspect of the process. Second, because detailed design is apparently easy, it is assumed that anybody can do it. Of course, this is completely untrue. This error is akin to believing that providing the engineers have successfully specified the engine, transmission and suspension of a car, then anybody can be left to design the body work, position the pedals, and lay out the dashboard!

Detailed design is sufficiently important to warrant a significant portion of this book, but at the same time we should remember its position in the overall process.

Character versus graphical user interfaces

It has been suggested that the rules and guidelines discussed in this chapter apply equally well to character and block mode interfaces as to graphical interfaces.

Although in principle this is true, in practice the limitations of a character interface mean that many of the goals identified in this chapter are not realistically achievable.

A character screen has a limited grid of (typically) 80 by 24 characters, with a choice of at most 256 different symbols. Compared to the typical graphical screen's 1000 by 1000 pixels, individually set to anything from 16 to millions of different colours, the character screen dramatically limits the potential visibility — the more functions you make visible, the more you restrict the amount of data presented to the user. This leads to poor mappings, typically arbitrary function keys or sequences of function keys. Functions are often left completely invisible. Feedback is similarly restricted by the limited visual bandwidth.

There have been several attempts to emulate GUI controls such as checkboxes and radio controls with character constructs such as (o) and [X], as well as presenting multiple sizable, moveable windows, but these are rarely satisfactory. The major problems lie in the area of affordance: it is difficult for the user to determine how to operate these 'pseudo-buttons' in the absence of a mouse. The mechanisms for navigating around the screen are also often convoluted. Furthermore, these interfaces tend to be highly modal — you can be in 'menu mode', 'move window' mode, 'normal' mode, for instance — and the functions to move from one mode to another are often themselves invisible and arbitrary. If interfaces were vehicles, character mode would be a train, GUI a sports car. You do not put a steering wheel on a train.

In my opinion, it is unreasonable to expect to be able to build really good user interfaces without the flexibility and richness of the graphical environment. Of course this does not mean that if you are obliged to build for character mode, you should ignore these principles. Consistent, well-chosen functions and as much visibility as possible will help, but you should not be surprised that such a narrow 'information channel' is difficult to work with.

In my professional life I am often asked about the practicalities of deploying a single application across both graphical and character interfaces, particularly as many development tools claim to be able to deploy an application unchanged to both environments. My advice depends on how much resource you can devote to the interface: if you can, design two separate interfaces for the two environments. If this is not practical, design for the character environment and restrict yourself to its limitations. I have yet to encounter a successful application designed for the graphical environment and deployed to character terminals.

Summary

Much of this chapter has focused on errors of design as the most effective illustration of underlying principles. Let us summarize what we have said so far by making some positive assertions about good design. In this chapter we began with two fundamental principles of all design: simple tasks deserve a simple interface; complex tasks require guidance and elucidation. We then attempted to explore these rules in more detail, by trying to identify elements that contribute to simplicity on the one hand, and to guidance on the other.

The well-designed interface exhibits fundamental characteristics of high visibility, appropriate feedback, concrete mappings and strong cues. By appropriate choice of level, form and language of expression, the design reduces the input and output gaps between the user and the system, thereby reducing the burden of interpretation placed on the user.

A good user interface is designed to support cognitive processes such as memory and learning. It avoids overloading short-term memory, and makes effective use of long-term memory by promoting recognition over recall. The user is helped to learn by the provision of a coherent underlying model. Within the constraints of the real world, the design attempts to support the working style that we expect to be associated with the task in question.

This combination of principles is intended to lead to improved productivity, higher satisfaction and greater effectiveness on the part of the user.

2   Conceptual models

'Technology is the knack of so arranging the world that we don't have to experience it'

Max Frisch

Introduction

As a programmer, one of the major benefits of programming in a high-level language is that you are isolated from the hardware, to a great extent, so that you can focus on the algorithm. (If you don't believe that this is a benefit, you are reading the wrong book!) When users choose to use your application they expect similarly that they will be isolated from the software and will be free to focus on the task in hand.

As discussed in the previous chapter, the graphical environment provides us with the opportunity to isolate the user from the technical details behind the scene. Ultimately, we can even construct a fantasy for the user that is so convincing that the computer itself disappears. This is the illusion of a good user interface. We want the users to interact with the user interface in such a way that they experience the illusion that they are manipulating directly the objects of interest. Perhaps the best-known example of this illusion is the Apple Macintosh desktop: to delete a file, you drag an icon representing the file to the wastebasket and drop it in. As in real life, the file is not irretrievably lost until you empty the wastebasket.

In the jargon of user interface design, we say that the Apple Macintosh takes an office desktop as its *conceptual model*. Individual actions and objects on the desktop use *metaphors*, such as the wastebasket and the document, within the framework provided by the conceptual model.

The terms *conceptual model* and *metaphor* are widely used, but at the time of writing the suggestion that they are core concepts of user interface design is beginning to be questioned. Although they have proved very useful ideas in ground-breaking designs such as Apple's Lisa and Macintosh, at first sight they seem to have less relevance to the world of business applications. An early reviewer of this book asked: what is the metaphor behind a door handle? And a participant in one of my seminars asked, given that many business applications are merely form filling, is there *always* a conceptual model?

In fact these criticisms are coloured by the everyday meanings of these words, rather than the particular meanings intended in the world of user interface design. Because of the meanings associated with these words in everyday English, it is hard to talk about metaphors that are in fact very literal, such as form filling, or conceptual models that are barely abstracted from the real thing. For this reason I intend to use a terminology that is less prejudiced (to the mainstream developer) by previously encountered meanings. This terminology also allows us explicitly to differentiate between various kinds of model. I shall also explain the more commonly used terminology and its relation to the terms I use here. It is important to emphasize that the current backlash is against the terminology used, not the ideas expressed!

Metaphors and models

We introduced the idea of a conceptual model at the end of the previous chapter. The conceptual model is the Big Idea, the unifying vision behind an application. We now turn to the related idea of metaphor. A metaphor is an external representation of a component of, or an action in, the underlying system. We have already seen several examples of metaphors, notably the Apple Desktop and its wastebasket metaphor. Metaphors can be used to represent both data and actions within the system. A metaphor answers the question: what is this like, that the user already understands?

A conceptual model is, in one sense, the highest-level metaphor of an application or system, the metaphor that characterizes the whole system. For example, Lotus Organizer takes a Filofax® or personal organizer as its conceptual model. The conceptual model provides a framework, a set of consistent guidelines, into which all the lower-level models and metaphors fit. Within the personal organizer model, Lotus Organizer includes metaphors based on day planners, month planners, task lists and so on.

One of the roles of the conceptual model is to provide a consistent interpretation across an application. In a well-designed application, each metaphor will fit well into the framework. This allows the user to transfer the model that he has learned from one place to another. One of the great strengths of the Apple Macintosh environment is the common desktop model that is shared by the operating system and all applications. Because every application (at least in theory!) draws on the desktop metaphor, new applications and tasks are more easily learned.

One of the characteristics of poorly designed applications is that they contain metaphors that individually may be strong and useful, but collectively contradict each other or the conceptual model, or have no obvious relationship to the conceptual model. Isolated metaphors are not necessarily useful. They are an example of the incomplete or false rules discussed in the previous chapter. Microsoft Windows, discussed below, exhibits many problems associated with such mixing.

Many people, myself included, use the terms metaphor and conceptual model interchangeably, relying on the context to make the distinction clear. The difference is essentially one of perspective. Let us now turn to a more detailed examination of conceptual models.

Models and the user

The fax software that I use under Windows on my PC uses printing as its metaphor or conceptual model. The fax driver presents itself as just another printer in the Print Setup dialog. To print a document, I simply select the fax as the print destination, then print the document as normal. Notice how the metaphor represents something new, unfamiliar and technically complex — faxing a document — in terms of something already familiar — printing a document. The complexity of the underlying communications software is completely hidden (at least, until something goes wrong!).

As this example illustrates, a metaphor or conceptual model need not be related to a physical object in the outside world, such as a wastebasket. The critical objective of a metaphor is to relate to a referent that is already familiar or readily understood. The referent may be a physical object in the external world, an abstract idea in the user's mind, or an established idea in a computer system, as in the fax example. The key requirement is not that the referent be a physical object. A good choice of referent is one that:

- Is already well understood by the user
- Has a broad range of characteristics that have a correspondence in the application

Selection of a good metaphor requires absolutely that you know who your audience is, and what it already understands. The fax as printer metaphor works well for me only because I already understand how to choose between different printers under Windows. To many of the salespeople that I work with, this would be completely unfathomable.

Given that we accept the proposition that the user interface should present an abstraction of the user's task, rather than a more-or-less detailed representation of the data, the question naturally arises, how should that abstraction be chosen?

Defining the model

Key to answering the question posed above is the absolute requirement that we must understand the user's point of view. If the task involves dealing with orders and invoices, no mention of databases and transactions should erupt into the user's view. On the other hand, if the application involves controlling a modem to connect to a bulletin board, it may be necessary that you expose the technical details of serial ports, modem control strings and dial instructions to the user. Otherwise, the user will not have sufficient control to be able to complete the task. Even in this case, however, a good application will provide some isolation. For example, you might ask the user: do you have a standard Hayes-compatible modem, in which case the application defaults everything, or do you need customized control? (Tognazzini (1992) provides an excellent discussion of this topic.)

The fine balance that we need to achieve is to abstract to the user's point of view and present the world at his level, in his terminology, without hiding anything that is necessary for the user to complete the task successfully.

The user interface should represent the work task as the user understands it, not the data model as the designer understands it. There is a vast difference between the designer's *system model*, which is concerned with issues such as representation, storage, access, integrity and efficiency, and the *user model*, which is concerned with issues such as interpretation, manipulation, search and retrieval. Our goal is to model the application at the level of the user task.

What makes a model?

If a conceptual model is to be useful to the user in forming a consistent internal model of the system, it first needs to guide the *designer* in structuring the overall organization of the application. It also sets some guidelines for the choice and implementation of metaphors and models lower down the model. Having chosen a model, we ought to be able to ask of each component of the design, which component of the model does it correspond to? A strong model is a tool for the designer to communicate her vision to the user.

One of the key tasks in choosing a model is to centre the model. For example, the Mac begins with the document as its primary concept; actions are grouped around the document. The user has the illusion that the capabilities of the system (printing, editing and so on) are brought to each document. This is a typical data-centred model.

A business application for order entry might deal on an equal basis with invoices, orders and delivery notes. It would be hard to choose one of these as the central concept. In this case it is attractive to put a task or process, namely Order Processing, at the centre. The application can then guide the user, or indeed several users, through the process, bringing the required documents or forms to the appropriate user as the progress of an order requires.

It is also possible to design applications that are centred neither on data nor processes, but on external entities. For example, a support system for a medical practice might be centred on the patient. Around this centre the user might find both documents, such as patient records, and processes, such as scheduling an appointment at a specialist clinic.

It is fashionable to talk about user-centred design for applications. As the examples above show, this is a more complex goal than it might seem at first sight. Having put the user at the centre, we still need to determine whether then to focus on the user's data or on the user's tasks. We also need to decide who we mean by the user: do we mean the person pushing the keys, or do we mean that person's customer (the doctor's patient, in the example above)?

One of the strengths of the Macintosh is that a single model pervades (almost) the whole system. Under other systems, for example Microsoft Windows, each application is left to choose its own model, or centre. Some applications are document-centred, some are process-centred, and some have no discernible centre at all. In consequence, the user is left to discover the orientation of each application that he uses. If you are responsible for designing a suite of applications, rather than a single application, you should consider carefully the benefits that will accrue to the user if you can find a unifying theme, or model, that can be used consistently across all of your applications.

A second key task, closely enmeshed with the first, is to choose a domain of expression. For example, the Macintosh takes the Desktop as its domain: all of the metaphors and models are expressed in terms of this domain. Lotus Organizer elects the personal organizer. Most business applications adopt form filling. The strength of a choice of domain comes from extending that choice throughout the application or system. The weakness of many business applications is that the user fills in forms as if working on paper, but nothing else in the system resembles in any way a paper-based system, neither its strengths nor weaknesses. Instead we present the user with abstract commands such as 'commit', the relationship of which to either the movement of paper or to business processes may be totally arbitrary.

It is important for the user that the domain of expression is able to describe both input and output. The example mentioned above, the fax machine, illustrates the difficulties that occur when this is not the case. Although the model for sending a fax is clear enough, the model does not extend well to receiving faxes, as we shall see later. If the domain of expression is not used consistently through an application, whether because the chosen domain is not sufficiently expressive, or simply because of a failure to apply the domain consistently, the benefit to the user rapidly becomes diluted.

In summary, the choice of centre and the choice of domain of expression are the two key factors that will determine whether the application is perceived by the user as a coherent and consistent system, or as a jumble of forms and commands.

Common models and metaphors

One of the best ways to learn about good and bad design choices is to examine some real examples. We shall look at some common examples of metaphors or conceptual models, and we shall also compare several different models of a single system, namely file management.

If you examine the applications commonly used in an office or warehouse, you may well find the following metaphors and conceptual models.

Card index

A very common metaphor for simple personal data storage systems, such as contact names, is the card index. Windows comes with the free 'Cardfile' application (Fig. 2.1), which is widely left unused. This is probably because it is actually harder to use than a paper system. Without sophisticated linking, cross-indexing and searching capabilities, an electronic card index does not repay the effort of entering dozens of business cards or other information.

Although a pure card index application has not proved widely useful, it is still a useful model in two ways. First, it can underlay more sophisticated models such as Hypercard or other hyper-linked tools. Second, it can be embedded within a

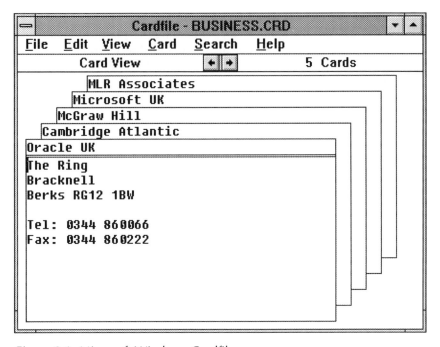

Figure 2.1. Microsoft Windows Cardfile

more complex application as a metaphor. For example, within many business applications it is necessary from time to time to enter the name of a supplier or customer. We might use a card index metaphor to aid the user's selection of a name, as an alternative to presenting the user with a simple list or wildcard search.

Calendar or diary

Most simple diary applications present a representation of a monthly diary and daily planners. Their effectiveness depends on the ease with which one can perform tasks that are difficult, error-prone or tedious with a paper diary, such as scheduling repeating appointments. Unfortunately, in many such applications the user cannot perform even straightforward tasks such as moving appointments from one date to another.

It is instructive to note that the difficulty in performing such tasks, which are almost trivial in terms of system requirements, occurs purely because the designer has failed to provide an adequate user interface to perform the task. This failure in turn stems from a poor model. The designer may be thinking too physically — the diary is essentially an interface into a table listing appointments, and appointment time is part of a non-updatable unique key. Alternatively, the designer may be thinking too literally — the actions available are modelled too closely on what is possible on paper.

Personal organizer

Almost universally, applications combining diary, scheduling, contact management and 'to do' lists model themselves on the personal organizers that were popular in the 1980s. Some are modelled very literally, even down to the physical appearance of an open binder. Others are less literal-minded, but still adopt the same categories of information: appointments, 'to do' lists, daily, weekly and monthly plans.

The effectiveness of these applications depends not on the physical representation of a ring binder, but on the ease with which the user can find, sort and prioritize information, and see information entered in one view transformed into a different view.

Spreadsheet

Although most people are unaware of the fact, before the hegemony of the personal computer, spreadsheets were actually produced with pencil, paper and lots of erasers. The first electronic spreadsheets were based in a very literal way on the paper version (except, of course, for the erasers).

The ease with which changes could be made in an electronic spreadsheet quickly guaranteed their popularity with users of the paper version. Later, users began to discover innovative and creative uses for spreadsheets that would be impossible (or at least hopelessly impractical) on paper. Nowadays, the spreadsheet is so firmly embedded in our experience as computer users that the electronic spreadsheet has itself become, in turn, a metaphor for new applications. For example, Oracle Corporation's Data Browser, a tool aimed at non-technical users for accessing relational data, boasts of its 'spreadsheet-like interface'.

The desktop

The Apple Macintosh famously uses a 'Desktop' as its conceptual model. On the screen the user organizes folders, documents, disks and printers. The mouse pointer acts like an electronic hand, allowing the user to point to objects on the desktop, pick them up, and move them around. Of course, the metaphor is not taken too literally. For example, few people actually keep a wastebasket on top of their desk! But such pragmatic breaking of the boundaries seems to cause no difficulty to users.

Lessons

Notice how the more effective models in this selection are not limited by the choice of model. Where it is appropriate, they extend the capabilities of the application in ways that are not possible in the original. This may seem an obvious remark: if the application does not go beyond the thing being modelled, why use the computer at all? In a personal organizer application, you would not expect to have to enter an appointment into both the day view and the week view; the application should do that for you. Yet I know of several business applications that require the user repeatedly to enter the same name and address information. It is amazing how often limitations of the original are needlessly mimicked in computer systems.

Some applications are actually *less* capable than their real-world model. I know of several online help systems that are actually harder to use than a paper-based equivalent. They are no easier to search than the original tabbed ringbinder, and you cannot fold down the corner of the page or write in the margin of the electronic version. It is hard to imagine that a designer can be so dull-witted as to build a computer system that is actually worse than the manual system, and still have the audacity to inflict it on users!

File system conceptual models

Having introduced a number of commonly used conceptual models, let us now contrast several different approaches to a single problem: the storage and organization of files, or in other words, file systems. Note that we are not interested here so much in how the file systems are actually organized on the storage subsystem (the representation) as in how they are perceived by the user (the presentation).

Traditional mainframe and minicomputers

Traditionally, a mainframe has an unsophisticated presentation along the following lines:

- The file system is composed of libraries.
- A library contains files.
- A file contains members.
- A member may be a dataset or a program.

If we compare this to the real world, it seems to be a reasonable model. A library in an office will typically contain files or folders, each of which contains in turn a number of documents. So the metaphor, although not particularly sophisticated, is straightforward and readily understood.

The system also differs from the model in some important ways. For example, a real folder or file has a particular physical size, and so is limited in the number of pages (amount of information) it can contain. In a typical file system implementation, the limit is not the amount of information but the number of programs or datasets that can be held in a single file.

Access permissions are a critically important extension that have no obvious correspondence in a real library. One consequence of this is that different file systems based on this model have widely differing presentations and mechanisms for file protection.

In summary we can conclude that this is, for the most part, a readily understood, if somewhat limited, model.

Apple Macintosh

The metaphor of the Macintosh is tightly bound to the desktop itself. Its key characteristics include:

- The desktop has folders and documents arranged on it.
- A folder contains documents or other folders.
- Folders may be opened to reveal their documents or closed to hide them.
- Documents can be opened; dropped on the printer; thrown in the wastebasket; moved from folder to folder, etc.

If we were to compare this with the mainframe system, the biggest difference is that the Mac is *document-centred* (Fig. 2.2). All of the actions are modelled around the idea that the primary concept is the document, and other concepts are arranged around the document to support it. By contrast, the mainframe system is centred on the file system, with the file itself coming at the bottom of a hierarchy.

One immediate consequence of this model is that the metaphor is very easy to extend. For example, to fax-enable applications, Apple simply adds an icon representing a fax machine to the desktop. To the Mac user, it is immediately obvious how to fax documents.

The Macintosh designers were also confident enough of the strength of their model to break the rules when necessary. As we noted above, the wastebasket

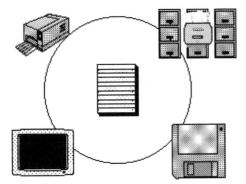

Figure 2.2. The Macintosh is document-centred

does not generally sit on one's desktop, but the interpretation of the metaphor is reasonably obvious.

Even the Macintosh, however, is not perfect. There is one infamous example: to eject a floppy from the drive, you drag it to the wastebasket. How does 'throwing away' the floppy represent ejecting it? Apple is perfectly well aware of this 'blemish', which crept in at the beginning of the Mac's development, but for various good reasons have stuck by it (see Laurel (1990) for the whole story). To the embarrassment of HCI purists, once you are used to it, the action works remarkably well!

Microsoft DOS

MS-DOS suffers from its long history. Having started out as an adequate system for organizing a small number of files on removable disks of limited capacity, it has over time grown by accretion, flirted with Unix and collided with networking. The result is a bit of a mess:

- Each disk contains a file system. Drives are identified by letter, although the same letter may identify different physical disks at different times, and a single disk may be identified by different letters.
- A file system may contain directories, but not necessarily.
- A directory may contain files and other directories in a hierarchy.
- A file may be a data file, a program, a library or something else entirely. Files have obscure names limited to eight characters.
- A file may be marked as Hidden, System or Read-only, although critical files vital to the operation of an application are rarely protected against deletion in this way.

Some years ago I was teaching a DOS-based word processor to a roomful of secretaries. We completed the first exercise, a job offer letter, and saved our work. One secretary chose the file name 'personne' (she really wanted to call it 'personnel', but DOS does not permit that). Then we completed the second exercise, and she saved her second letter — in the same file. In the office, this would have been perfectly reasonable: two documents in a single file. In DOS,

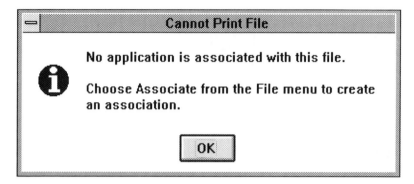

Figure 2.3. Microsoft Windows 3.1 exposes its mixed metaphor

she had just destroyed her first letter. Who is at fault here? The user, for believing that something called a file would behave like a file? Or the designer, for choosing a name that misleads the user into expecting a metaphor where none exists?

Microsoft Windows

Microsoft Windows Version 3.1 adds some aspects of the desktop metaphor to the DOS file system, but not all. For example, some documents can be printed by dropping them on the Print Manager, but by no means all (and there is no obvious way to tell merely by inspection). Figure 2.3 shows what happens if you attempt to print a file that has no associated application. (At the time of writing, Microsoft was promising a dramatically revised desktop for Windows 95, but the release date was at least six months away. For the purposes of this chapter I wanted to discuss an interface that would be well known to most readers, and also would provide a good contrast to the Macintosh.)

There is also a basic confusion between groups, as organizers of the desktop, and directories, as organizers of files (contrast with the Mac, which deals simply with folders). Files can be dragged from the File Manager and dropped within groups in the Program Manager, even when this is meaningless (the file has no 'association') — but group files ('.grp') cannot be dropped on the Program Manager, although it seems perfectly obvious to me what the intention of dropping a group file must be. In short, Microsoft Windows suffers from a badly *mixed metaphor.*

If the Macintosh is document-centred, it is difficult to see what Windows is centred around. Some aspects of the system are apparently device-centred, some are application-centred, and a few are document-centred.

Expressions and transformations

The examples above have been presented in the commonly used terminology of conceptual model and metaphor. However, as I suggested at the beginning of the chapter, this terminology is proving rather strained. For example, what is the metaphor behind the Microsoft Windows Clock "applet"? It seems less than useful to say that Clock takes a clock as its metaphor!

For this reason I prefer to talk about *expressions* and *transformations*. In other words, how is some aspect of the application *expressed* to the user? And how is the user presentation *transformed* from or to the system representation?

Expressions

Broadly, we can divide models into concrete, symbolic and abstract expressions. The idea conjured up by the word 'metaphor' corresponds most often to a symbolic expression but, as we shall see, most business applications juxtapose a concrete expression of data with an abstract expression of actions. We shall examine each of these models in turn, before contrasting these three types of expression by considering how the process of faxing might be presented in an abstract, symbolic or concrete expression. It is important to note that these distinctions are not hard and fast; rather, this is a way of *characterizing* different kinds of expression.

Abstract expressions

We are all familiar with abstract expressions. Most character or block mode transaction processing applications use abstract expressions. Function key driven applications are abstract; all command interpreters are abstract; and menu accelerators in Windows applications are abstract.

Abstract expressions are easy to identify. They have no direct or compelling correspondence to the object or action that they express. For example, the word processor I am using right now expresses the 'Save' command as 'Shift+F12' and the 'Print' command as 'Ctrl+Shift+F12'. Why 'F12'? And why should the 'Ctrl' key turn 'Save' into 'Print'? (See, for example, Fig. 2.4.) There is no compelling reason for choosing these key mappings over any other, so the expression is *abstract*. It is clear that it is hard to apply the word 'metaphor' to such mappings, which is why I use the word 'expression'.

Even the Apple Mac contains some abstract expressions: Cut, Copy and Paste are Cmd-X, Cmd-C and Cmd-V. The keys were apparently chosen because of their position on the keyboard rather than for any relationship to the commands implemented.

Command interpreters are abstract. Faced with a prompt, how do you determine the command for, say, 'delete a file'? It might be 'del', 'erase', or almost anything else. Although to us as experienced computer users some words seem like obvious choices, who would guess the Unix commands 'rm' for 'remove', or 'man' for 'help'? To the average user, words like 'del' are just as arbitrary. Away from your keyboard, what do you ever 'delete' in the real world?

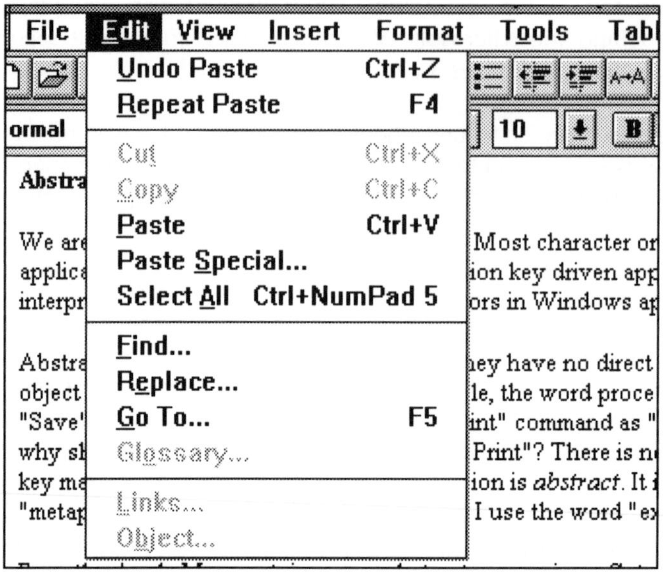

Figure 2.4. Abstract mapping: why 'Ctrl+NumPad 5'?

In terms of the fundamentals we identified in Chapter 1, abstract expressions are nearly always poor or arbitrary mappings. Even superficially 'obvious' choices do not stand up to close examination. For example, in the Mac world there was a long-running confusion over whether Cmd-P should mean 'Print' or 'Plain text'. In my word processor, 'Ctrl+S' is 'Style', not 'Save'. Abstract mappings are only 'obvious' with hindsight. Abstract expressions also often exhibit poor visibility. In an unfamiliar command interpreter, how do you determine what commands are available? There may be online help available, but first you have to find out what the name of the help command is! Many of us have suffered the frustration of moving from one Unix system to another and discovering that our favourite commands are missing or renamed.

On the other hand, abstract mappings are not automatically a bad thing. For the experienced, regular user of an application they can provide very rapid access to frequently used actions. As the examples above suggest, though, such mappings should be treated cautiously. An abstract expression is particularly dangerous when it is the *only* expression of a given action.

Although the 'sin' of abstract expression is nearly always committed against actions, it is fair to describe some expressions of data as abstract. Generally this is a sin of omission: the designer fails to translate from the system model to the user model. As a developer you may occasionally encounter a message of the form 'Memory Protection Exception at 0C3E:12D6'. The data — the offending instruction in the code — is expressed in terms that are meaningful to the system (an address) rather than to the programmer (a source code line number). Difficult as it may be for us to see it, this is frequently how we treat our users.

Symbolic expressions

When we first hear the word metaphor, symbolic expressions are perhaps what first comes to mind. In practice, symbolic expressions are quite rare. Symbolic expressions are precisely those expressions where one thing — data or action — is expressed as being *like* another. The example mentioned earlier, that faxing is like printing, is one example. Actions within the expression have some of the characteristics, but not all, of the symbolic referent being modelled.

The Mac's 'eject disk' action — drop the image of the disk on the wastebasket — is a symbolic action. It is easy to see that this is not as immediately compelling as the more concrete metaphors to be found elsewhere in the Mac, such as deleting or printing. On the other hand, once the symbol has been understood, few users have difficulty with this symbolism.

Cut, Copy and Paste are an almost universal symbolic representation of the idea of moving information from one place to another. The idea begins in text editors with a concrete expression for moving text around: paste-up in the publishing world uses a physical form of Cut and Paste (in those shops that do not yet use so-called electronic paste-up). The concept of Copy is then added, with the symbolic expression that Copy is like Cut, except that the source is undisturbed. Copy has no obvious analogue in the physical print shop, but the symbolic expression makes it clear. The idea is then symbolically extended into applications other than text editors. In a spreadsheet, you can Cut and Paste cells. (On a paper spreadsheet, you would erase and rewrite: this would be a concrete expression.) In a presentation graphics package, you can rearrange the slide order using Cut and Paste. (If you were dealing with a physical set of transparencies or acetates, you would pull a slide out and slide it in elsewhere to rearrange order. Thus Cut and Paste is again symbolic.)

Symbolic expression pervades the Unix input/output model. The learning user begins with a model of the file system. This model is itself moderately complex and (for ordinary users) difficult to acquire. For example, many non-technical people never feel entirely comfortable with the idea of links. Once the model has been more or less understood, it becomes the basis for a symbolic expression of devices. Reading from and writing to a terminal is (with certain limitations) like reading and writing a file. Inter-process communication through pipes is (again, with subtle limitations) also like file input/output. Using Berkeley sockets, even cross-network communication can be modelled on files. The power of this approach is that it allows a programmer easily to extend her knowledge of part of the system to a completely distinct part. As we noted in the previous chapter, it is often said that Unix is relatively easy to learn for the system programmer, compared to other operating systems. In our terminology, we would attribute this ease of learning to a consistently applied symbolic expression in the conceptual model.

The difference between symbolic expressions and concrete expressions can be blurred. In general, concrete models express things as behaving like the thing they actually represent (the Wastebasket is like a real wastebasket: the user doesn't 'delete' a document, he throws it in the wastebasket); whereas symbolic models express things as being like something other than the thing they actually represent (the fax machine is like a special kind of printer). In the Unix example, communicating with a terminal is like using a file, not like using a terminal under another operating system.

Concrete expressions

The most frequently quoted example of a metaphor is one already much visited in this book, and it happens to be a very concrete expression: the Macintosh desktop. To 'delete' a document, you throw it away. To move a document from one folder to another, you pick it up and move it. Actions within the metaphor correspond very directly to the action they represent in the 'real' world.

Microsoft Window's File Manager contains a number of concrete expressions. For example, files can be moved around the file system by picking and dragging. Unfortunately, only a small subset of actions within File Manager have such a concrete expression. There is no concrete expression for file deletion, for example. We shall examine the implications of this a little later.

Most business applications contain a large element of concrete expression, at least for the data. Filling a form on the screen can be almost exactly equivalent to filling the same form on paper. It is this concrete expression that led to the question quoted earlier: 'Is there always a conceptual model?' My answer would be yes, although sometimes the model is very literal, and so it becomes hard to see.

Many business forms need to be passed from hand to hand and actioned by a number of people. Order processing is a classic example:

- The customer's credit is checked.
- The order is filled and shipped.
- The customer is invoiced.
- Eventually, payment is collected.

In most business applications, the Shipping department will fill out a form (paper or electronic) and, once the order has been shipped, they will indicate this to the system through some symbolic or abstract expression of 'commit transaction'. If the designer had constructed a model that was consistently concrete, this action could be expressed by dropping a representation of the order (a document icon, perhaps) onto an iconic 'Out Tray'. This idea then extends naturally to include an

'In Tray' where incoming orders arrive; and a 'Pending' tray for orders that cannot ship for some reason — shortage of stock or credit pending approval, perhaps. Unfortunately, in practice we tend to build applications in which only the data, or documents, are modelled concretely; actions are modelled symbolically or abstractly, or often are missing entirely.

As the examples above suggest, concrete expression of actions (as opposed to data) often relies heavily on *direct manipulation*. Icons or symbols representing documents are moved to icons representing devices, other people's work queues, and so on. Consequently they are programmer-intensive, demanding a far higher degree of expertise than simple form-filling applications. (At least, they are under Microsoft Windows, which provides a very low level interface to the programmer who wants to build such capabilities.) GUI development tools aimed at the transaction processing market are only now beginning to provide good support for constructing applications that exploit direct manipulation.

However, it is not absolutely necessary to program 'drag and drop' or other difficult direct manipulations to provide some concrete expression. Consider the following description. The interface presents a list of orders in progress. The user can 'pick up' one or more orders by clicking in the list to select them. The cursor shape will change to indicate to the user that he or she has an order or orders 'in hand'. The order can then be 'dropped' on any of the target areas: the out tray, if the order has been filled; the printer; the supervisor's work queue; and so on. In terms of implementation, this is barely more difficult than a traditional application, but the expression, for the user, is far more concrete. All we are doing is raising the expression of what we are doing to the level of the user's terminology.

The great danger in concrete expressions is in copying not only the strengths but also the weaknesses of the model. A good example of this error can be seen in Lotus Organizer. This application presents the user with a graphically very precise representation of a personal organizer, right down to the rings in the ringbinder and the holes in the paper! Different sections of the organizer, such as 'To Do' lists, are accessed by clicking on tabs that resemble the tabbed file dividers of a physical organizer.

Unfortunately, the behaviour of real tabs has been modelled too closely. When you are at a section in the middle of the organizer, some tabs (those for sections in front of the current one) are on the left of the image of the binder, and some tabs (those for sections after the current one) are on the right. This is just as you would see the tabs in a physical binder. If you move to a section at the 'back' of the binder, all the tabs move to the left. Again this is exactly the way a real binder would appear. Unfortunately, it makes it very hard to find the tab you want: the tabs move around, from left to right, as you move around the different sections of the organizer. It would actually be easier to find the section you wanted if the tabs behaved *less* like the real thing, and just stayed in one place (like ordinary buttons, in fact!).

The ease of use of concrete expressions arises from drawing most directly on knowledge that the user already possesses. If you know the properties of a wastebasket, a folder, a printer or Form E45 in your business, you can transfer that knowledge to the application. The power of concrete expressions is greatest when the designer avoids the trap of limiting the model by copying the real world too literally.

Case study: Models of faxing

For purposes of comparison, it is interesting to see how a single task, namely faxing a document, might be expressed in each of these three ways.

The simplest model of faxing is a concrete expression, as it might be implemented on a Macintosh. A fax machine icon is presented on the desktop. To fax a document, you simply drop it on the icon, just like placing a real document in the feeder tray of a fax machine. The number to be dialled is specified as a property of the fax machine icon. If a particular fax number is used frequently, it can be 'memorized' as a speed dial, or a specific icon can be added dedicated to dialling that number. Faxing in the model becomes just like faxing in the real world, with the bonus that you can have as many fax machines as you like. Faxing also strongly resembles other document-centred actions such as printing or deleting. This benefit arises from the strength of the overriding desktop model.

Under Microsoft Windows I have a symbolic expression: faxing is like printing. This enables me to fax from any document that can print. I select, through the Print Setup dialog, the fax modem as my print destination, then print as normal. When I select the print action I am presented with a dialog that asks me to specify the number to dial, the addressee's name and so on. (This is a slight departure from the model: would it not be more consistent if these details were specified in the Print Setup Options for the pseudo-printer?)

This model is far from perfect. Although very convenient for sending, it has no natural extension to receiving faxes, the behaviour of which is not at all like scanning a document, the obvious inverse to printing. Reviewing the status of failed or pending faxes in the fax log also has no obvious correspondence to the printer model.

We might also propose other, equally valid, symbolic expressions. For example, the fax machine might be represented as a pseudo-directory in the file system, rather than as a pseudo-printer. Faxing would then be like saving a file, rather than printing. This suggests a natural expression for incoming faxes, which appear as files in an 'Incoming' directory. Outgoing faxes would quite naturally be found in a 'Sent', 'Pending' or 'Failed' directory according to their status. As this example shows, it is quite typical of symbolic expressions that a number of alternatives, with different strengths and weaknesses, will be possible.

Under Microsoft DOS, faxing has a purely abstract expression. I use an application called BitFax, but other applications will be very similar. To send a fax from another application, such as a spreadsheet running under DOS, the manual tells you to do the following:

- At the DOS prompt type: BF4 /TSRB (this loads the application into memory and prepares it for print capture).
- Start the DOS application.
- Select Laserjet or Epson printer within the application. (If the application does not support one of these, you are lost!)
- Print the document as normal. A dialog box then appears, telling you that the printer output has been 'captured', and asking you to press enter.
- The 'send fax' dialog then appears, allowing you to specify destination fax number and other details.

The manual also informs me: 'To temporarily disable Print Capture so you can print a document to your printer, press Left Shift-Q. To re-enable Print Capture, press Left Shift-P.' There is no obvious reason for these choices, nor is it obvious how you determine from within your application whether print capture is currently enabled or disabled. This is not a criticism particularly of BitFax: most DOS applications have an equally abstract expression.

Selecting a form of expression

Although the best choice of expression is very much dependent on particular circumstances, and especially on the nature of your user constituency, we can still make some useful broad generalizations. Usually, a concrete expression is more readily understood than other forms of expression as it relates more directly the message that we wish to convey to the user. We can infer that we would expect concrete expressions to be more readily learnt. Note the difference in ease of comprehension between a desktop such as that of OS/2 Version 2.0, with icons representing *each printer*, and one with a single icon representing a *print manager*. The former are concrete objects in the user's world, the latter is an abstract concept. If you drag and drop a file on the print manager, which print queue does it go into?

Their very solidity, on the other hand, may make such expressions more constraining than symbolic or abstract expressions. By definition, a concrete expression is weakened every time we step outside its bounds for the sake of expediency. A symbolic expression or abstract expression tends to have more scope for expansion.

It is tempting to suggest that concrete expressions are always better than symbolic expressions, and symbolic expressions in turn are better than abstract expressions. Although this is often true, it is not automatically the case. One only has to observe the fluency with which most users can edit using keystrokes for cut, copy and paste to see that some abstract expressions are very useful. Table 2.1

	Selection	*File masks*
Type of expression	Concrete	Abstract
User effort	Potentially many key clicks	Brief, compact specification
Mapping	Direct, choice is explicit	Indirect, choice is implicit
Visibility	Choices are highly visible, easy to backtrack and change selection	Low, choices must be listed before beginning specification
Feedback	Good feedback during selection process	Effect can only be verified after the action

Table 2.1

contrasts two mechanisms for selecting multiple files for an action, such as delete or move: selection by clicking in a list of files, and specification through a wild card or file mask.

For most users, the lack of visibility before the act and the postponement of feedback until after completion make deletion of multiple files by specifying a file mask a task involving high anxiety. The selection mechanism seems to score over file masks for all but highly confident users who want to be able to specify actions rapidly against large numbers of files, and are willing to bear the risk in return for that high productivity. Of course, you may be designing for a constituency of users who are already, or are expected to become, highly fluent in the application in question. In this case the gain in productivity may outweigh the possible losses due to the lower visibility and associated higher potential for damaging and costly mistakes. Once again, you must know your users well.

Mixed levels of expression

Although it is a tempting simplification, it would be wrong to conclude that only one form of expression should exist within a single application. One need only look at the Macintosh to see that abstract expressions such as Cut, Copy and Paste can co-exist happily with an otherwise concrete model. This is perfectly reasonable when the different forms of expression are used at different levels of the interface. On the other hand, it is definitely a good idea to try to use a single form of expression at any given level or within a given area of an application. For example, it would be a mistake to have an abstract expression for Cut without an abstract expression for Paste. The Windows fax software discussed earlier shows the effects of this error: it has a symbolic expression for sending a fax, but an abstract expression for receiving. As a result, it is difficult for the user to reconcile the two aspects of the application in her internal mental model.

Another example of this mixing can be seen in Lotus Organizer. This application has a very strong concrete model that covers almost every aspect of the application, with one notable exception: when the user wants to cancel an appointment or discard the task, he drags it to a small wastebasket icon. Now, in real life you do not 'throw away' an appointment. A concrete expression might involve 'picking up' an eraser and bringing it to the appointment, or taking a 'pencil' and striking off the task. This one symbolic expression looks oddly out of place.

File Manager illustrates well some of the dangers of this kind of mixing of levels. If you consider various file management tasks, then look at how they can be effected in the DOS/Windows environment, you find that certain tasks are best carried out by direct manipulation. Examples include moving files from one place to another, and especially moving a directory subtree from one place to another. Other actions that might naturally be performed by direct manipulation, most notably file deletion, are in fact performed using a menu command. Then there are actions that can only be performed by dropping out to a DOS prompt. Chief among these is printing multiple files. It is difficult to understand why File Manager cannot, at the very least, process this by attempting to print each file in turn. Yet even DOS does not provide a complete set of capabilities: there are actions that cannot be performed at the DOS prompt, such as renaming a directory. Regardless of his wishes, the user is obliged to mix levels.

The result of this kind of mixing of levels of expression for actions that, to the user, are apparently part of the same action set (i.e. actions against files) is that the user can build no consistent expectation of how any given action might be carried out: by direct manipulation, through the menu, or at a command prompt. The user is expected to commit to memory such peculiarities of the tool as the fact that a single file with an appropriate association can be printed through File Manager, but not a file without an association, nor multiple files with or without associations (Fig. 2.5).

Whose viewpoint?

It is important to emphasize that these characterizations of expressions are not absolute; in fact they are generally relative to a particular person's point of view. For example, the wastebasket metaphor is a concrete expression for the user, but very abstract for the system programmer who has to implement it. The print driver metaphor for faxing is symbolic for the sender, but concrete for the programmer of the driver.

Technical teams in discussions about user interface design choices often find themselves at loggerheads, with user representatives and designers completely unable to understand the others' points of view, and insistent that their own suggestions are 'easier' for the user. Usually nobody has any real evidence for

Figure 2.5. File Manager cannot print multiple files

his or her point of view. In many cases these failures to communicate can be attributed to the fact that each person is arguing from his own perspective; what is concrete for one is abstract for the other. Once again, testing by real users is vital.

If you are familiar with the common usage of the word metaphor and want to retain it, I would suggest the following equivalencies. If you use the word 'metaphor' for concrete expressions, you will be consistent with most of rest of the world. By extension, symbolic expressions may fairly be called 'similes' ('this thing is *like* that thing'). Finally, abstract expressions can charitably be called 'ciphers'. You need to know the key to the code before you can make any sense of them.

Transformations

One widely known example of transformation concerns a game for two players, involving the numbers 1 to 9. Each player in turn chooses a number; once a number is chosen, it cannot be taken by the other player. The goal of the game is to acquire three numbers that add up to 15. For example, if you have taken the numbers 9 and 1, your opponent had better take 5 to stop you winning on the next turn. The game seems quite complex until you lay out the numbers in a grid like this:

8	1	6
3	5	7
4	9	2

Now play the game by indicating your choices with an X, and your opponent's with an O. Suddenly the game is seen to be identical to noughts-and-crosses or tic-tac-toe, a trivial game for most of us. Any solution to the first game gives a line of Os or Xs; and any line adds up to 15. A simple transformation dramatically changes the difficulty of the game.

Transforming an aspect of the user interface can be equally powerful. In this sense, much of user interface design can be thought of in terms of finding appropriate transformations. It is useful to divide transformations into those suitable for output, those suitable for input, and those suitable for data both entered and displayed. (For the mathematically minded reader, these three kinds of transformation are analogous to mathematical functions, which we can describe as being Into, or Injection; Onto, or Surjection; and One-to-One Into, or Bijection. Let me warn you in advance, though: the correspondence is not intended to be exact. It is just a useful metaphor if you happen to have a mathematical background!)

Output transformations

Not every transformation is a complete correspondence like the one in the tic-tac-toe game. Instead the user representation presents less information than the system actually contains. This may seem like a heresy: doesn't this violate the widely espoused principle of WYSIWYG? In practice, losing or hiding information can be a great service to the user. For example, replacing the message 'N records written' with 'Work saved', regardless of the value of N, is a typical *output transformation*. Each message, value, or state in the user model corresponds to at least one message, value or state, and potentially to several, in the system domain.

If we consider an application that forms part of a stock control system, we might highlight items currently deliverable from stock (whatever their stock level) in green, and items that are not deliverable (for whatever reason) in red. All possible levels of a stock item are mapped onto just two presentations. Clearly, transformations which 'lose' information in this way are only useful for output from the system, not for user input. After all, if the user were to set the status to 'Red', how would the system know which of the possible system states that map to red is intended by the user?

It is a characteristic of output transformations that by definition some system information may be lost from the user presentation, so (in general) there is no means for the user to map the presentation back to the precise internal representation (which 'Red' status precisely?). This implies that an output transformation is appropriate when and only when the user does not need to determine that system value or state. 'Work saved' is a perfect example. Choosing a good output transformation is always a question of reducing the information presented to the user to everything that she needs to know, but no more.

You may be wondering how this suggestion that we present the user with less information than is actually available corresponds to our assertion in the previous chapter that the user should easily be able to determine the state of the system. The solution to this apparent paradox is to recall the difference between the system model and the user model. The user needs to be able to determine which state in the *user* model the system is in, not which state in the *system* model. So in fact, reducing the number of states presented to the user to Red and Green, rather than presenting the many possible system states, actually makes it *easier* for the user to determine the user model state. Less can be more!

Input transformations

We can also envisage transformations which map system values to some subset of the possible user interface presentation. Each message, value or state in the user model corresponds to at most one message, value or state in the system domain. Some user model values or states may not be mapped from any value or state in the system model.

This may not look very useful at first sight: if some of the user interface presentations are never mapped from internal representations, how can they ever be used? The power of such a transformation becomes clear, however, if we consider the mapping in the opposite direction; in other words, if we consider how user input might be mapped.

Consider one extremely common requirement, the need for a user to enter a date (delivery date, order date, expiry date, etc.). Some possible formats for the date 14 October 1994 might include:

- 14/10/94
- 14/10/1994
- 14-10-1994
- 14-Oct-1994
- 14 Oct 1994
- 14th October, 1994
- October 14, 1994

All of these possible formats represent the same date, but (in many applications) it is difficult for the user to determine, other than by trial and error, which one format the application accepts. In reality, the internal representation will almost certainly be none of these; typically a database will store a date as a day number offset from some arbitrary starting date. Since the application must perform some conversion, is there any technical reason why the application cannot accept all of these formats, recognizing the one that the user has chosen and performing the appropriate conversion? This is an ideal candidate for an *input transformation*.

Naturally, when the date is later presented back to a user, only one of these formats will ever be used. It would be very confusing for users if the system could present a single piece of information, unpredictably, in different formats, depending on who had entered it. It is a characteristic of input transformations that sometimes information can be returned to the user differently from the way the user entered it. A classically simple example is an input field that forces its input to upper case, regardless of which case the user types in.

We can imagine another kind of input transformation, this time of actions rather than of data. In a command line interface, part of the difficulty for the user arises from the fact that of all possible ways that the user might express a command, only one (typically) is acceptable to the command interpreter. For example, to remove a file, the command might conceivably be 'delete', 'del', 'erase', 'remove' or 'rm', among other possibilities. The user has to memorize and recall the command appropriate to the particular interpreter. This becomes especially difficult if, like me, you use several different interpreters in a working day. Yet it would be almost trivial for an interpreter to recognize any of the above commands as the remove command. This is an excellent opportunity to implement an input transformation.

In practice, input transformations are rarely found. This may be attributable to several causes, not least the fact that input transformations are often difficult to program, requiring considerable thought and effort from the programmer. If the user only ever uses one date format, he may not even notice the effort that the programmer has made. So unlike output transformations which are usually directly visible to the user, input transformations often go unappreciated. The fact that input transformations usually improve input, rather than output, may also be significant. Thimbleby (1990) points out that most user interface design seems to focus heavily on output to the exclusion of input.

One-to-one transformations

We call the kind of transformation illustrated by tic-tac-toe above a *one-to-one transformation*, because there is a one-to-one correspondence between the two presentations, in both directions. Everything in the user model has a unique representation in the system model, and vice versa.

In the user interface, replacing a yes/no question with a check box would be a simple one-to-one transformation of input. Presenting the descriptive names, rather than catalogue numbers, of stock items in a delivery note would be a more complex one-to-one transformation, this time of output. It is clear that both transformations contribute to the clarity of the user interface. Because of the one-to-one mapping, such transformations can be appropriate for input or output, but are especially useful where the same information is both captured and presented back to the user.

One-to-one transformations are more appropriate for input than pure input transformations in those cases where it is useful to force the user to a single way of expressing an input. For example, replacing a yes/no question with a check box eliminates the user's doubt over whether the question can be answered with a simple 'Y', or requires 'Yes' in full, or is case-sensitive.

One-to-one transformations are probably the most commonly encountered, because they are the easiest to design. They avoid the difficult questions presented by output and input transformations, which require the designer to understand the user's needs sufficiently well that a good mapping can be established. One-to-one transformations can often be implemented with a simple change of terminology or mapping. However, the designer should be careful not to assume too easily that a one-to-one transformation is actually useful to the user. When I pointed out the '7 records written' problem to one designer, he suggested as a serious solution that the message be changed to '7 rows saved'!

Summary

As the examples above show, the ideas of expression and transformation operate throughout all levels of the user interface. One of the purposes of the conceptual model is to guide the choice of transformations so that we present the user with a model of the system that is coherent and internally consistent. At the highest level, the conceptual model is itself a transformation of the user's task from the system domain, typically editing tables, to something else. Choosing that 'something else' is the subject matter of this chapter and the skill of the designer.

Case study

The case study below is one that I use in seminars. After reading through the scenario, you may want to sketch your own proposed solution before reading the discussion of the solutions offered.

Scenario

Acme Consulting is a small company employing around 400 consultants. The consultants are divided geographically into four geographical regions and within each region into five industry groups (Finance, Manufacturing, Pharmaceuticals, Defence and Retail). Each team (that is, an industry group within a region) has a secretary dedicated to them for administrative support. All secretaries and consultants have access to PCs with VGA or SVGA screens, and the secretaries have dedicated laser printers.

The company has identified a number of problems in the area of time management. The current paper-based office diaries/schedulers, held by team secretaries but occasionally updated by other team members, are proving unreliable. Often the diaries are hard to find, because people take them away to update them and do not return them. As a result, people are only entering around 50 per cent of their time commitments into the diary. This results in a number of problems:

- The secretary may double-book people because the diary incorrectly says they are free.
- People are hard to find when they are out of the office.
- It is particularly difficult to organize meetings (such as project reviews) between consultants because the diaries are so unreliable.

- The vast majority of meetings are between members of the same team, but some meetings are cross-team.

The company would like to improve the scheduling of meetings, but does not want to go to the expense of building a full-blown 'personal organizer' system for all 400 individuals.

Given this scenario, I ask seminar attendees to outline the conceptual model for the user interface of an application to meet this requirement. They may assume that a satisfactory data store can be constructed to support any specification they come up with! They are also allowed to assume that the development tool supports any (reasonable) capabilities they require, for example to support direct manipulation.

Popular solutions

This exercise is designed to promote discussion so that the participants will gain experience in critically evaluating different user interface options. There are several models that are likely to be proposed; here are, in my experience, the commonest three, with some suggestions as to their relative advantages and disadvantages.

The simple list

The application shows the user a list of meetings, for example as a multi-column list box showing a description of the meeting, together with its time, date and place. The user can add, modify and delete meetings. Add and modify take the user to a detail window that shows time, date, place, and a list of meeting attendees. A Filter or Search facility helps in the location of a particular meeting.

Although surprisingly popular, this is the answer to avoid. It is the data-centric solution: present the meetings table to the user to edit. There are many shortcomings with this model, not least the fact that the model (the underlying database) is completely abstract for the user. To see the impact of this poor model, try answering questions like these through such an interface:

- What is John Smith doing on the 14th of this month?
- When is the next time John is free for five days in a row?
- Who is available for a meeting on the 7th of next month?

All of these questions show that the burden of interpretation is on the user, rather than on the application, where it belongs.

The desk diary

This is the most commonly presented solution. Taking a desk diary as the conceptual model, the user is shown a diary page that gives appointments and meetings for the day or for a week.

In more sophisticated versions of this proposal, the user is able to open several 'pages', showing different dates and different users. A nice addition is to be able to 'turn the page' of several people's diaries in synchronization, to aid searching for a slot when everybody is free.

From here the user is provided with a 'meeting planning' function, which shows a date and time; a location; and a list of participants. Pop-ups for a list of participants to select and add, available locations, and a pop-up calendar for choosing the date aid the user in constructing a meeting. When the user is working in any of these pop-ups, the others use strong visual feedback to show availability. For example, if the user goes to the calendar window and picks a date, the lists of participants and locations grey out those people and locations unavailable on that date. If the user goes to the participants list, the calendar greys out dates on which any of the people selected are unavailable, and rooms too small for the number of selected people. The feedback between all the different selection windows helps the user to hunt towards 'fuzzy' requirements such as 'I want a project meeting sometime in the week of the 15th; I don't need the whole team, but at least six people must be available to make the meeting worthwhile'.

There are a lot of attractive features in this suggestion, particularly in the way that it can guide a user in the search process. It uses a familiar model, the diary, and has strong visibility. However, there is a stronger solution that addresses the original requirement more directly.

The wall planner

Take a 'Sasco' style wall planner as the conceptual model. This is a very creative solution that few people propose: many people find it hard to imagine such a graphical, direct manipulation kind of solution. Remember that the original specification said that people were consultants, so their time is mostly booked in whole days. Also the major problem is concerned with booking several people together.

This application presents the user with a view like a wall chart: a list of people down the side, dates across the top, and coloured blocks representing different commitments (project, vacation, internal meetings, etc.) at the intersections, exactly like a real wall planner.

Unlike the real thing, though, electronic planners can be customized by the user, who is able to decide which people will be listed (by selecting entire regions or teams, or picking individuals) and the granularity of the time scale (e.g. days or half-days). The order of listing can be altered by picking and dragging people up and down.

To create a booking, the user points at the people and date or dates. Note that the set of dates need not be contiguous: any dates can be selected. To modify a booking, the user clicks on the appointment for any person. All participants and dates for that meeting will be selected, and people and dates can be added and removed by selecting and de-selecting. To remove a booking completely, the user picks it up and drags it off the planner. The booking will be removed from the diary for all participants and all days.

For designers who can break out of character mode thinking, this is easily the most effective solution. If we look at it in terms of fundamental principles:

- The conceptual model is very familiar to every office worker.
- Direct manipulation of the planner is just like filling in a real wall planner, so mappings are strong.
- Visibility is good: available slots are easy to see, and people's diaries are easy to compare.
- Direct manipulation of the planner gives instant feedback.

One objection to this approach is that this represents a considerable programming effort in any tool. This is true, but remember that ease of construction was never part of the brief! After all, should it be hard for the computer or hard for the user?

Summary

We have now explored the ideas of models, transformations and expressions in considerable detail. We saw that a model contains both a point of reference, or in other words a centre, and a domain of expression. We have identified some of the characteristics of a good choice of model. Good models are derived from something that is already familiar to the user. The derivation may be concrete, symbolic or abstract, and we have explored the benefits of striving for consistency of expression within related areas of an application.

Good models are not limited by the referent model. Taking the model too literally can mislead the designer into transferring its weaknesses as well as its strengths to the application, as well as missing the opportunity to extend the model. The skill of design is in extending the model in ways that are natural and fit well into the model, rather than in ways that are arbitrary and so dilute the model.

A good choice of model is the foundation for all that follows. If the model is weak, the application will almost inevitably turn out to be an agglomeration of unrelated 'features', a pile of bricks with no mortar, rather than a building. A strong model is the best defence against creeping featurism.

3   Taskflow

'I must — I will — I can — I ought — I do'

R.B. Sheridan, *The Critic*

Introduction

Before we begin to specify dialog flows in detail — that is, to determine specific windows and dialog boxes, and fix their relationships and modality — we need first to understand the user's taskflow; in other words, the ways in which the user carries out her tasks. It is an important discipline to separate out these two aspects: we first determine *what* we want to do before we address *how* we do it. Taskflow is one of the most difficult aspects of user interface design: it is now that we must begin to express the user's needs and the business requirements in a form that can ultimately be implemented as one or more applications. Taskflow is the interface between real world requirements and application specifications. While still firmly maintaining a user-centred viewpoint and a principle-based approach, we must begin to take account of the real world limitations of information systems and especially of their users.

Unlike the conceptual model, there is no single well-established terminology for this stage of design. I have chosen to use the word taskflow to describe this stage because of the analogy with workflow. The latter term describes the way in which work moves around an organization, involving both manual and automated processes, and also 'external' processes, where the work moves entirely outside the organization and passes through the hands of customers or suppliers. Taskflow is the equivalent process within the user interface. Taskflow can also be thought of as those aspects of workflow that involve an interaction between a user and a computer system.

Taskflow is concerned with the way in which an application or system handles a unit of work. It involves specific issues of implementation such as how much freedom is given to the user in the order and manner in which he handles tasks; how much the application guides or constrains the user; and to what extent the user is forced to perform tasks serially or is allowed to perform them in parallel.

The importance of taskflow cannot be overstated; the decisions taken at this stage will strongly determine the whole character of the application, and if a user works frequently with your application, this means that your choice of taskflow will have a dramatic impact on the nature of that person's job. This is a serious responsibility. In this chapter we aim to discuss the issues involved in designing taskflow, illustrate some of the traps and dangers for the designer, and examine several mechanisms for controlling taskflow.

Design principles

Throughout this chapter we talk about choices between various kinds of taskflow. It is important to bear in mind that a single application will typically exploit different kinds of taskflow in different places: at some times it may be appropriate that the user is strongly constrained, at others that she is allowed plenty of freedom; some tasks may be inherently serial, others may be serial or parallel at the user's preference. This chapter is devoted to illustrating the designer's options, and identifying the trade-offs involved. We will begin by examining the external issues that need to be considered by the designer of taskflow. We will then look at the idea of closure, one of the most significant considerations in implementing taskflow. Finally we will look at freedom and ask is too much freedom merely anarchy?

Components of taskflow

Taskflow is influenced by a number of sources, not least of which is the business workflow and data flow that is the concern of the systems analyst. For the purposes of this book we shall begin from the assumption that this analysis has been performed, and that it is our job to implement the processes identified. In reality, particularly in small organizations, the systems analysis may be carried out by the same person who carries out the user interface specification, and even the implementation. If this is the case, the designer is obliged to enforce a rigid self-discipline with regard to each role. It is all too tempting in your role as user interface designer to specify elements that you know will be easy to implement, rather than ones that will be easy to use.

The processes identified directly in data flow diagrams are not the only considerations. A second major component of taskflow comes from the business rules. These rules will influence the way in which workflows are broken down into taskflows and allocated to particular systems and users. Issues of privilege, authority, and responsibility for particular tasks will come to bear. A third major component is the working style of the users, or of the job in hand. As we noted in the opening chapter, personality type will influence the way in which people prefer to work. Taskflow is the most significant single component of design in matching the character of the application to the preference of the user. Those preferences can only truly be determined through representative testing.

Identifying tasks

As part of our work at this stage, we need to specify in more detail the processes identified by the systems analyst. Recall the example from Chapter 1, where we identified workflows associated with accepting a delivery into the warehouse. From the systems analyst's point of view, this will be a process on a data flow diagram (Fig. 3.1).

One of the difficulties of working within this kind of specification is that it is frequently written from the 'wrong' viewpoint. Many systems analysts are former programmers and designers who have 'climbed the ladder' to analyst. As a result they often create specifications that reflect the system from the point of view of the data, not from the point of view of the user. In consequence, their diagrams may be of little use in designing for the user's viewpoint.

As far as the analyst is concerned, the diagram shown in Fig. 3.1 may well be the lowest level of her decomposition; we are free to implement this process as we wish, providing only that the right changes are made to the Stock datastore, and the correct data is passed to the Invoicing process. We can break down the task-flow through the Stock Control process in more detail, as we did in Chapter 1:

- Identify the delivery (supplier, order number, etc.)
- Compare the delivery note with the original order
- Compare the actual delivery with the delivery note
- Accept (fully or partially) the delivery into the warehouse
- Enter the delivery details into the stock control system

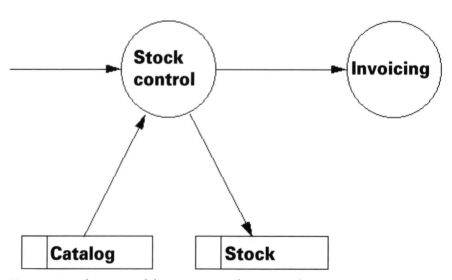

Figure 3.1. A fragment of the systems analyst's specification

As we look in more detail at these tasks, additional tasks will in turn be identified. For example, we may identify such tasks as:

- Maintain the list of suppliers
- Maintain supplier catalogs
- Maintain stock management tables (shelf life, re-order levels of stock items, etc.)

Notice how some of these additional taskflows arise directly from our decision to construct an application to support a particular workflow: stock management tables are purely an *artifact* of the decision to computerize the stock control. This adornment is typical of the process of translation from processes to taskflows.

Some of these tasks are inherently serial in nature; for example, 'Enter the delivery details...' must be the last step in the flow. Others are potentially parallel; the two steps 'Compare the delivery note with the original order' and 'Compare the actual delivery with the delivery note' can be carried out in either order, or even simultaneously. This does not automatically imply, however, that all of the parallelism available in the task should be made visible to the user. We shall return to this topic in considerable detail later.

Business rules

As we noted above, the systems analysis will be the major factor in identifying taskflows. The rules and standards of the business will then limit the choices that are available to us in turning processes into taskflows. One major aspect of this limitation is privilege: once a task has been specified, we need to identify which users (or strictly, which *roles*) are permitted to carry out a particular task. For example, altering re-order levels and stock levels of parts in store is a privilege reserved for a stock control specialist, who understands the potential costs and impact downstream in the business of raising or lowering the levels of stockholding. These restrictions will guide the designer either in partitioning separate roles into separate applications, or in constructing applications that respect the roles of each user. We address this question of privilege in more detail below.

Business rules may constrain the *sequence* in which particular tasks may be carried out. For instance, suppose that an order arrives from a new customer, one that we have not done business with before. There is no technical reason to bar this customer from being added to the customer database, the order from being fulfilled immediately, and the customer being invoiced in the normal way. The business rules, on the other hand, will almost certainly prohibit a new customer from being granted credit: they will be obliged either to pay up front or to wait until their credit references have been checked. So whereas for an existing customer we will ship, then invoice, then chase payment, for a new customer we get the payment (or a reasonable guarantee of payment) first, then ship.

If the systems analyst has done a thorough job, you may well find that she has identified these business rule dependencies, but there is no guarantee of this. Even if she has identified them, it will usually still fall to the user interface designer to identify appropriate mechanisms to implement them.

Tasks, data and roles

As we noted above, the issue of privilege is a key aspect of business rules. The questions that need to be asked of each task are:

- Which roles have the *responsibility* to carry out this task? For example, many people including stock control clerks may enter delivery details.
- Which roles have the *authority* to carry out this task? For example, only managers are permitted to modify the list of authorized suppliers.

It is not unusual to find that a role has responsibility for a task, but may lack the authority for certain aspects or subtasks. For example, if the clerk receives an order to enter, but the supplier is not in the existing list, we have a role conflict. One of the most subtle aspects of taskflow is identifying and dealing with such conflicts.

These conflicts arise because the question of privilege involves a three-way relationship between the tasks to be carried out, the data to be acted on, and the roles that carry out those tasks:

- A user acting in a particular role is responsible for carrying out a particular task.
- A task acts on (reads, updates, etc.) data in ways identified by the systems analysis.
- Actions upon the data are restricted according to role.

A useful design exercise is to construct three matrices corresponding to these relationships: Roles against Task Responsibilities; Tasks against Data Requirements; and Data Permissions against Roles. The first two matrices can then be used to deduce a fourth matrix, Roles against Data Requirements. A comparison of these two matrices, Data Permissions and Data Requirements, can then identify potential conflicts between authority and responsibility.

In complex systems it is useful to make use of another cross-reference, namely tasks that trigger other tasks. For example, the 'Stock Entry' task may trigger the 'Maintain Suppliers' task. It is useful to record explicitly that the 'Stock Entry' task only reads from the suppliers list, but may trigger the 'Maintain Suppliers' task, which can update the suppliers list. This approach leads to greater clarity than simply bundling all of the implied data accesses under the first task. By separating out the accesses specific to the triggering and triggered tasks, the designer exposes the triggering event that raises the authority/responsibility conflict. Once the point of conflict has been identified, the designer can make a well-informed choice to resolve it. We shall see examples of such choices in this and the next chapter.

At first sight, the designer might hope that by beginning with data and tasks, and using those matrices as the basis of role definitions, it might be possible to construct conflict-free roles. Unfortunately, in realistic cases, such as the missing supplier above, we will often find that a role may have appropriate authority for a task in nearly all cases. Allocating a task to a role of much higher authority merely to deal with a small percentage of exceptional cases is rarely acceptable from a business point of view. Such a solution would imply either granting too much authority to clerical workers, or alternatively allocating mainly clerical work to senior people.

Working styles

One of the major conflicts in any application is balancing freedom against constraint. Free taskflow allows the user to work as he finds best. Constrained taskflow guides the user to a successful conclusion. Freedom allows the user to organize his work to his own taste, leading perhaps to greater satisfaction on the part of the user. It may also allow a creative user to be more effective, finding innovative ways of working. Constraining the taskflow can improve the user's productivity by preventing the user from following dead ends, leading him to perform the right tasks in the right order, and may lead to greater satisfaction on the part of the user from an increased feeling of security through knowing that he has completed all the requirements of a task. Some users will feel frustrated by constraint; others will feel insecure without it. Much will depend on the personality of the user.

A great danger in this kind of decision is the natural tendency to project our own preferences onto users. As we noted earlier, users are not necessarily like us. Given the distribution of personality types discussed in Chapter 1, the commonest mistake is to offer the user the freedom that we would want, not the freedom that he needs. What may seem like restraint to us may feel like supportive guidance to him. Users may not necessarily enjoy or even benefit from being given all the freedom that is possible. One danger, as suggested above, is that too much freedom may make the user feel less secure. I have often witnessed conversations along these lines:

> *Designer:* OK, now you can enter the order.
> *User:* Do I enter the shipping address first, or the line items?
> *Designer:* You can do it either way.
> *User:* Yes, but which way *should* I do it?

This user clearly finds it hard to trust the designer's assurance that the two paths are equivalent. This distrust may be soundly founded on experience of previous applications!

Taskflow as automation

One danger that you must always beware of is the temptation simply to automate existing manual taskflows. In many cases, existing taskflows reflect the limitations of older technology (or even a complete lack of technology), rather than the actual requirements of the business's workflow.

I was involved in an analysis for an insurance company that had systems at its head office and also at a number of regional offices. Our analysis of processing for investment and savings policies revealed a taskflow that goes something like this. An agent, usually an independent financial adviser, sends in an application for a new policy to a regional office. This office enters the minimum details into its local system, and puts the policy and a printout from their system in the mail to head office. Overnight, details of all new policies are downloaded electronically to the head office system, and details and changes relevant to locally issued policies are uploaded to the regions.

Once the paperwork arrives at head office, the policy is reconciled with the information received electronically from the regional office, and full details are entered into the central system. Many errors in policy applications are picked up at this point, resulting in requests for clarification being sent to the regional office. Other updates are made as the application progresses through credit and reference checks, until eventually a policy is issued. During this period, which might last several days or even weeks, changes might still be made to the policy application in the regional system. Typical changes include corrections to the spelling of a name, addition of missing details such as date of birth or, with reasonable frequency, outright cancellation of the policy application.

Inevitably, this process led to frequent conflicts between changes to the data stored centrally and changes made regionally. Whenever a policy was changed both in the region and at head office on the same day, the overnight reconciliation meant that the region's changes were discarded in favour of the version held at head office. Local changes would then have to be identified and re-entered.

The insurance company in question had recognized that this process of checking and re-entering local changes was tedious, time-consuming and error prone. They wanted us to design a user interface that would make it easier for the administrators in the regional office to identify policies that had been updated from the centre, and to reconcile the local and central changes. They had in mind something that would allow the user to view the two versions side by side and somehow merge the changes into a single version.

In fact, what this process really needed was a thorough re-design to eliminate the conflicting updates. Better sharing, rather than duplication, of data; properly identified data ownership; and identification of sensible procedures for applying updates would all help to remove the problem. Trying to improve a fundamentally 'broken' process with a little visual magic is often a tempting cheap fix but ultimately is a mere palliative.

Summary

Translating processes into taskflows is a complex task, and the ideal designer will draw on her knowledge of both business needs and user needs to identify a design that satisfies both. In the section that follows we examine one key aspect of that satisfaction, namely closure. In principle closure should be driven by business requirements and user expectations, but all too often it is subordinated to technical ease of implementation.

Closure

If you work in any word processor or spreadsheet, you probably make regular use of the 'File/Save' command. This is a very simple example of a concept that I call *closure*. The act of closure is associated by the user with a subconscious sense of satisfaction, or of resolution of tension. In this specific instance, the user receives an affirmation that the work that she has done so far is safe, regardless of what might happen in the future, and so is released from concern of loss of work.

We can also think of closing a sequence of actions: the point at which the several steps that make up a single task are all completed is a point of closure. The point at which the user above chooses to perform 'File/Save' may correspond to reaching the end of a section, and choosing to 'make safe' that section before beginning the next. When working in my word processor, I always save my work both before and after performing a spell check; I do not feel secure that the corrections have been 'accepted' until I do so.

A third aspect of closure is represented by entering and leaving a region of 'high risk'. For example, as I type in this word processor I am in a region of low risk. If I hit an incorrect key, as indeed I frequently do, I can simply backup and correct it. This allows me to work at a relatively low level of concentration, at least as far as the actual typing is concerned. On the other hand if I begin a cut and paste operation I enter a region of high risk: one wrong keystroke, and potentially I can lose the contents of the cut buffer or clipboard. If I have cut a large piece of text, for example several paragraphs, the cost is significant. So while I am in this region of high risk, I experience a sense of tension and must concentrate more intensely on each keystroke to avoid a costly error. At the moment when I paste the buffer, I can lower my level of concentration, and once again there is a release of tension. Closure is a term used in psychology to describe the feeling of satisfaction or relief that a person feels in completing, or closing, a task. At the point of closure one is able to discard the component details of an open process from memory (particularly short-term memory): the process becomes defined in one's mind by its start and end points only. In that sense, closure is the point at which separate bits of information become a chunk. For our purposes closure has a somewhat broader meaning; I use the term closure to describe all of the following related scenarios, for which I have offered examples above:

- The user saves work in progress, thus setting a limit on the worst possible loss.
- The user completes a task or subtask, thus allowing short-term memory to be unburdened of the requirements of that task.
- The user leaves a 'risky' region and enters a 'safe' one, thus allowing the concentration level to be lowered.

What these have in common is that they are all associated in the user's mind with a sense of release and resolution. Closure is an extremely effective simplifier of tasks, reducing the burden on both short- and long-term memory. The desire to close is so strong in most people that it is exploited in various guises in all kinds of structured mental processes, which are consciously organized (either by the 'designer' or the 'user') to offer points of closure:

- *Computer programs are constructed from calls to functions and procedures for which the internal details, in principle, are hidden*   One of the reasons that complex computer systems are so hard to construct, debug and maintain is that in practice most programming environments offer very poor closure. It is very hard to make use of another piece of code without knowing all of the internal details; knowledge of the parameters and result of a function rarely provides full closure. Subprograms so often have hidden internal states or unadvertised external side-effects that they provide only a kind of 'leaky closure'. I suspect that one of the reasons for the appeal of object-oriented programming is that (at least in principle) it provides much stronger support for closure.
- *Mathematical theorems are constructed as a sequence of sub-theorems and lemmas, and draw on results known from other, already proven, theorems*   As each sub-theorem is proven, the reader need only retain its assumptions and its implications, not the internal arguments that led from the former to the latter.
- *Effective sales presentations are organized into major and minor points*   Once the listener accepts the assertions presented within each major point ('Our product is faster and lighter than the competition') he can discard from active memory the arguments that convinced him of it ('We have pioneered the use of high-technology alloys').
- *Musically minded readers will recognize a strong relationship to resolution and modulation in a musical piece*   The composer deliberately builds in the listener an expectation of, and a desire for, resolution. When the resolution is finally delivered the listener experiences an intense sense of release of tension and of satisfaction.
- *Amusing logical fallacies are often constructed by deliberately mis-applying previously closed steps*   Only the elephant and the whale give birth to offspring weighing over 50 kilograms. The president of the United States of America weighs over 50 kilograms. Therefore the President's mother is either an elephant or a whale.

Closure is so widely exploited that users have a natural expectation that an application, like any other complex process, will offer points of closure. It seems reasonable therefore to expect that a design that directly supports this expectation through a user interface that provides visible, concrete, frequent points of closure, will appeal to users. Such a design will emphasize the user's sense of security and satisfaction. Let us begin an examination of this idea by first looking at some examples of the consequences of failing to provide adequate closure.

Failure to close

As a user works in any application or tool, the amount of unsaved, uncommitted, or incomplete work builds up. As well as the other tensions of memory demands and concentration, this leads to a growing feeling of discomfort in the user's mind because, either consciously or subconsciously, the user is aware that the 'open' work is somehow at risk:

- Some kind of unexpected system failure may cause unsaved work to be lost, especially if the environment is unstable or unreliable. Even when the environment is stable, the user's perception, perhaps from past experience, may remain one of instability, leading to anxiety.
- Work may accidentally be lost through some sort of simple user error, such as closing a word processor document without saving changes. The user may be distrustful of the application's ability adequately to protect against such errors.
- The user may be afraid that under some circumstances she will be unable to proceed to closure.

For example, she may be entering the details of a delivery. She may know from experience that the data that is provided to her occasionally contains incorrect item catalog numbers. If she comes across such an error, she will be unable to complete entry of the delivery. As she progresses through the line items, her anxiety will increase, not decrease, as she has more unsaved work at risk. On the other hand, she may experience an enormous sense of relief if she does manage to commit a large piece of work!

A classic example of failure to close occurs with the DOS 'Backup' command, used to store backups of files to floppy disks. When you insert each disk, you are reminded that the contents of the floppy will be lost, and you are asked if you are sure you want to continue. This is an excellent question, with only one drawback. The only way you can be sure that you want to continue is to verify the contents of the disk; and the only way you can verify the contents (unless you have a spare computer!) is to interrupt the backup. The backup will then have to be restarted from the beginning. In other words, if the user has any doubt about the contents of a disk, he is unable to proceed to completion. Thus, as the user performs a large backup with a pile of floppy disks at his side, he will become increasingly anxious that the ever-dwindling pile of disks may be insufficient, knowing that the cost of failing to close is extremely high.

This example may seem laughable to users of multitasking operating systems: in a 'proper' operating system the user can just start up another session and examine the disk. Before we get too smug, we should note that many transaction processing applications present the user with an equally painful inability to close. The problem occurs in any application that employs the update strategy known as 'optimistic locking'. For those unfamiliar with the term, this is a strategy in which the user works against data fetched from the database *without* locking it, thus allowing other users to access the data. Only at the point when the user is ready to save (commit) his work does the system attempt to acquire locks on the records in question, checking that they have not been changed in the meantime.

There are many reasons to choose to implement an optimistic locking strategy, both technical and commercial, but it carries a significant risk of inability to close. The user may receive a system message that effectively says: 'Another user has changed these records. Re-query and try again'. The user cannot close, and so must discard his work, and try again. Worst of all, there is no guarantee that the user will be able to close the repeated work, as the same problem can occur again. Although the loss of work is in itself regrettable for the short-term loss of productivity, a longer-term issue is the lack of confidence that will be engendered in the user. In this kind of application, every update becomes an adventure; users can never be sure that they will be able to proceed to closure.

Affirming closure

I had the misfortune to work with the 'Beta' release of a major upgrade of a certain MS-Windows development tool. Like much 'Beta' code, it had an occasional tendency to crash, losing any unsaved work in the progress. To protect myself, I habitually saved my work every few minutes, and particularly after any large number of changes. Unknown to me, this tool had a highly unfortunate bug: the 'File/Save' command, while appearing to write to the disk, was not in fact saving anything! I discovered this only when the tool crashed, and I reloaded my application to find that over four hours' work had been lost. After that, I saved only to floppy disk (for the reassurance of hearing the disk spin) and checked the file's size date stamp through File Manager after each save.

This experience illustrates an important principle of closure. If the user is to experience the sense of resolution associated with closure, he needs to receive affirmative feedback that closure has occurred. In my case the sound of the disk and the sight of the date stamp provided the feedback I required.

Closure is not the same as save or commit: work must not merely be saved, it must be seen to be saved. The word processor that I am using right now has an 'autosave' feature (Fig. 3.2). This ensures that in the event of a power cut or other catastrophic failure I can never lose more than a few minutes' work. The autosave occurs very discreetly; if the document is on the network, I do not even hear the disk spin. In consequence I am generally unaware that a save has occurred, or how much time has passed since the last save. This discretion has certain advantages; for one, it does not interrupt the flow of my work. Unfortunately, without the affirmation I experience no sense of closure, so I save manually every few

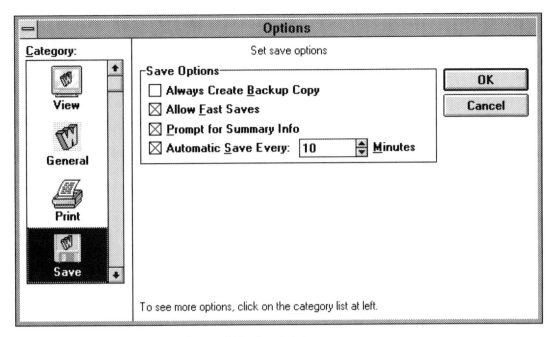

Figure 3.2. Microsoft Word Version 2.0 Autosave

minutes anyway. By contrast, another word processor that I use pops up a dialog box that interrupts my work and forces me to make an explicit save. This can be distracting, but does at least give an affirmative closure (Fig. 3.3). There is no easy resolution to this dilemma. As a designer, this is the kind of trade-off that you will often have to consider. Allowing each user to set a preferred level of affirmation is one solution; user testing of different scenarios may also help.

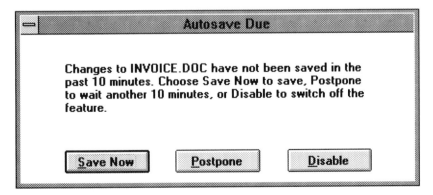

Figure 3.3. Affirmative autosave

Commit is not closure

In the example above, as with any word processor or similar tool, closure is (at least in theory!) under the explicit control of the user. While this may be highly desirable in many cases, it is not always appropriate. In many transaction processing applications, points of closure will be determined by business rules and transaction integrity. If this is the case the designer needs to ensure that the user is made aware of where closure points occur. Ideally this will be done by matching actual points of closure to the user's natural expectation of closure points; that is, closure points will correspond well to business units of work. If this is not practical the designer has an obligation to make points of closure explicit to the user.

As an example of matching closure to the user's expectations, consider the ATM or cash dispenser. The early design of these machines involved this sequence of actions:

- The customer inserts his card
- He enters his PIN code
- He specifies the sum of money required
- The cash is delivered
- The card is returned

This sequence frequently led to the customer walking away leaving his card in the machine. The problem is that the task in the customer's mind is 'Get Cash'. This task is closed for the customer when the cash is delivered, making it very easy to forget to retrieve the card. The modern design reverses the last two steps; the customer does not receive his cash until he has retrieved his card. In this rearrangement, the system exploits the customer's expectation of the point of closure to ensure that all the actions have occurred.

It is very often the case that for practical reasons such as the need to commit a transaction, we cannot easily match the system's need to close with the user's expectation of closure. Often this involves forcing closure before the user is ready for it. An order entry application that I have used allows the user to browse through orders in the system, making changes as she goes. She can modify as many order headers as she desires without committing, but as soon as she modifies a line item, she must commit her changes before she is allowed to browse another order.

Although there are solid technical reasons for this, to the user the distinction between modifying an order header and modifying line items is baffling. Indeed, the system's demands for commits can appear to be completely random. The user can sometimes postpone closure to match her expectations, but on other occasions is forced to close before she is ready, with no obvious difference between the two cases. It might well have been better in this application had the designer forced the user to commit each change, whether to header or to details. The user would then have been able to form a consistent theory, or expectation, of the system.

The opposite problem occurs when the user is not allowed to close, even though she is ready to do so. This usually involves not being able to save what the system regards as incomplete or partial work. A CASE tool I used to work in refused to allow the user to save an incomplete data flow diagram; because of the validation defined within its internal repository, it could not save data stores with no inflows, for example. Once I entered a diagram and began to edit it, I knew that I could not exit without returning to a valid state. On more than one occasion I found myself at the end of the working day facing a diagram in some disarray. Given the prospect of fixing up all the flows so that I could save and exit, I usually found it easier to delete the offending objects and re-enter them the following day!

This example may sound unusual, but in fact many transaction processing applications suffer from the same inability to save work in progress. In the application mentioned above the user may want to save the work in progress after entering a number of line items (simply for comfort) but without actually submitting the order. Unfortunately, the application does not permit this: the only two options open to the user are to submit the order, or to discard it.

It is a very common error for a designer to equate the system's need to commit a transaction with the user's expectation of closure. When the two cannot coincide, it is the designer's responsibility to make the mismatch explicitly visible to the user.

Breaking work down

The example above is one instance of a more general need for users to close before the system is ready. Users often need or want to be able to save work, even though they have not completed what the system or the business regards as a transaction. They simply want to 'hold' what they have so far, and put it beyond risk.

One way that the application can meet this need is to allow the user to divide a long and complex task into smaller components, each of which can be closed individually. There are two major ways to structure support for work breakdown: serial closure and hierarchical closure. Serial closure provides 'savepoints' or 'marks', by which the user can save work up to a given point against any risk of loss. Hierarchical closure divides a task into a set of nested component tasks. Once each of these components is committed, the overall task can be closed. This process of decomposition can be repeated to as many levels as necessary.

Broadly speaking, serial closure is preferential to hierarchical closure because it places fewer demands on short-term memory. Consider a task broken into steps A, B, C and D. At the first closure point the user closes A. At the second, he closes B, and can forget A entirely. He need only remember that he has completed the task *as far as* B. This continues for C and for D. At each stage, only the most recent closure is relevant. This is precisely what happens when you periodically save your work in a word processor or spreadsheet: only the most recent save matters.

Contrast this with a task divided into steps 1, 2, 3, . . . with substeps 1.1, 1.1.1, and so on. When the user gets to step 2.2.3, for example, he has to maintain a 'mental stack' of closed and open steps. More likely, he has a notepad next to his desk to record his state. This is not to say that hierarchical organization of tasks should be ruled out; only that it should be used with respect for the user's short-term memory limitations. Ideally the interface designer will make an appropriate representation of the 'closure stack' explicitly visible to the user.

In practice it is perfectly possible to combine both nested and serial closure points. Consider for example a more complex version of the order entry application. In this version, the user can choose to:

- Save each line item as it is entered or modified, without submitting the order to the system
- Save several line items, without submitting the order
- Save a partial or incomplete order, without submitting it, for later completion
- Modify several orders without submitting any of them, so that the user can view several associated orders and make related changes to all of them
- Return to an unsubmitted order and continue where it was last left
- Submit a completed order, when the user is ready
- Retrieve an incorrectly submitted order, if it has not already moved on in the process

This last point is particularly challenging. In the GUIs that I use most regularly, I can retrieve a file deleted in error, at least for a reasonable period. But this is just about the only serious mistake that I can rectify! Anything else I do of any consequence, most of which involves working against a relational database vastly more sophisticated than the MS-DOS file system, cannot be revoked once submitted. Many is the time I have wanted to recall a badly worded e-mail message sent in haste!

It is instructive to relate this proposal to support incomplete work to the idea of conceptual models discussed in the previous chapter. The order entry screen is usually a concrete expression of an order entry form with the 'advantage' that, unlike the paper form, which can be picked up and put down at any time, and left in any state of completeness, the electronic form can only be either discarded or completed. If order entry were truly modelled on its paper referent, it would allow the user to 'put it down' — to save work without loss — at any point. It is interesting to ask ourselves why anyone should be expected to use a computerized system that has less flexibility than its paper equivalent.

Of course, the capability to support incomplete work would be more challenging for the developer to implement, but it would correspond much more closely to the user's needs from the system. It could be achieved reasonably easily by allowing work in the system to have a status of 'incomplete' or 'in progress'. It is remarkable how many applications only allow for completed work in their models.

Summary

As a user works in an application, somewhere in his conscious or unconscious mind he is holding a closure goal, and is seeking to achieve that goal, with an accompanying resolution of tension. It can be difficult to tell if your design supports the user's closure points well, but some clues will quickly tell you if they do not.

Observe the users at work. Do they need a notepad at their side? Are they constantly jotting notes of what they have done, where they have got to, and where they are going? Do they make lists of tasks and tick them off one by one? If so, it is a fair bet that the application's closure points are not matching those of the users.

Closure is the mental goal of an application user. In the next section we discuss degrees of freedom; in other words, how many paths should we offer the user between initiating and closing a task?

Degrees of freedom

How would you feel if you had to shut down your computer before you could use your telephone? This would make for an extremely frustrating office environment. Yet this is precisely how many applications are constructed: once you have entered into a particular path of execution, such as enter an order, you are trapped in that path and can only either complete it or abandon it. Buying office supplies recently, I watched the sales clerk discard an almost complete order entry because he did not have the price for one item in my order. To run the on-line price catalog, he had to abandon the transaction in progress.

On the other hand, if the application provided no visible constraints at all, it would be extremely difficult to become productive. The application would be like playing the famous 'Adventure' game. You are faced with a prompt, and are left to guess how to progress. This is known as 'Black Cave' syndrome, and is always a possibility when the user is presented with too many choices or too little apparent guidance. These two extremes represent tyranny on the one hand, and anarchy on the other.

An anarchic application with total freedom itself represents another kind of tyranny: the tyranny of the blank screen. Many word processors, spreadsheets, and other office applications acknowledge this problem, and attempt to provide the new user with some more structured entry into the application.

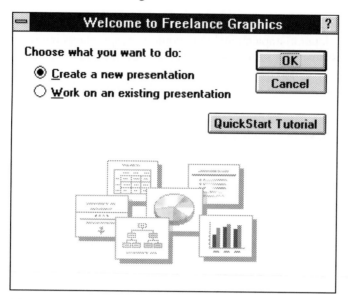

Figure 3.4. Lotus Freelance Version 2.0 startup screen

The screen in Fig. 3.4 is presented to the user when launching Freelance. It is an excellent example of guidance. (Unfortunately, it is also a very poor example of detailed design, as we shall see in a later chapter!) The user is presented with a direct choice between the only two possibilities: she either creates a new presentation, or works on an existing one. If she chooses to work on an existing presentation, the 'File Open' dialog is presented. If she chooses a new presentation, she is asked first to choose a 'Smartmaster' set (a graphic style for the presentation), and then a style (such as 'Title' or 'Bullet') for the first slide. In other words, the application leads her through the steps she would have had to carry out manually.

In a later section we shall discuss in more detail mechanisms such as this for implementing guidance and expressing the paths available to the user, but first we need to determine how much freedom to offer. We begin by looking at how much freedom is actually available, then consider reasons for restricting the freedom.

How much freedom?

Given a process to implement, the first job of the designer is to identify the constituent tasks. Having done so, she can then proceed to identify the degrees of freedom available. One useful approach is to examine dependencies between tasks. Dependencies may be simple, such as one task must be performed before another, or after another, or may be more complex: one task may be a subtask of another. Dependencies may be quite subtle: two otherwise unrelated sets of tasks may need both to be completed before a third set of tasks can be begun.

Useful questions that the designer can ask herself to identify these dependencies include:

- *Does a process contain tasks that must be carried out in a particular order?* In other words, are there tasks that are inherently serial? The contents of an order's delivery note cannot be checked against the original order until the order has been identified. On the other hand, the delivery note can be checked against actual delivery independently of any other task.
- *Does the user need to suspend a task in progress to carry out a related task?* The user might need to look up or add a name and address to be able to complete the entry of other details.
- *Does the user need to suspend one task to carry out an independent task?* The user might be recording details of one telephone call, when another more urgent call arrives, requiring him to suspend the call in progress and return to it later.
- *Do tasks or sequences of tasks need to synchronize at particular points?* The user may be able to enter an order header and its constituent line items in either sequence, but both must be entered before proceeding to the next step.
- *Does a task contain subtasks?* All of the above questions may be applied recursively to the subtasks of a task!

This kind of taskflow analysis, when applied to a large system, can lead to enormous complexity. It is important to apply it appropriately. The systems analyst is responsible for a 'first level' analysis of the business into related processes and data flows between them. Taskflow analysis can then be applied to each process. In practice, there will inevitably be an interplay between these two levels. The taskflow analysis may reveal coupling (dependencies) between processes that appeared to be independent; such processes might better be combined into a single process. Conversely, taskflow analysis might reveal that a process is composed of two entirely independent elements that might better be represented separately.

Discipline and restraint

It might seem tempting to conclude that we want applications to be as free as possible, within the limits set by the business rules and technical requirements. Unfortunately there are many cases that are not so straightforward. For example, one Windows application that I use involves recording details of customer service calls. I can enter the name and company of the caller, the time and date of the call, and details of the discussion in any order. However, if the caller is not in the database I must add him, which I can only do by discarding any call details that I have already entered, adding the caller's name, then restarting the call. A similar (character-based) application that I also use always requires me to enter the caller first, adding him if necessary. Only then can I proceed to enter the call details.

The second application in this comparison is more constrained, more serial, than the business rules strictly require. However, it is this less free application that in practice is both more comfortable and more productive in use. The comfort comes from the reassurance of knowing that I shall always be able to reach closure. There are really only two acceptable implementations of this taskflow: a completely free flow, in which I can work in any order *under all circumstances*, including entering a new customer; or a tightly constrained flow in which I am only allowed to work in sequences that always lead to successful closure.

The first application falls between these two possibilities: it allows as much freedom as the designer could easily provide, but unfortunately this corresponds poorly to the freedom that the user needs. As a result the user is allowed to enter a path that cannot be closed. Rather than allowing the user more freedom, in fact all we have done is mislead the user into making an additional mistake.

We noted earlier an example of an order entry application that might also benefit from less freedom. We wanted actions that (from the user's viewpoint) are directly comparable to offer the same degree of freedom. In that case the action was editing order headers and order line items. Although to us as designers it may be perfectly reasonable that data based on master and detail tables should behave differently, to the user it seems nonsensical that a restriction should apply to one part of the order form and not to another. We have an obligation to hide that difference from the user. If we cannot (within reasonable cost of implementation) make editing details as free as editing the master, then we should make editing the master as restrictive as editing the details. The user would be able to form a more consistent model of the system if he were obliged to commit each changed order, regardless of the particular change, before moving to another.

A third reason for limiting the user is simply to avoid overload of the user's mental capabilities. Consider an insurance organization selling home cover policies over the telephone. The telesales operator needs to take the following details from the user before offering a quote and issuing a policy:

- Name and address
- Type of residence
- Level of cover required
- Previous history of claims and cover
- Method of payment

Technically, these sets of details are independent, and could be collected in any order. If the user is left to work through them at whim, he may easily miss something. By contrast, if the application leads him methodically through the steps, while still allowing him to backtrack without loss if necessary, the likelihood of error is reduced. Does implementing all the parallelism available actually help or hinder the user?

As these examples show, restricting the freedom offered to the user can offer benefits in a number of ways:

- We *may* eliminate paths of execution that might not lead to closure
- We can increase the consistency of usage, which *may* help the user to build a consistent mental model
- We can reduce the concentration demanded of the user, which *may* reduce the burden of responsibility and improve accuracy

It is important to note the word 'may' in all of the above statements. Much will depend, as always, on the nature of the task and the types of people who will use the application.

Expressing dependencies

Another way of considering the first example above, recording customer service calls, is to note that the (apparently) unconstrained version actually promises more than it delivers. It hides a constraint, namely that the caller's details must already be recorded, and so gives the user a false expectation. Although it implies that the user can work in either order, there is a *hidden dependency* in the logic that is not expressed in the user interface.

This is an extremely strong instance of the visibility principle: the user interface *must express explicitly* every dependency that actually underlies it. Few things are more frustrating to the user than a hidden dependency.

Summary

In determining the freedom to be offered to the user, the designer needs to:

- Identify technical and technological limits
- Uncover business and process dependencies
- Make allowance for user limits and expectations

Finally, every dependency that the designer implements should be clearly expressed to the user.

Modes

There are two well-established and widely held principles when it comes to modes:

- Modes are fundamentally evil and should be avoided at all costs.
- Modes provide support and guidance and should be provided wherever possible.

Part of the problem is that it is very hard to define exactly what is meant by a mode. Most of us think we can recognize one when we see one, but it is very difficult to put down in writing a definition that is both useful and consistent. Modality of windows in an application is easy enough to define, but there are many other kinds of mode.

The Unix editor 'vi' presents one of the most infamous examples of modes. The user operates in one of several modes, most commonly 'insert' mode or 'command' mode. In insert mode, each keystroke is treated as a character to be added to the file. In command mode, (almost) every keystroke is treated as a command: 'x' deletes a character, 'l' moves the cursor one character to the right, and so on. Many users, even experienced users, make mistakes with vi as a result of not knowing what mode they are in. It is impossible to tell merely by inspection (in most implementations of vi). The only test that is certain is to type a character, and the only safe character is 'Escape', which exits from insert mode to command mode. If you are already in command mode, 'Escape' just beeps. If you watch vi users at work, you will often see them hit 'Escape' several times, until they hear the reassuring confirmation of the beep.

This gives us our first definition of a mode: the same keystroke (or more generally, user action) has *distinct* meanings according to the mode. By contrast, my pocket electronic personal organizer is modeless. I can enter the details of an appointment onto the screen, then choose to either search for an appointment that matches (by hitting the 'Next' key) or enter the appointment into the diary (by hitting the 'Enter' key). There is no 'enter query' prefix, there are no separate query or edit modes, and all commands are available at all times.

Which of these two approaches, modal or modeless, is preferable? In fact this is an unanswerable question, and this is another reason for most designers' ambivalence towards modes. The two approaches simply allow the user to make different mistakes. In vi, I can easily mistake which mode I am in, and begin typing characters when in fact I am in edit mode, with unexpected and potentially disastrous consequences. Conversely, with the modeless personal organizer, I occasionally fail to save appointments. I enter an appointment, then hit the 'Next' key, intending to move to the next day in my diary, without first hitting 'Enter'. The organizer interprets my action as 'Search for a match', and my entry is lost. In a modal implementation, the 'Next' key would be ignored until after I have committed my changes.

Granularity of modes

Any worthwhile statement about modes must include some idea of level or granularity. For example, this word processor is *modeless at the level of documents*. In other words, if I am working in a document and am not in a 'restricted' state such as a modal dialog, I can choose to work in any of the other open documents. If I enter a modal dialog mode, it is equally modal with respect to all open documents. This paradigm is typical of the MS-Windows Multiple Document Interface (MDI), discussed in more detail in Chapter 4.

By contrast, a typical form-filling application might be modeless within a given form, but modal with respect to other forms: the user must complete one form before she is allowed to work in another.

It turns out to be remarkably difficult formally to define modes in a way that excludes 'trivial' types of modality but includes 'proper' modes like those above. For example, if I press 'S', in my word processor I get the character S, unless I am holding the Control key down at the time. This may not seem like a mode; in the normal sense, we would prefer to think of 'Control+S' as a different action, rather than the action 'S' while in 'Control' mode. However, without the idea of granularity it is all but impossible to give a formal definition of a mode that excludes such low-level, transient modes.

Modes are pervasive. Even the most modeless application is modal at some level of granularity.

Definitions of modes

Given that definitions of modes are extremely difficult, let us see how close we can get. Let us begin with the following first attempt:

- Version 1: A system is modeless if a user action has the same interpretation whenever and wherever it is attempted.

This definition implicitly includes the restriction that every action is always available. A little reflection shows that this definition is useless for all practical purposes. Any graphical application will have various areas of the screen where clicking the mouse has distinct meanings. For example, the present word processor has an area where the text is presented, button bars, a menu bar, and a status line, as well as 'non-client' areas such as a title bar, minimize and maximize buttons, and scroll bars. Clicking the mouse (the simplest conceivable action) in these different areas is interpreted completely differently by the system. So we need to qualify our definition:

- Version 2: A given *space* within a system is modeless if a user action has the same interpretation whenever and wherever it is executed within that space.

In other words, it is more practical to consider the modality of separate portions of the screen than of the whole application, especially when we consider that mouse actions and movements have such widely different meanings.

It is important to note that the idea of a space is to be understood conceptually, not physically. For example, double-clicking the background in MS-Windows brings up the Task Selector. Which physical locations of the screen count as the background depends on what concealing windows are open. A space is to be thought of in terms of ideas like 'inside', 'outside' or 'over', rather than a particular physical position. This definition of a conceptual space also encompasses pop-up windows, drop-down menus and other dynamic display items, as well as direct manipulation of displayed objects.

One benefit of this definition is that it disposes quite handily of the trivial modes present in every application: when the cursor is on a given item or control, keystrokes or mouse clicks apply to that control and are interpreted by it. Typing 'D' when the focus is on a pushbutton labelled 'Delete' is clearly quite different in meaning from typing 'D' when the focus is on a text field. Given the second version of the definition, we only care whether, for example, double-click always means the same to a text item, not whether it means the same to a text item and to a button.

Moving between spaces

One question immediately arises from this definition: how does the user move between spaces? For example, consider the action of opening a drop-down menu. In MS-Windows, this can be done by clicking on the menu item, for example 'File', putting the user into 'select from menu' mode. The selection can then be made with the mouse, cursor keys or the keyboard. The menu remains until either the user makes a selection, or until he dismisses it. He can do this by hitting the 'Escape' key, or simply by clicking in another space.

In this case it is so easy to move in and out of the menu space, or mode, with the mouse that many people will not even have identified it as a mode. The fact that it really is a distinct space or mode becomes clearer if you attempt to drive the menu exclusively through the keyboard. On the other hand, if you enter the space of a modal dialog box, such as Fig. 3.5, you can only enter another space by resolving the dialog, either by OK or Cancel.

In terms of modality, what distinguishes this dialog from the drop-down menu? To dismiss the menu mode, the user clicks in the space outside it; to dismiss the

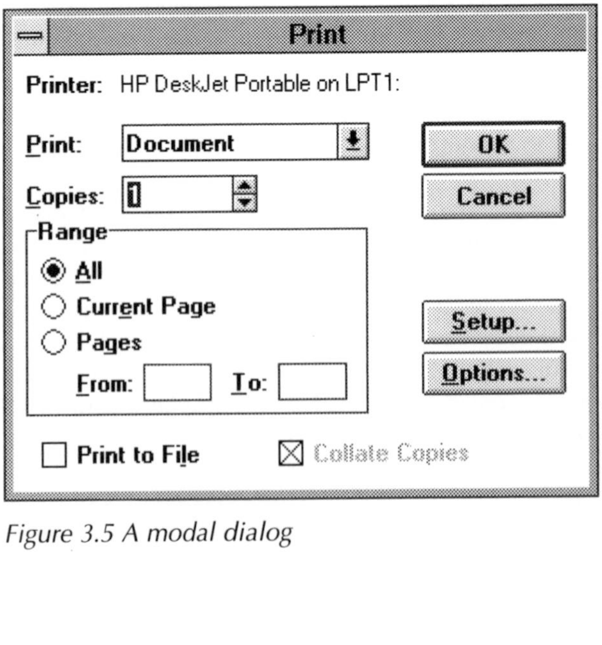

Figure 3.5 A modal dialog

modal dialog mode, the user clicks on a button. Modality is apparently related to the ease with which one can move between the spaces. It is at this point that the definition begins to get subjective:

- Version 3: An application is considered modeless if it consists of spaces that are themselves modeless, and the user can move 'easily' between spaces.

At this point modality becomes a subjective experience of the user interface. Whether or not a space is modeless depends on what level of granularity you examine it at. Whether the spaces are modeless with respect to each other depends on the user's understanding of 'easy'.

Principles for modality

Modeless applications are something of a Holy Grail, to be sought even if never achieved. Modeless design can sometimes be an excuse for abdicating the designer's responsibility to support the user's taskflow. The user is simply given complete freedom, and left to work out her own taskflow. Entering a mode is one of the ways in which the user can inform the application of her intentions ('Enter a query'), which allows the application to guide her to that goal. Modes have an important role to play in the design, but need to be designed carefully if they are not to be damaging.

Many transaction processing applications use modal forms: each form can be used either to perform a query by example against the database (query mode), returning a set of records that the user can update; or the form can be used to insert and modify records previously queried from the database (edit mode). Typically, there is a magic key that introduces a query (enters the mode) and another to perform the query (exits the mode). Ambiguity arises when the user specifies a query that returns no records. What mode is the user now in? Should the user be returned to edit mode with an empty set of records, or left in query mode and asked to re-specify the query? Many applications assume that a query returning no matches implies that the user simply made a mistake and needs to make a small adjustment to one of the query criteria. Other applications assume that the user's intention was to verify that the item she is about to enter does not already exist. Very few applications make it clear to the user which mode she is left in.

Despite all of this uncertainty, it is still possible to propose some rules that will make modes more useful and less harmful, regardless of the level of granularity that is being considered.

- *Use modes consistently*   From the user's point of view, similar 'spaces' should behave in similar ways. For example, in Microsoft Word Version 2.0, the spell checker is modeless but the thesaurus is modal.
- *Do not initiate modes unexpectedly*   In certain transaction processing appli- cations that I use, all data entry forms are completely modeless, allowing me to

navigate freely around the form until I enter a mandatory field. At this point I am 'trapped' in that field until I supply a value for that field. The mode arises without warning.

- *Make it clear to the user that she has entered a mode* Well-designed applications provide feedback that is highly visible without being obtrusive. The vi editor offers no feedback at all. For example, given that the user cannot click outside a modal window, it would be appropriate to change the cursor shape when the user moves the mouse outside the boundaries of the active area.
- *Make it clear to the user how she escapes from a mode* Again, vi gives no visible clue that the Escape key terminates Insert mode. If the user prepares a query in a transactional application, make it clear how she either executes the query or cancels the mode without querying. If the query returns no records, make it explicitly clear to the user which mode she is left in.
- *Always make it possible for the user to escape from a mode harmlessly* In the simplest case, this means that modal dialogs always have a 'Cancel' button.

Modes operate at all levels of the user interface. We have introduced them here as an aspect of taskflow, but they will also form a significant component of dialog flow (Chapter 4) and detailed design (Chapter 5). Modes can be a very powerful mechanism for guiding the user to perform correct actions in the correct order, but only if they are used in a way that respects the fundamental principles of visibility, feedback, mappings and cues.

Design conflicts

As you design taskflow, you will rapidly become aware of a number of conflicts. We have already discussed the differing needs of different classes of users in terms of the jobs they undertake, the responsibilities they are given and even their personality types. In addition to all this, the needs of experienced users and those of novice users, frequent and infrequent users, power users and those with a simple job that they need to get done as rapidly as possible, are often in contradiction with each other.

Immediate use versus long-term use

In particular, two properties frequently asserted to be key benefits of graphical user interfaces are very often in opposition. These are ease of learning (or immediate use) and ease of (long-term) use. Ease of learning suggests immediately intuitive design with plenty of visibility, lots of guidance, and simple, easily understood tasks. Ease of use implies providing the user with efficiency of expression, uninterrupted flow and powerful, complex commands available at the touch of a button. One of the great dangers of usability testing is that it is generally carried out with subjects who are unfamiliar with the application, and so we end up testing ease of learning only. For the experienced user,

- *Too much guidance will become obstruction* If the user is obliged to pick her way step by step through a process that she knows by heart, confirming every 'dangerous' action, she will quickly become frustrated.
- *Too much feedback will be perceived as instability* If the user interface lacks fixed 'points of reference', it becomes difficult for the users to learn. For example, at one point the designers of the Macintosh experimented with 'scaled' scroll bars in text boxes and document windows. 'Normal' scroll bars have a moving scroll button or slider of a fixed size, whose position indicates the position of the visible window relative to the whole document. A 'scaled' scroll bar, on the other hand, has a variable size slider, the size of which indicates the proportion of the document that is visible. For example, if almost all of the text is visible, the slider will almost fill the scroll bar. As the text gets longer, the slider shrinks as the proportion of visible text gets smaller. To the experienced user, the size of the slider provides additional feedback. Experiments at Apple revealed that this was at the cost of ease of learning: new users, most of whose documents are small, took longer to learn how to use the slider; some failed entirely to discover its function.
- *Too much visibility will overload the user with information* Some applications bombard the user with a menu, a status line, button bars on all four sides of the window, floating palettes, several scroll bars, etc. From all of this information, how is the user expected to pick out the relevant elements?

Having said this, it should be borne in mind that the majority of applications in use today are in no danger of providing too much anything! One of the most frequent questions I am asked by designers, all of whom of course are expert and experienced users, is: 'Won't all of this be obstructive to the expert user?' My reply is always: most user interfaces are so difficult to learn, hardly anybody ever becomes an expert user.

Conflicts of this kind are not unique to the question of taskflow design. Just as the principles of visibility and feedback apply at every level of the interface, so these potential conflicts also arise at every level.

Design notations

It is useful to be able to sketch on paper a schematic representation of the task-flow that you have identified. As in any other part of analysis and design, it is a useful discipline to the designer that allows her to be thorough and systematic. It also allows her to communicate her proposals with her fellow designers in a concise and complete manner. A good notation will also help the designer to identify areas where it may be beneficial to reduce the amount of freedom available to the user, for example by exposing areas which are at a similar 'level' to the user, but which for technical or business reasons have different degrees of freedom.

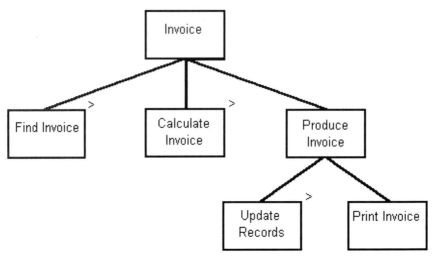

Figure 3.6. A sample Jackson structure diagram

Structure diagrams

Many formal or informal notations can be used by the designer, provided the notation allows her to express parallel and serial processes, alternate and optional paths, synchronization, points of closure, and decomposition into subtasks. Jackson structure diagrams (Fig. 3.6) and similar techniques can be used to good effect. Whatever technique you choose, whether formal or informal, it is advisable to annotate your diagrams freely. This is clearly essential when using an informal notation in order to resolve ambiguities. It can be even more important to add explanatory notes in a formal notation: in my experience, the more rigorous and complete a notation, the less readily is it understood by people!

Beware of state diagrams

There is one notation that I would strongly advise against, which many people often seem tempted to use. That notation is state diagrams, or anything that resembles them. They are at first sight an attractive way of describing user interactions, and work reasonably well for the kind of very simple examples that fit neatly into textbooks, but are unusable for interactions of any reasonable complexity. The reason is simple arithmetic. In any process that has paths that are not strictly serial — in other words, flows that can be followed either in parallel or optionally — the number of states tends to grow exponentially with the number of steps on those paths.

Recall the insurance telesales example above, which had five independent sets of questions that the telesales agent had to ask. Assuming that order of execution is not significant, and that each set of questions can only be in one of two states (completely asked or completely unasked), if we describe a fully parallel taskflow this process requires 32 states and 80 transitions between them! Yet the process is trivial to describe in words or draw as a structure chart. Demonstrably, state diagrams are not appropriate at this level of specification. Anyone who remains unconvinced is invited to draw the diagram in question, then ask another designer to deduce what it represents!

Summary

In the first part of this chapter we have identified a number of goals that the designer seeks to achieve in designing taskflow. Let us remind ourselves of those goals:

- Implement the tasks and flows identified by the analyst.
- Enforce business rules that impact and restrict those flows as they apply to different roles and users.
- Support the user through a consideration of closure, degrees of freedom and modality.

In the second part of this chapter we turn our attention to mechanisms that can be used to implement these goals, mechanisms that can raise the visibility of closure, open or restrict freedom, and guide or restrain the user.

Mechanisms for implementation

There are many mechanisms that can be used to achieve the goals that we have identified, though from a cursory examination of many business applications, their designers might be surprised to discover that there are more subtle methods of guidance than modal windows.

We shall suggest a number of techniques, all of which have certain advantages and disadvantages, and are appropriate in different circumstances. A typical application will make use of a selection of these techniques, not be restricted to a few or to a single choice. It is only with experience that you will develop your own repertoire of techniques and a sense of appropriate choice of the right tool for the right job. The list presented here is by no means exhaustive, but should give you enough ideas to avoid the omnipresent modal dialog and its OK or Cancel.

Guidance

We have already seen one example of guidance earlier in this chapter, in the Freelance startup screen. There are many opportunities to lead a user step by step through a complex process. Some common forms of guidance include:

- *Windows installation programs*   Instead of being given a complex list of instructions (disk copies, file moves, directory creation, and edits to system files) to carry out, the user follows a series of dialogs that perform the operations in response to answers to questions about the user's intentions.

- *Wizards* Many applications contain automated sequences that carry out complex tasks on behalf of the user, such as inserting and formatting a table, or creating a reference to a figure in a word processor. The user is automatically presented with each window that needs to be completed in turn. Disparate commands are linked together to achieve the user's task.

- *Coaches and tutorials* Coaches can provide on-screen instructions to the user, tracking his process, and telling him what to do next. Though helpful, coaches are often inflexible if the user ignores or misinterprets the instructions and leaves the correct path. On-line tutorials can be useful, but are often of less value than coaches. Tutorials are generic and act out of context, whereas coaches are specific and act in context. Some tutorials include animations that demonstrate a command in action, and these can be a powerful method of teaching a user to carry out a task for himself. Unfortunately they are generally difficult and complex to construct, so you need to be convinced of their value before undertaking such a development effort.

Guidance can be very useful in applications that inherently have a lot of freedom, such as a word processor, and where productivity can benefit if the user can be encouraged to learn more of the capabilities of the application. Well-designed guidance is characterized by these features:

- The guidance can be enabled and disabled readily; it is under the user's control.
- The experienced user can bypass it completely.
- It encourages the inexperienced user to learn for himself, rather than to become dependent on the automated wizard.

Locks

There are many occasions when steps must interact or synchronize, and locks are an effective way of enforcing this. Locks can be very flexible, ensuring that only valid sequences of actions occur, but without tripping the user up unnecessarily. The user is allowed to perform actions in any order, the system then ensuring that events occur in the right order. A well-designed lock is like a good watchdog: it doesn't bark in the night without good reason.

Strict lockouts are the strongest and commonest form of lock. They are mechanisms that prevent an illegal event from occurring, or prevent the user from making a mistake in the first place. Examples include disabling of commands (such as an 'OK' button) until all required information is supplied.

Interlocks are more subtle, and they guide a user to perform the right actions at a synchronization point. A common example is demonstrated when you attempt to exit Windows without saving work in an application. Windows offers each

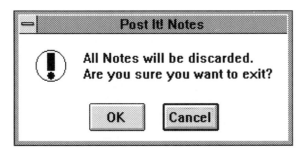

Figure 3.7. An interlock in action

application the opportunity to respond to the exit, or in other words to synchronize. Each application in turn can present the user with the chance to save
outstanding changes, or even prevent the exit altogether, as in Fig. 3.7.

Interlocks may be implicit or explicit. The interlock in Fig. 3.7 is an explicit
interlock: the application reminds the user of the interdependency and offers the
opportunity to act on it. An implicit interlock, once established by the user, works
silently. For example, the user may set up an interlock that automatically saves
her changes without asking when she exits from the spreadsheet.

Forcing techniques

Guidance and locks can be subtle non-blocking mechanisms for implementing
flow. Sometimes it is appropriate or even necessary to be more forceful with the
user; to offer him a very narrow range of choices, or even a single path. There are
a range of forcing techniques that are suitable for such circumstances.

Forcing can occur at the level of windows. Modal dialog boxes are one example
of this, and can be used individually or in stacks to ensure that a series of actions
is performed in a narrow and restricted channel. Figure 3.8 presents a typical
example. The disadvantage of modal dialogs is that they lock the user out of all
other parts of the application. If the user of this application decides at the last
moment that he needs to double-check the page layout he must cancel all the
way out of this stack, make any changes, and re-enter it.

Alerts are an even more forcing form of modal dialog. Both modal dialogs and
alerts will be examined in more detail in Chapter 4.

Mandatory or required fields also have a role to play in forcing the flow,
preventing the user from exiting a window or moving forward until he has provided all the information required. Similarly, commands and other items can be
dynamically enabled and disabled:

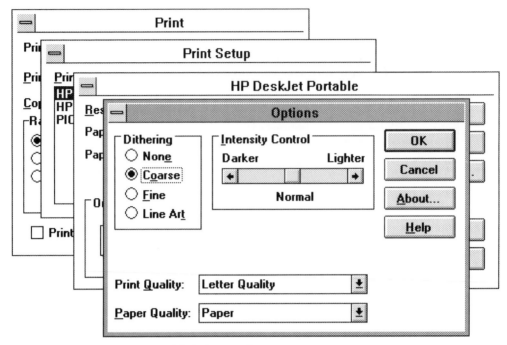

Figure 3.8. A modal dialog stack

- The user can be prevented from choosing inappropriate or unavailable options.
- The user can be given a visual indication of completed work by enabling commands progressively as information is supplied.
- The user can be led through a complex process by enabling options in turn as he progresses.

Work queues and task lists

One of the least forcing and potentially most attractive mechanisms for controlling taskflow is through work queues, also known as task lists. If the implementation is well designed, such mechanisms can be highly generic and data driven, allowing them to be reused easily across an application. The user of the application is presented with a list of tasks or steps to be carried out. All the steps presented at any one time are modeless with respect to each other; they can be completed in any order, or even simultaneously. The example in Fig. 3.9 shows a simplified example for use in an´ organization that offers personal loans by mail. The user can select any step and execute it; completed steps are indicated by a check mark. The user can work serially through the steps, or open several steps at once. Once the steps presented have been completed, the next step in the process appears in the list, and so on until the

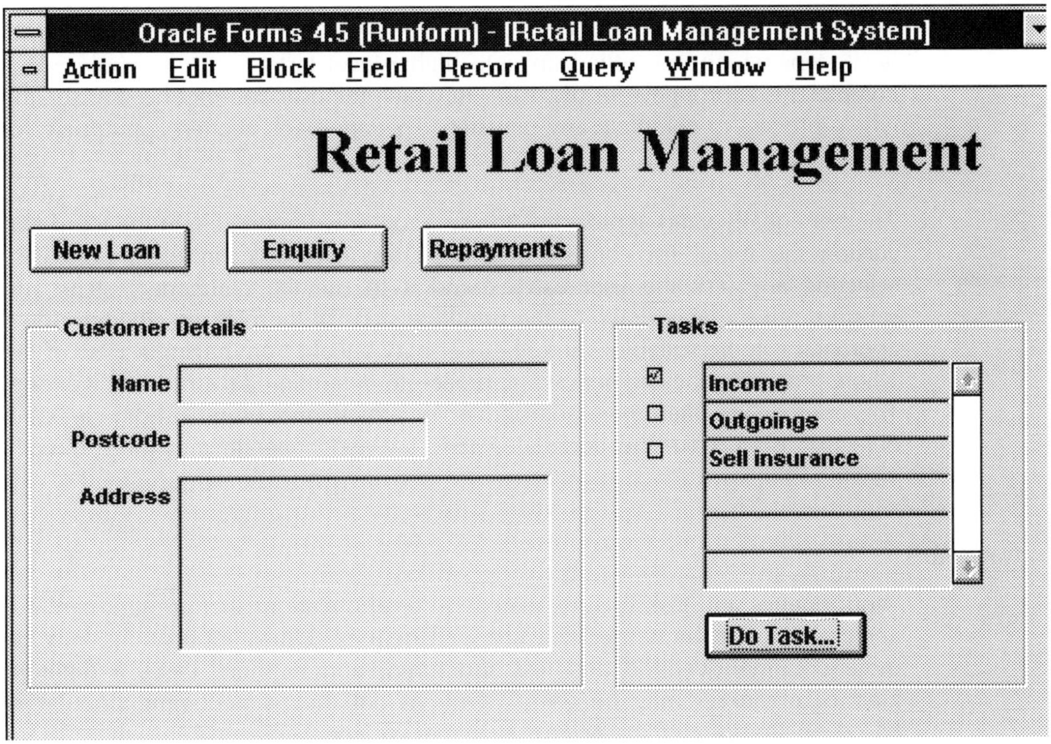

Figure 3.9. Steps in granting a personal loan

whole process is completed. This kind of mechanism has a number of highly attractive features:

- The implementation mechanism can be data driven, and so is easily modified to match changes in business practice, and can be self-customizing for different classes of user or business roles.
- The required flow is made explicitly visible to the user at all times, as is the user's progress.
- The flow can be made as modeless as the business permits, or as modal as the user prefers.
- The interface provides strong support to short-term memory as the user is not asked to maintain a mental stack; the 'task stack' is explicitly visible.
- The interface strongly supports closure by providing multiple serial closure points, including feedback at each closure.
- The model is able strongly to support partial work by saving the information entered so far together with the state (complete, partially complete, and incomplete steps).

This kind of bottom-up approach, where the user is initially presented with low-level steps which are 'rolled up' into higher-level tasks until the whole job is complete, is appropriate for processes in which the user does not need to see the whole process to complete any one step. This approach is often appropriate for clerical tasks.

Another equally valid approach is to use a top-down approach. In the top-down version the initial list consists of the highest-level tasks in the process. By selecting any task the user can expand it to see the component steps and substeps, all the way down to the primitive steps of the process. The top-down approach is more suitable where the user may benefit from having a view of the whole process, choosing her own approach to determining the order of working. This approach is often more appropriate for professional users. In both cases the objective is to make the underlying taskflow and dependencies more directly visible to the user.

Navigators

Work queues and task lists are excellent for applications that are task-centred, and the steps to be carried out are well defined. Other applications may be more document-centred and less structured, and in those cases a different kind of organizer may be useful. One model that is becoming popular is based on the idea of the Microsoft Windows File Manager tree, where branches can be expanded and collapsed under the user's control. In some applications, all the leaves of the tree must be populated; in others, the user decides when the tree is sufficiently populated; in still others, the tree may contain parts that must be populated and others that are optional. This kind of application is epitomized by GUI development tools such as Oracle Forms, shown in Fig. 3.10.

A module consists of components such as windows, blocks, items, and procedures. Each category can be expanded or collapsed at will, allowing the user to control the complexity of the view that she sees. The user can also choose alternate presentations, such as a 'visual hierarchy': windows contain canvases which contain items. Although there is no fixed order of working nor any predetermined definition of completeness, this kind of navigation tree provides substantial guidance to the user in reviewing and tracking her work. Outline view in word processors and presentation graphics packages, in which parts of the work can be collapsed and expanded, are also examples of this idea.

We can imagine a similar approach, as an example of a more structured application, for medical records. The top of the tree will now present the doctor's patients. Under each patient will be personal details (required), and a series of treatment records (optional). Under each treatment record might be a medical history, including treatments provided, consultants visited, appointments atten-

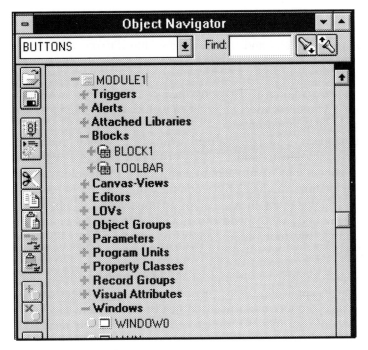

Figure 3.10. Oracle Forms Version 4.5

ded, referrals, and so on. The physician can browse and navigate this tree, opening all of those records relevant to the current illness, and closing (hiding) those
not relevant. This might be significantly easier to use than the traditional tree of
menu functions oriented around the corresponding database tables.

Customization and macro languages

At the time of writing it is fashionable to allow the user a degree of control over
his own user interface. The user may be given the ability to rearrange menus and
button bars, or choose which elements are displayed. Macro languages that
provide keystroke recording and playback for frequently used actions have been
around since long before the advent of the GUI; and in the most complex cases,
the user can write full-blown programs with their own dialogs in a macro
language.

Customization is superficially attractive for a number of reasons:

- All users will be able to optimize the interface to their own personal needs.
- It relieves us from much responsibility for the interface.
- We can meet the needs of different classes of users with a single application.

In practice, customization is often in danger of being a dangerous gimmick:

- Rearranging buttons and menus makes little difference if the actions available to put behind those buttons and menus are poorly defined in the first place.
- If users are so good at designing their own interfaces, why employ professionals? If you allow users to modify a well-designed interface, they will probably only make it worse.
- What happens to a personalized interface if several people use a single machine from time to time?
- It is highly tempting for certain individuals to devote a disproportionate amount of time to developing complex macros that is out of all proportion to the value of those macros to their work. I am sure that we all know somebody who spends hours writing Word Basic programs that total and format his monthly expenses, or dBase macros to compute prime numbers.

Customization does have an appropriate and important role to play, especially when a single application must meet the needs of different classes of user, or when a single product must meet the needs of many organizations. Like every other aspect of user interface design, it must be carefully designed and implemented in accordance with business and user needs. It should not be seen as an opportunity to abdicate our design responsibilities. Too often I have encountered the attitude that it does not matter if we do the design badly now as the user can put it right later!

Summary

As noted earlier, the mechanisms suggested above are by no means an exclusive list. There are many other mechanisms by which the user can be guided or constrained; the application can make the underlying taskflow explicit; and dependencies can be made visible to the user. Some of those mechanisms may be far more complex and sophisticated than the ones presented here. These suggestions should give you some inspiration in finding an appropriate degree of guidance and constraint, rather than the black and white choices represented by the rigor mortis of modal dialogs on the one hand and the anarchy of unconstrained forms on the other.

Major classes of taskflow

Although there are many possible forms of taskflow, two patterns recur so frequently in transaction processing and business applications that it is useful to discuss these two broad classes. These classifications should be taken as very gross characterizations of different classes of applications: after all, characterizations do not get much broader than dividing all business applications into one of two categories!

Many business applications consist of carrying out a well-defined set of tasks and steps in an order that may not be completely fixed, but is at least in principle highly restricted. Such applications are often found in clerical work, supporting service representatives, aiding telephone selling, fulfilling orders, processing invoices and so on. Such applications are *task-oriented*.

These applications are characterized by a taskflow in which the user works through tasks, steps and substeps, reaching closure points determined by the application, under the control and guidance of the application. Little if any personal initiative in determining the task content is required or even permitted.

By contrast, other applications provide a set of 'tools' such as editors and filters to the user, who must synthesize her own tasks from these building blocks. Such applications typically have few or no predetermined tasks; the user is expected to be able to compose her own tasks. Such applications are typically provided to professional users, knowledge workers and others whose tasks are difficult to predetermine or which are inherently ill defined. In many cases it may simply be impossible to provide 'tasks' that correspond to all of the possible actions the user might want to carry out. I call these applications *subject-oriented* (the term object-oriented already having been taken!).

These applications are characterized by a taskflow in which the user first performs a search for the invoice, patient record, letter, document, or other subject to work on, usually aided by various kinds of filter appropriate to the domain in question, then selects and acts upon that subject. The actions are typically very simple, such as discard, rename, move, duplicate, or edit the contents. The user then returns to search for another subject for her actions. I call these two phases discrimination/identification and selection/action.

Characterizing taskflow

If we compare these two classes of application side by side, certain characteristics emerge (Table 3.1).

Typically, a subject-oriented application *supports* the user's job, whereas a task-oriented application *is* the user's job. In designing taskflow for these two classes, the emphasis from the designer's viewpoint falls quite differently. For a task-oriented application, the key is good identification of tasks and well-chosen closure points. For a subject-oriented application, it is most important to choose the correct subjects to represent (invoices, orders, credit histories and so on) and to provide an effective discrimination mechanism.

If we accept this broad classification, the question naturally arises: should these styles be mixed in a single application, or should an application exclusively use

	Task-oriented	*Subject-oriented*
Fundamental metaphor	Performing tasks	Editing documents or other subject matter
Typical taskflow	Hierarchy of tasks, subtasks, steps	Identification/ discrimination followed by selection/action
Definition of tasks	Well-defined by analysis, mostly static	Inherently ill-defined, highly variable
Source of tasks	User carries out predefined tasks	User synthesizes own tasks
Types of action	Complex, business oriented	Simple, document-oriented
Closure points	Determined by application	Chosen by user

Table 3.1

one or the other? My advice would be to avoid mixing styles at any given level of the application. For example, it would be acceptable to design a subject-oriented application, such as a word processor, in which some of the tools are themselves task-oriented. These tools are often what are known as 'wizards', and this designation is a clue that the designer herself realizes that these particular tools are somewhat 'outside' the model. On the other hand, when the two classes are mixed at the same level, it becomes very hard for the user to follow. One classic example is Mail Merge in most word processors. Here is the online help from Microsoft Word Version 2.0:

> With the Print Merge command, you can set up the main document, data file, and header file to print form letters or other merged documents.
> Note: If you already have a main document and data file, skip the procedure below and move on to Printing form letters or other merged documents.

> To set up a print merge operation

>   1   Do one of the following:

>   If you do not have a main document, choose New from the File menu (ALT, F, N), and then choose the OK button to display a blank document.
>   If you already have a main document, open it.

>   Note: Follow steps 2 through 11 to create and attach a data file. When you do so, the print merge bar appears so you can complete the main document.
>   2   From the File menu, choose Print Merge (ALT, F, M).
>   3   Choose the Attach Data File button.

4   Choose the Create Data File button.
5   In the Field Name box, type a field name.
    A field name corresponds to one type of information you want in the data file. For
    example, type name.
    Note: Field names can contain a combination of up to 20 letters, numbers, and
    underscore characters. Word does not allow spaces, and the first character must be
    a letter.
6   Choose the Add button.
7   Repeat steps 5 and 6 for each field you want in the data file.
    Note: To delete a field, select it, and then choose the Delete button.
8   Choose the OK button.
9   Specify a filename and location (drive and directory, if needed) for storing the data
    file, and then choose the OK button.
10 Fill in the data under the appropriate field names.
    See Working and moving in a table.
11 From the File menu, choose Save (ALT, F, S).

    If the Summary Info dialog box appears, fill in the summary information you want,
    and then choose the OK button.
12 To return to the main document, do one of the following:

    From the File menu, choose Print Merge (ALT, F, M), and then choose the Edit Main
    Document button.
    From the Window menu, choose the document name.
13 Type the text of the main document. When you want to insert a piece of informa-
    tion from the data file, choose the Insert Merge Field button (ALT+SHIFT+F), select
    a print merge field, and then choose the OK button.
14 To name and save the main document, choose Save from the File menu (ALT, F, S).

To begin the print merge operation. . .

and so on. This task is both hard to carry out and hard to understand. This is due, at least in part, to the mixture of document- (subject-) oriented actions and task-oriented steps.

Another example can be seen in many fax applications. The accepted model under MS Windows is that faxing should be like printing. While this is an effective model for sending a fax from another application, the model becomes confused when we move into the fax application itself. Incoming faxes appear as imaged documents in the fax receiver application itself; from here they can be saved, printed, edited and so on. Outgoing faxes, however, appear as entries in a status log. The status can be viewed, and individual faxes can be held or released. In other words, incoming faxes are handled using a subject model, outgoing faxes using a task model. This becomes extremely confusing when the two overlap; if the user needs to edit an outgoing fax, to send a failed fax to an alternate number, or wants to forward an incoming fax to another fax machine, it is far from clear in most imple-mentations whether the user deals with the fax using the 'incoming' or 'outgoing' model. It becomes very difficult for the user to determine whether the action is even possible.

Different classes for different users?

This classification raises one very interesting point. One of the greatest difficulties in designing an application is in catering for different classes of user. If we consider, for example, a service line dealing with queries about insurance policies and claims, we might identify two classes of users: service representatives, who are the first point of contact for incoming calls, and supervisors. Service representatives can perform a well-defined set of tasks such as explaining the cover included in a policy, helping a caller complete a claim form, or updating a caller on the progress of a claim. Anything outside these bounds, such as a complaint about service or an incorrect payment, is dealt with by a supervisor, who can perform unrestricted, arbitrary changes to a policy document or claim document (within the limits of his authority).

It is traditional to design a single application for such needs, probably using different roles to try to meet the needs of different classes of user, and typically providing little support to either. What the analysis above suggests is that what is really called for is two *distinct* applications driven by quite different metaphors: a task-oriented application for the service representatives, in which their various tasks are explicitly represented; and a subject-oriented application for the supervisors, in which they can locate and edit any policy or claim document. Perhaps much of the debate and difficulty that often surrounds the question of designing for different user roles is caused by trying to force two different needs into a single model.

Summary

Good taskflow supports business processes, data integrity, and human needs. Some guidelines that characterize good taskflow have been established in this chapter:

- Match points of closure to the user's needs, not the system's, whenever possible.
- Affirm successful closure to the user.
- Avoid allowing the user into a path that may not be closable.
- Make hidden dependencies visible; express constraints.
- Support incomplete work and work in progress.
- Do not automate bad workflow.
- Allow the users as much freedom as they can profit from, not as much as is technically feasible.
- Eliminate unnecessary restrictions; discard unhelpful freedoms.
- Different classes of user may need different classes of taskflow; there is no single right answer, even for a single application.
- There are many degrees of freedom between tyranny and anarchy.

The attentive reader will have appreciated that good design is far from formulaic. It requires creativity and skill from the designer in balancing tensions and resolving conflicts between opposing requirements of the interface. Success comes from natural ability, practice, and studying other applications, both good and bad. Most of all, success comes from listening to the criticisms of your users, both during the development process through representative testing, and after implementation by actively seeking feedback from users.

4   Dialog design

'Unless one is a genius, it is best to aim at being intelligible'

Anthony Hope

Introduction

In the previous chapter we introduced the idea that a well-designed application supports the taskflow of the user, presenting the user with a set of tasks that correspond well to his or her real world tasks. We also discussed the role of guidance in enabling the user to work through those tasks rapidly and effectively. In this chapter we will develop these ideas into specific, practical GUI constructs in order to answer such fundamental questions as: how many windows are appropriate to implement the taskflow? What kind of windows should be used? And how should those windows relate to each other?

In order to discuss dialog design, it is important that we begin by agreeing the definitions of some basic terms, namely dialog, dialog resolution and dialog flow.

A *dialog* is a set of related windows used to carry out all or part of a work task. Examples include the MS-Windows *Print dialog*, which includes the *Print, Print Setup* and *Setup Options* windows. A dialog may contain both modal and modeless dialog boxes as well as other kinds of window, defined below.

A dialog is said to be *resolved* when the user completes all actions in the dialog and dismisses the dialog box. *Resolution* may be positive, for example the user clicks the *OK* button, or negative, by clicking the *Cancel* button. When designing dialog flow, in the sense of considering possible paths through windows, we are often unconcerned with whether the user has chosen a positive or negative resolution, only that the dialog is resolved. For example, in the *Print* dialog the user may pass through many windows, but ultimately he will return to the initial *Print* window and choose either *OK* or *Cancel*. Resolution typically returns the user to a normal or base mode (in the sense of the previous chapter) of the application. Resolution is also frequently a point of closure for the user.

The possible paths or sequences of windows that a user may pass through before ultimately resolving a dialog constitute the *dialog flow*. Elements of dialog flow include the number, arrangement, and modality of windows.

Detailed design and dialog design

Although it is desirable to try to isolate dialog design from detailed design, in practice the two are closely linked. For example, we need to find a balance that can keep related fields together without overcrowding the display of a particular window. This is an issue of dialog design, but it is inseparable from detailed issues such as particular choice of controls: a list box take up more window space than a simple text. Error handling is another area rife with such interconnections.

Should we then give up and simply plunge immediately into detailed design? I would advise against this. From a purely economical point of view, it risks having to discard large pieces of detailed design if the dialog design changes. It is not uncommon for entire windows or even complete dialogs to be discarded as design of dialog flows is refined, or for one model to be jettisoned in favour of another. Not only is this wasteful of resources, there is also the risk that your judgement will be influenced by a natural desire to retain pieces in which you have invested a lot of effort. On the other hand, it is all but impossible to proto-type or use popular iterative techniques without investing in some detailed design. Users find poor detailed design very distracting, however much you ask them to focus purely on issues of dialog flow. How then to resolve this paradox?

This is an area where our purist intentions must give way to pragmatism. A reasonable approach is to accept from the outset that there will be a substantial number of iterations between these two stages of design, and limit your invest-ment, and potential loss, accordingly. Always begin with at least one iteration of dialog design, possibly on paper. Resist the temptation to sketch controls until you have a well-formed idea of at least 80 per cent of the windows. (I exclude here message boxes and other extremely simple windows.) In the first few rounds of design, invest as little as possible in detailed decisions. Use standard controls and default fonts. Do not construct custom controls until you are certain that they will be used somewhere. Substitute simple buttons where iconic buttons will appear in the final product. As the iterations proceed, and the boundaries between those parts that have solidified and those that are still in flux are pushed outwards, you can refine the detailed design towards the highest level of quality.

Dialog flow supports taskflow

Dialog flow must serve two purposes. Primarily, dialog flow is the mechanism that we use to control or manage taskflow. Dialog flow also has a secondary role of adapting the desired taskflow to the realities of a particular interface. For example, our analysis of taskflow may ask the user to provide a set of data that, on paper, would fill two or three pages. The dialog design is then responsible for organizing and presenting this data collection to the user in such a way that it is as easy as if she were completing a paper form. (Hint: a very large scrolling window is not the solution!)

As we noted in the previous chapter, there are a number of ways of implementing taskflow. We examine the relationship between those approaches and dialog design in the second part of this chapter. Before that, we shall attempt to elucidate some general principles of dialog design. Let us begin with a case study as illustration.

Case study: Stock control

Let us consider a stock control application, where deliveries into stock and orders taken from stock are recorded by the warehouse staff. Suppose the warehouse supervisor is entering the details of a new delivery into the system (Fig. 4.1). Conscientiously, the programmer checks that each stock item's catalog number exists in the catalog held in the database (a referential integrity constraint). Now in real life, there will be times when the catalog is out of date. How should the dialog flow of the application respond to this exceptional situation?

Supporting the data rules

Figure 4.2 shows the response of a typical application when a nonexistent catalog number is typed by the user. What should the warehouse supervisor do now? If she enters only the items whose catalog numbers exist, it may not be possible to update the delivery later. Did the programmer include the facility to enter part of a delivery now and update it later? Did the design specification foresee this possibility?

In all probability a typical design specification will say only: 'Each stock item must reference an entry in the stock catalog', with no advice on the recovery

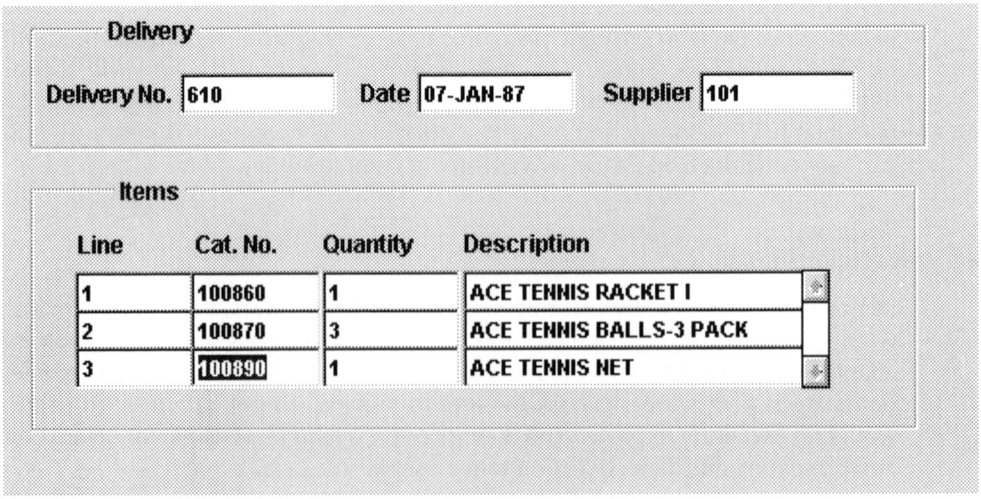

Delivery

Delivery No. 610   Date 07-JAN-87   Supplier 101

Items

Line	Cat. No.	Quantity	Description
1	100860	1	ACE TENNIS RACKET I
2	100870	3	ACE TENNIS BALLS-3 PACK
3	100890	1	ACE TENNIS NET

Figure 4.1. Entering details of a stock delivery

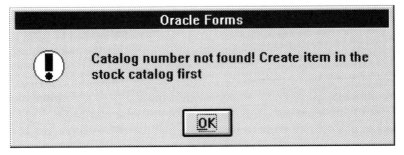

Figure 4.2. Typical unhelpful response

strategy when a stock item is missing from the catalog. If the user enters only part of the delivery, the online system will temporarily become out of step with the physical warehouse stock; similarly, the online system will also be incorrect if the warehouse supervisor cancels out and sets aside this entire task until after the catalog has been updated. In the worst case, an order could be delayed or lost because a shipping clerk is unaware of the 'invisible' stock, and so mistakenly believes that an order cannot be fulfilled.

Ultimately, the cause of the problem here is that the programmer or designer has divided the system into *two distinct tasks* which the user must carry out in a predefined sequence: maintain the catalog, and update stock levels. Unfortunately this is not the way that the work always flows in the real world. In real life, the two tasks may be reversed or even simultaneous. This first attempt merely supports the data integrity rules of the business, not the taskflow. It is *data-centric*.

Supporting the process rules
Figure 4.3 shows the programmer's second suggestion. This is certainly an improvement over the first version. The application does now acknowledge that occasionally an item may be delivered that is not yet in the catalog! However,

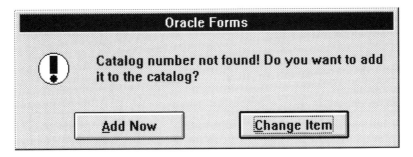

Figure 4.3. Add the missing item to the catalog?

problems may still arise: suppose the catalog cannot be updated? The warehouse supervisor may not be *authorized* to update the catalog; that responsibility may be reserved to the purchasing department. Even given the authority, she may not have all the *information* required to enter a catalog item (such as the depletion level that triggers an automatic re-order, or the name of the preferred supplier). So, although our second version models the user's process more closely, it still does not implement the taskflow in the sense of the previous chapter. It fails to take into account the business integrity requirements. It is *process-centric*.

Supporting the business rules

Figure 4.4 shows the programmer's third (and final) version. Now the warehouse supervisor has the choice of adding the item to the catalog herself, or of setting it aside to be added later. In the latter case the application may place the catalog item in a work queue of items to be added by another user with appropriate authority. In either case the warehouse supervisor can continue and completely enter the delivery into the system, even though the order line item breaks the data integrity rules. Notice that the default choice is to return to the entry screen and change the item number. We guess that the most likely cause of error is that the user simply mis-transcribed the number from the paperwork.

This final version supports the data integrity rules, the process flow, and the business integrity requirements. It is also oriented towards trapping the kind of 'mistakes' that real users encounter. It is *user-centric*.

Lessons from the case study

This case study demonstrates three important, and related, aspects of dialog flow design. First, good dialog flow design presupposes a complete understanding of the required application taskflow. This can only come from a really thorough task analysis of the user's business tasks, as we discussed in the previous chapter.

Second, one cliché of user interface design is that the application should prevent errors rather than cater for them. However, as this example illustrates, many so-

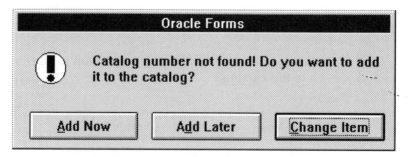

Figure 4.4. Add the item to somebody else's task list?

called errors are an inherent part of the way any reasonably complex organization does business. They should be considered not as user errors, but as dialog flow *exceptions* or as *mistakes*. It is naïve to suggest that such business issues can be 'designed out' by tweaking the application's user interface. The user interface must deal with the exception when it arises. We shall discuss designing for error in considerable detail later.

Third, traditional analysis methods are often inadequate for the specification of user interface behaviour. Often, task analysis identifies the process requirements of the system, but has little or nothing to say about the handling of exceptions to those processes, especially time-dependent behaviour such as we see illustrated here. (This is an area where object-oriented methods may prove particularly effective.)

It is a fair criticism that the third version will be more complex (and therefore more costly) to build than the first. However, we should ask: what is the cost to the business of not being able to enter deliveries promptly? The business in our case study lives and dies by stock level information. If orders are lost because, mistakenly, the system says that the order cannot be fulfilled from stock, that is likely to be considerably more expensive than even a large extra effort in the design and construction of the user interface. In general, good user interface design may not merely be more expensive, it may be *substantially* more expensive than data-centric design. It is important, therefore, for the designer to keep in mind the business benefits of improved design.

Dialog decision flow

One of the goals of good dialog design is to organize tasks so as to minimize the effort of the user. Applications designed for the simple terminal traditionally present all actions of a similar nature at the same level of descent into a dialog, without regard to how common or uncommon those actions are. Similar actions get grouped together. Regardless of which device the user wants to use, whether it is the laser printer he uses many times a day or the plotter he uses once a month, the device he just used, or one he has never used before, he must go through the same sequence of decisions. Whether he wants to use exactly the same setup as the last time he printed, or choose an unusual orientation or scaling, he must still pass through the Setup window. The mainframe-hosted e-mail client that I occasionally use is typical of this design. When I print a message, the system always asks which printer I want to use, whether I want landscape or portrait output, and whether I want to print any attachments along with the message. The answers to these questions rarely change, yet must be provided every time (Fig. 4.5).

Contrast this with the 'minimum effort' dialog in Fig. 4.6: here the decision tree is organized to place the commonest choice at the top of the tree. If the user wants

Figure 4.5. Equal effort decision flow

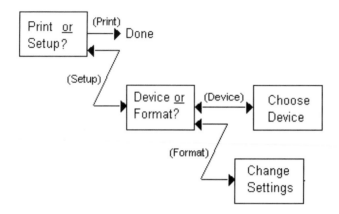

Figure 4.6. Minimum effort decision flow

to print in just the same way as last time, he simply accepts the current setup (visible in the first window). Only if he needs to make a change from the previous choice does he visit the lower windows. If the tree is designed correctly, the user will be able to perform the task with a single action in the most common cases.

I also use a Windows client to the e-mail system mentioned above. In this client, I simply choose the 'Print' iconic button, and the message is printed to the default printer using all the same settings as the last time I printed. This idea of minimum effort can be implemented in the interface in a number of places, for example in the hierarchy of menu commands, or in the organization of 'Options' and 'Setup' windows within a dialog. Installation programs that allow the user to choose between Standard and Custom installation settings are a common example.

Of course, there are trade-offs to the minimum effort design. If the user needs to access an unusual option or setup, he must descend into lower levels, then return to the top level; potentially this is slower than the straight line approach. The simple equal effort flow is a more appropriate choice in dialogs where no particular path is clearly more frequently used than any other.

Designing for minimum effort may also conflict with the natural instinct on the part of the designer to keep related fields together. For example, when the user chooses a font in a word processor, she typically will choose a particular font family, such as Arial; a size, in points; plus optionally some combination of bold and italic styles. In fact, the underlying system provides many more possibilities than these but, for the author of a word processor document (as opposed to a graphic designer working on a professional page layout), the other options are very rarely used. The choice of another six typeface 'weights' besides normal and bold is unlikely to be of interest. What should the designer do? Is it more useful for the user to see only the commonly used settings? To see all the settings together? Or to see the commonly used settings on the initial window, with the full functionality available on demand on a second window? Only a thorough task analysis will provide the answer.

Where is the most common path?

The problem above is just one example of a more general difficulty in dialog design. Identification of the most common path can be made early in the design process only if you have a very good understanding of the taskflow, and hence of the likely relative popularity of the different paths through the dialog. Prototyping and user testing can help, but there is a risk that the user's choice of paths will be skewed by limitations in the prototype itself, so that the prototype becomes a self-fulfilling prophecy. If a specific feature were more easily available in the prototype it might be used more; but paradoxically, if the feature is not used much in testing, there is little motivation to make it more easily available. In practice, it is often the case that the most common paths only emerge in use. For example, consider a certain GUI design tool. In its first release, this tool implemented the following dialog flow for setting the visual appearance or style of a field (or other control):

- Select the field
- Open its modal 'Properties' dialog window
- In this window, click on the 'Text' button; a 'Text Properties' modal dialog window is opened
- Set the visual appearance properties (font, colour, size, weight, etc.)
- Click on OK to accept the visual appearance
- Click on OK to save the properties
- Repeat for each field

Given that a typical application has many tens or even hundred of controls, this is an extremely tedious process. It is also error prone: it is very easy for the user of this tool to click on OK in the 'Text Properties' dialog, then Cancel in the 'Properties' dialog, invisibly losing the changes in the 'Text Properties' dialog. It is also all too easy for the designer to miss a field. Clearly the designers had not sufficiently investigated the implications of building an application using any visual appearance other than the default. In the second major release, in response to user feedback, the dialog has become:

- Select all of the fields to be changed
- Open a modeless property dialog showing their common properties
- Set the visual appearance properties

This second version is dramatically more efficient. There are three factors that contribute to this improvement:

- The ability to change many fields at the same time represents a tremendous saving for large applications.
- The fields describing the visual appearance, which are changed very frequently, are on the first window visited.
- There is no need to provide additional confirmation of the changes (resolving the modal window); each changed property is accepted as soon as the change is made.

The only disadvantage of the second version is that, without a Cancel button, changes made to a field or control cannot be discarded. On the other hand, user feedback showed that users nearly always changed only one or two properties at a time, in which case 'Undo', which reverts the changes to one property, has almost the same effect.

Prototyping and user testing will help, but there is a risk that the user's choice of paths can be skewed by limitations in the prototype itself, so that the prototype becomes a self-fulfilling prophecy. If a specific feature were more easily available in the prototype it might be used more; but paradoxically, if the feature is not used much in testing, there is little motivation to make it more easily available. This is not to be taken as a suggestion that user testing is a waste of time, only that it must be carefully designed. Particular care must be taken if the results of *brief* testing sessions are extrapolated to predict the suitability for *long-term* use or experienced users.

Summary

As we illustrated in the case study, dialog flow needs to support three aspects of taskflow:

- *Data integrity*   The dialog flow is responsible for ensuring both that individual fields satisfy the validation rules, or *value integrity*, defined for them and that related fields satisfy the *referential integrity* defined for them.
- *Process flow*   The dialog flow should allow all sequences of action identified as necessary in the task analysis, while protecting the data integrity. As the case study shows, process flow is closely aligned with managing the response to violations of data integrity.
- *Business rules*   These rules often combine aspects of both data and process, and are often time or sequence dependent. They answer the question: is this action valid given the current data, the current state of the system, and the current user? Such rules may be arbitrarily complex; for example:
  - Only the warehouse manager may update the stock catalog.
  - Nobody below the level of senior manager may re-order a stock item that is currently marked as overstocked.

– Only a sales manager may authorize shipment of the last *n* items of stock, except in the last two weeks of each quarter, when any salesperson may authorize shipment of any stock to make quota.

To put it another way, data integrity determines merely what data is *ultimately* valid. Process flow determines the theoretical routes by which we may arrive at valid data. Business rules modify the process flow and data integrity according to the requirements of the real world.

This kind of business-dependent flow occurs frequently in the real world. For example, in financial trading systems it is vital that the user, a trader, be able to record details of a trade very rapidly. The user interface for such a person will perform the absolute minimum of validation, often accepting data that, strictly speaking, violates many value and referential integrity rules. This information will be corrected and completed later, probably by someone other than the trader, in a back office.

Designing for minimum effort is not simply a question of nitpicking, minimizing the number of key clicks that the user must provide. Avoiding visiting unnecessary windows can give the user the illusion that the task is simpler than it actually is, by hiding complexity unless it is required. The *Print/Print Setup* dialog is an excellent example of this. This concealment can dramatically improve productivity and reduce errors, and we shall return to the subject later in this chapter. Well-designed dialogs retain changed settings from the lower, more complex levels, making those the new defaults at the highest level, as for example when the user descends into print setup. This allows the application to 'tune' itself to each user's preferences.

Data entry applications

A special case arises in intensive 'heads down' data-entry applications, where the user is simply recording information, provided perhaps on mail-in cards, advertisement responses, manual logs, or print-outs from another system. If the information supplied to be entered is invalid, there is nothing the data entry clerk can do: he does not have the authority to change the data, nor does he have any mechanism to pursue the information provider and get the correct answer. In this kind of situation, a supportive application needs to quietly accept the data provided, and re-route the input to a rework file or a supervisor's work queue for resolution.

In some applications the designer may need to distinguish between two possibilities: a data entry error, in other words an error of transcription by the clerk; and an error in the supplied information. It is a matter of judgement for the designer to decide whether to disturb the user and offer the opportunity to correct the input, or simply to accept everything and make corrections later. In an ideal world, this decision would be based on concrete figures such as comparative work rates and productivity figures for the two approaches, and known error rates both in the data supplied and for the transcription by the clerks. Unfortunately, it is rare that we have access to such figures; you will not usually be offered the opportunity to build both versions and run them competitively against each other! The decision may also be overridden by other business issues; one common requirement is for supervisors to track the error rates of individual clerks.

Dialogs and windows

In seminars and consultancy, the single question I am asked more often than any other is: 'How many fields should appear on each window?' Many people seem to hope that there is a simple answer, or at least a simple formula, that tells the designer when to stop adding fields to the current window and begin the next one. (In fact, this is precisely how certain application generators work!) While we can put an upper limit on the complexity of a window, in general this question does not have a simple answer. Dialog design involves aspects of taskflow, including ergonomics and efficiency, as well as issues of detailed design such as the amount of 'white space' required on a screen, the size of objects, and detailed mechanisms for linking related windows in a dialog.

We begin by examining principles of organization, in other words breaking down the application into small sets of windows, or dialogs. This allows us to define more carefully the questions that dialog design must answer. We can then turn our attention to detailed implementation questions such as the representation of different windows and the navigation between them.

Organizing window content

The first step in dialog design is to identify the dialogs themselves. This consists of identifying related information and actions, and grouping that information toge-ther into a single dialog. In theory, these dialogs should be closely related to the tasks identified for the application. In practice, as we suggested in the previous chapter, there will always be a proportion of additional tasks that arise purely as a result of implementation decisions. Table maintenance in a transaction proces-sing application is a typical example. Once dialogs have been identified, each dialog can be broken down into specific dialog flow.

Identifying dialogs

In this initial stage, we are only trying to identify related information; we are not yet allocating that information to particular windows. You may find it useful at this stage to imagine a single 'super window' containing the entire dialog.

Examination of some of these dialogs may identify common sub-dialogs, although in practice truly shared dialogs are rare, except at the very lowest level. Very common basic actions such as print, file save, choose font and so on may recur.

My word processor uses the same dialogs for setting the text characteristics of reusable styles as it uses for applying custom characteristics directly to text (Fig. 4.7 overleaf).

In general, a subject-oriented application offers more opportunities for reuse of generic tools, whereas a task-oriented application may present the opportunity to identify and reuse common subtasks. For example, you may design a common 'Delete' dialog that informs the user that deleting a particular subject will cause a cascade of related subjects to be deleted: removing a patient removes all the treatment records; removing a treatment record removes the treatment details; and so on. Whatever the subject chosen for the action, the user is shown the consequences in the same way and given the opportunity to recant (Fig. 4.8).

Dialogs and closure

A useful way to orientate yourself when identifying dialogs is to begin by identifying a 'base state', which is the point of departure and of return for most dialogs. In a subject-oriented application this will typically be the state in which the user is freely editing the subject (the document, spreadsheet, invoice, etc.). Conceptually, the dialog is a tool that is applied to the subject. In a task-oriented application, this is the state in which the user is presented with the list of tasks, and is ready to choose which task to perform next. Conceptually, the dialog carries out the task in question, and returning to the base state corresponds to closing the task.

This suggests a strong correspondence between resolving a dialog and closing a task. In general, we should attempt to design dialogs so that the point of resolution corresponds to a natural point of closure for the user. A particular question arises with dialogs made up of sequences or nests of modal dialogs. There are two ways to implement such a group, corresponding to the ideas of nested and serial closure discussed in the previous chapter:

- *Stack the modal windows*   Each new window is opened on top of the existing stack. The user resolves each window in turn, eventually returning to the window at the bottom of the stack, where the whole dialog is resolved by resolving the initial window.
- *Present the modal windows sequentially*   Each window replaces the previous one, as the user resolves each window in turn. The user may also be able to backtrack through the dialog. The whole dialog is resolved when the user resolves the final window in the sequence.

The first approach is suitable for simple dialogs, but becomes unwieldy when the stack becomes more than two or three windows deep. While the second approach demands fewer key clicks from the user, it is important that the user be made aware of the sequential nature of the dialog. Otherwise, the sense of closure will be missing when the user resolves the final dialog and finds himself unexpectedly back in the base state. One way of affirming the closure is to make the

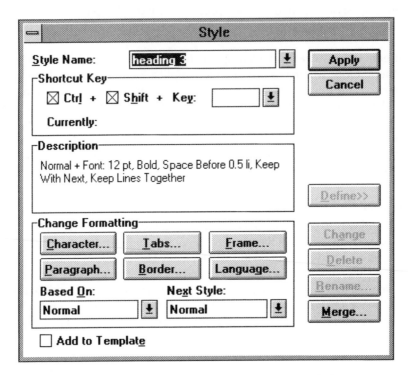

Figure 4.7. Style formatting reuses custom formatting dialogs

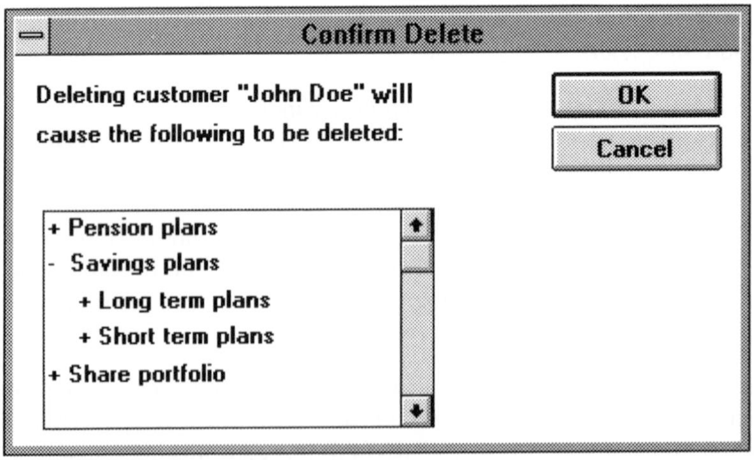

Figure 4.8. Common Delete dialog

last window a summary of all the previous windows. This indicates strongly to the user that he has reached a decision point. The installers for Microsoft Office and other complex applications provide an excellent example of this model. Microsoft Word Version 2.0 provides a very poor example:

- The Format/Paragraph command opens the *Paragraph* modal dialog window
- From here, the 'Tabs...' button opens the *Tabs* modal dialog window
- Resolving the *Tabs* dialog returns the user not to the *Paragraph* dialog, but directly to the document

The user is left with a sense that the *Paragraph* dialog has been lost, because it is never resolved. Were the changes applied in the *Paragraph* dialog applied or discarded?

Allocating controls to windows

Once we have identified dialogs, we can now begin to allocate particular functions and information to particular windows. At this point the designer must balance a number of conflicting requirements. Fundamental principles such as ease of use and ease of learning may pull in opposite directions. The requirements of the task and the comfort of the user may conflict. Detailed design issues such as the physical screen space available (or 'real estate' as it is sometimes known) may restrict the designer's choices.

We need to consider both the information presented to the user, and the actions (functions) available to the user. If we consider first fundamental principles as they affect the functions available to the user, the requirements of good visibility and strong mappings imply:

- To make a dialog easy to use, the number of controls should match the number of functions.
- To make a dialog *appear* easy to use, the designer should minimize the number of controls.

This is a terrible paradox for the designers of devices such as camcorders and stereos. Engineering limits and costs are a common barrier to excellent design in these areas. As software designers we are merely painting with light, and no such limitations apply. We can hide and reveal controls at will, as they are required.

If we consider also the information presented to the user, we arrive at the following guidelines for hiding and disclosing information:

- Present enough information and functions for the user to complete the task successfully in the commonest cases.
- Provide clearly visible cues that more detail is available if required, such as 'More' or 'Options' buttons.
- Never present an exceptional option in such a way that a user must learn it, in order to discover that he does not need it.

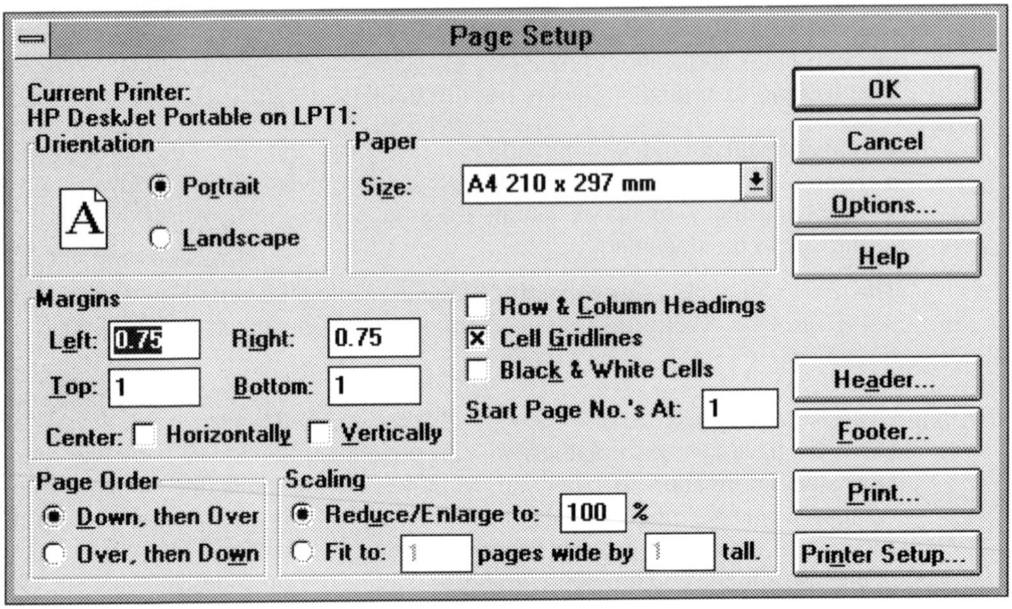

Figure 4.9. Microsoft Excel 4.0 Page Setup dialog.

Note that the designer needs to consider the requirements of both input and output. The user needs to be able easily to supply the input required in most cases, as well as being able to see system information that helps him complete that input and provides feedback about his actions. Once again, the fundamental principle of visibility should be uppermost in the designer's mind.

Microsoft Excel's *Page Setup* presents an excellent example of how not to design a dialog (Fig. 4.9). Options that are frequently changed are jumbled with others that may be rarely touched. And how does the 'Paper size' setting interact with the paper size selected through the *Print Setup* dialog? The overall complexity of the window makes it impossible for the user to judge the relative importance of different components, or their interrelationships.

The *Print* dialog of MS-Windows is an excellent example of good application of design principles. The first window presents enough information for the user to print all or part of the current document to the current printer in the current format. Only if the user needs to change any of these settings does she need to open further windows. Those windows are clearly indicated through buttons labelled 'Setup' and 'Options'. The only fault in this design is that it is not obvious to the casual user that to select a *different* printer, she chooses the 'Setup' command on the *current* printer.

Notice how the relatively modern 'fax as printer' conceptual model introduced earlier conflicts with this carefully thought-out and long-established design. The design of the *Print* dialog assumes, among other things, that the user switches to a different printer relatively rarely, so that action is placed on the second window of the dialog. Sending a fax, on the other hand, requires that the user *always* visit this second window and select the fax as her printer. She can then 'print' her fax. She must then remember to revisit the window to change back to her usual printer before she can print again. This conceptual model for the fax has the unexpected side-effect of violating the principle we discussed earlier, of presenting the most common path at the highest level.

As well as the problem of the additional windows that must be visited, this also leads to the kind of closure problem mentioned earlier. For the user, the task is closed as soon as she sends her fax. As a result she will frequently forget to re-select her usual printer, and she will accidentally send her next printout to the fax instead of the printer, followed by a scramble to correct the error before the fax should be dispatched.

Implementing the design

Having established some principles, characteristics and examples to separate good design from bad, we now examine in more detail some specific issues of dialog organization, such as sizing, and windows versus canvases. Before we do so, it is worthwhile reviewing some terminology. If your experience is in the Unix (Motif or OpenLook) world, you will find that you use different words for the same concepts as designers in the MS-Windows world or Macintosh world.

Terminology

We have already distinguished informally between *modal* and *modeless* windows. Formally, when a modal window is displayed, all controls in the application outside of the window are unavailable. In consequence, the user cannot use any other part of the application until she has resolved the modal window. By extension, we use the term *modal dialog* to describe a set of linked modal windows. As each new modal window is opened, it gains exclusive control at the expense of its parent.

By contrast, when a modeless window is displayed, both its controls and those of other open windows in the application are available to the user. In principle, any number of modeless windows may be open at a time.

Some windows can be resized, usually by clicking and dragging the border; and moved, usually by clicking and dragging the title bar. A window may also be *zoomed*, or *maximized*. This automatically increases the window to its maximum possible size. In MS-Windows, this is usually the physical size of the screen. As X-Windows based windows managers such as Motif usually run on much larger displays, it is rarely sensible for a single window to fill the screen, so a zoomed window usually has a maximum size much smaller than the screen size.

A window may also be *iconized*, or *minimized*. This reduces the window to an icon at the bottom of the screen. Confusingly, this is also sometimes called a window *close* in the X-Windows world. An iconized or zoomed window may also be *restored* to its size and position before it was zoomed or iconized.

The multi-document interface

MS-Windows supports a specific application style, or combination of window styles, called the Multi-Document Interface, or *MDI*. In this style, an application has a *frame* window within which all open modeless windows, representing documents, are contained. The frame acts as a 'holder' for work open in the application, carrying menus, button bars and so on, which apply to any document. Individual documents can be moved, sized, minimized and maximized within the frame rather than within the whole display. The frame itself can also be iconized, automatically 'taking down' all of its documents with it.

MDI was a very popular style in the 1980s, and contained the promise that it would make it easier for the user to 'keep associated work together' and 'manage several documents of the same type' easily. MDI has a number of advantages in terms of implementation, which may account for its popularity. It is very easy for the implementor to produce MDI compliant applications, delegating the arrangement of windows and icons to functionality provided automatically by the frame window (technically, by the frame window's default event loop procedure). The MDI style is also economical on screen space, as a single menu, tool palette, button bar, etc. can be shared by all open documents.

On the other hand, MDI has a number of conceptual disadvantages. The MDI model is *application* centred, rather than *task* or *user* centred. For example, if you are producing a report, it is unlikely that the report will consist of several word processor documents. It is more likely that the report will be composed from a word processor document, some spreadsheet data, some graphs, and perhaps some data from a database query. MDI does little to simplify such cross-application integration. The current Object Linking and Embedding (OLE) and the emerging OCX standards seem to be much more oriented to real user needs.

Window styles

Given all of these various possibilities for the choice of window style, it may be reassuring to discover that in practice the vast majority of windows fall into one of three categories: documents, modeless dialog boxes (tools), and modal dialog boxes (details, message boxes and confirmations).

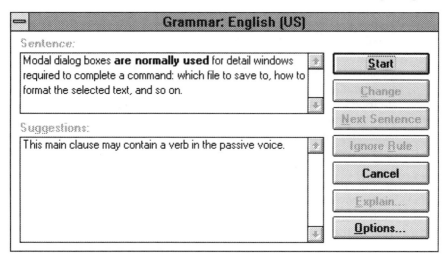

Figure 4.10. Grammar check, a typical tool window from Microsoft Word Version 2.0

Documents are the windows in which the subject matter of the application is presented: the word processor document, invoice, order entry form, and so on. Typically, documents are modeless, resizeable and minimizable. They may be maximizable, if the amount of information presented to the user can be increased by filling the screen (or frame). They may also be scrollable, both horizontally and vertically, again depending on the size of the document. In an MDI-style application, a document is always contained within the frame, and is clipped at the frame's borders.

In practice, many transaction processing applications permit the user to open only one document or subject window, but this is more often a limitation of the implementation tool or a consequence of the choice of a particular transactional model, rather than a natural implication of the conceptual model or a conscious decision by the designer.

Modeless dialog boxes are generally used to implement 'tools' that may be used alongside documents. Such tools may include spelling checkers and the find/replace dialog (Fig. 4.10). Floating toolbars and palettes are a special case of such windows, and are an excellent way of making a large number of functions easily available. Tool dialogs are not usually resizeable, since they are designed to show all of their components at a fixed size, so there would be no benefit in increasing the size of the window, but this is not a universal rule. Tools 'float' on top of any document windows, so that they are always visible, and they are not confined to any MDI frame. This allows the user to arrange tools so that they obscure the minimum of the document, while remaining readily available. Oddly, tools are rarely iconifiable, though it would be helpful in many cases to temporarily 'hide' a large tool window, such as a spelling or grammar checker, to reveal the document underneath.

Modal dialog boxes are normally used for detail windows required to complete a command: which file to save to, how to format the selected text, and so on. They are used to ask questions of the user, collect details, and also to confirm actions. Using a modal window for such dialogs obliges the user to pursue to closure the mental task that he has opened. Modal dialogs are rarely resizeable; they are usually designed to be large enough to show all the information required without resizing. Message boxes are a particularly simple kind of modal dialog box, and we will present some guidance for them a little later in the chapter. Modal dialog boxes may be invoked directly from the 'base state' of the application, for example the *Save As* dialog, or as sub-dialogs of tool windows, such as the *Options* window that can be invoked from Fig. 4.10.

Windows and modality

In practice, some distinctions between modal and modeless windows may have more to do with the low-level implementation details of the Windows interface than they have to do with subjective differences of usability. For example, in Microsoft Write, a basic word processor, the *Find* dialog is a modeless tool: the user can find a text, edit the document while leaving the dialog open, then return to the *Find* to search for the next occurrence. In Microsoft Word Version 2.0, on the other hand, the corresponding dialog is modal. After finding a match, the user must dismiss the dialog before he can edit the document. He can then recall the *Find* dialog, which will contain exactly the same find string and settings as when he dismissed it. I leave it to the reader to decide whether this is a design error, or whether there is a legitimate reason for this exception to the guidelines.

On the other hand, there are situations in which a modal implementation will definitely be significantly more restrictive in use. In particular:

- When it takes a long time to get into the mode, e.g. open a document or find and retrieve a database record to edit in a modal window
- When it takes a long time to get out of the mode, e.g. the user must resolve a large stack of modal dialog boxes

In general, if it is 'expensive' in time or effort for the user to get in or out of the modal window then, as in our discussion of modes in the previous chapter, the user will be aware of the modality as a restriction on his freedom.

Practical considerations of modality

Modeless dialogs are in general more complex both to design and implement than modal dialogs. The designer must concern himself with potential combinations of open windows that grow exponentially with the number of modeless dialogs. The only way to control this growth of complexity is to design each modeless dialog so that it is independent of other open dialogs. If modeless dialogs can be made truly independent, then from a design point of view the 'real' number of states grows only linearly, not exponentially.

From the user's point of view, it is also questionable whether multiple modeless dialogs that are *not* independent of each other will only serve to confuse. There is certainly a limit to the complexity that a user can comfortably deal with. The MDI interface is successful in part because every open document is independent of all other documents.

If you are unsure about the value of a modeless approach, a useful guide to determine whether a given modal dialog is worth the cost and effort of implementing as modeless dialog is to ask yourself the following questions. Look carefully at each question or field posed in the dialog:

- Could the user be unsure, and need to find an answer elsewhere in the system?
- If the answer is yes, what is the cost to the user of cancelling this dialog to go and find the answer?
- What is the balance between value added and cost if the dialog is modal or modeless?

It is important not to overlook the most significant cost: that of confusing the model. If some dialogs are modal and others are modeless, it will be far harder for the user to develop a consistent mental model of the application. (On certain window managers, the visual distinction between modal and modeless windows is too subtle to be noticed by many users.) The choice of modality should be driven principally by the obligation to present the user with a clear expectation and visible understanding of which actions and tasks are modal, and which are modeless, and only secondarily by technical constraints. If the designer fails to do so, users will probably learn simply to treat every dialog as modal, wasting all of the designer's efforts.

The distinction between tools on the one hand and detail gathering on the other is one attempt to distinguish uses of each style. If the designer follows such a model, he must ensure that he properly understands which dialogs the *user* understands as tools, and which as detail gathering.

Canvases and fold-outs

The example from Microsoft Excel above (Fig. 4.9) illustrates one of the problems of dialog design. When we have a large collection of closely related information, how do we avoid overwhelming the user with detail? We have already discussed the use of linked dialog boxes, either in sequences or stacks, as one way of reducing apparent complexity. Another technique is to make use of canvases — in other words, alternate display areas within a single window. Figures 4.11a and 4.11b illustrate the corresponding task from Microsoft Word Version 2.0.

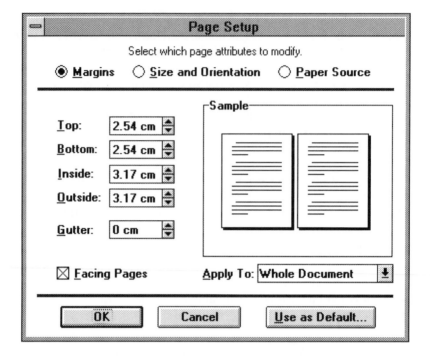

Figure 4.11. (a) Page setup margins; (b) page setup size and orientation

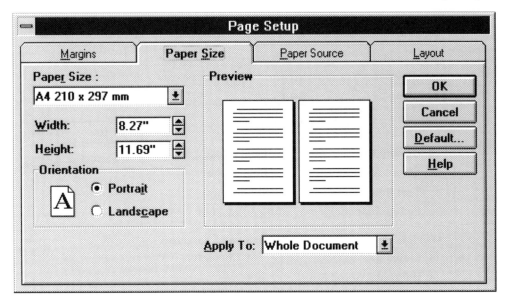

Figure 4.12. Tabbed dialog

A different set of detail information is presented depending on which radio button the user selects. The user need only visit the areas of page setup that she wishes to change. Of course, the same result could be achieved with three separate detail windows (Fig. 4.7 uses this approach: each of the buttons 'Character...', 'Paragraph...', etc. brings up a modal detail window), but this canvas switching version will be perceived by the user as being significantly less modal. In accordance with the principles established earlier in this chapter, the radio buttons are clearly labelled to indicate that more information is available.

A currently fashionable style of presentation for canvas switching on Microsoft Windows is the 'tabbed' dialog (Fig. 4.12). The 'tabbed' style has been common practice under OS/2 Presentation Manager, a much underrated user interface, for some time. One of the best-known, and most effective, implementations is in Lotus 1–2–3, where tabs are used to great effect to switch between several open spreadsheets.

The tab is visually more compelling (that is, it is a better cue) than the radio button group, and is rapidly becoming established as a 'standard' control. The metaphor of tab cards that can be brought to the front of the stack is very intuitive. As with many new ideas, especially one as visually attractive as tabs, there is a tendency to overuse tabs, and they are being put to some inappropriate uses. Remember that the aim of canvas switching is to reduce the *apparent* complexity when presenting a large amount of *related* information.

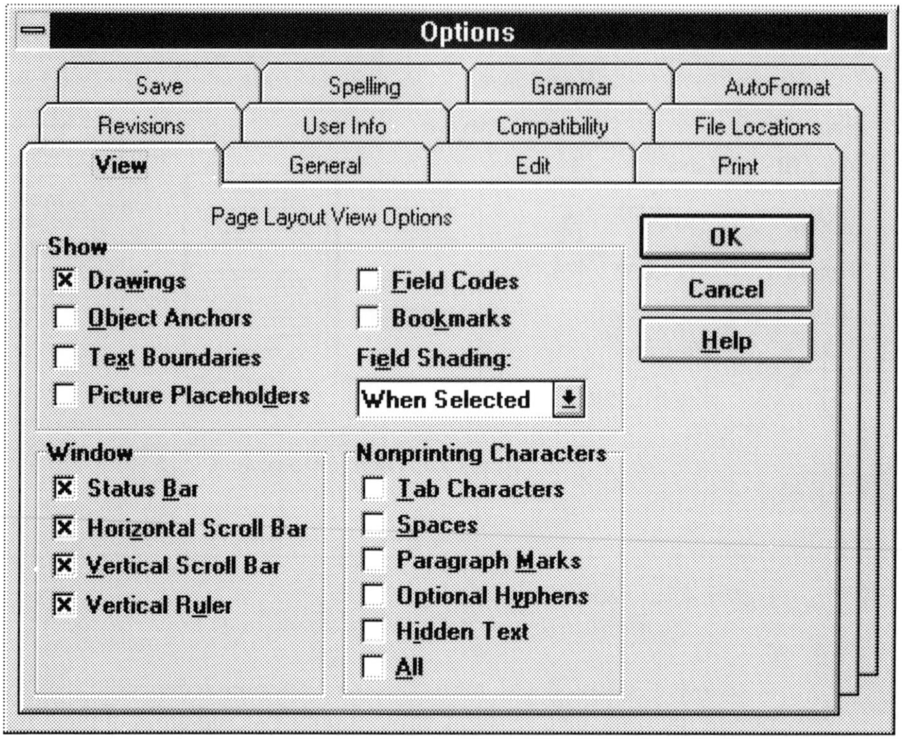

Figure 4.13. Overuse of tabs

Switching between multiple canvases should not be used simply as a way of lowering the implementor's workload by reducing the number of separate windows. In particular:

- *Do not use tabs where there are many choices, particularly when there are too many to present in a single row* Too many tabs simply become confusing for the user (Fig. 4.13). The tabs move around: when a tab is clicked, it moves to the front, along with all the other tabs in that row. This makes it difficult for the user to work systematically through the tab cards, and impossible for the user to learn the position of any given tab. Whenever she uses this dialog, the user must hunt for the position of the tab she wants.
- *Do not use tabs to gather information that is only related in the designer's model, not in the user's model* What is the connection, from the user's point of view, between 'Spelling' and 'Compatibility' (Fig. 4.13)?
- *Do not use tabs to represent steps in a process* The tab metaphor cues the user that she may visit as many or as few of the tab cards as she deems relevant, in any order. The metaphor does not suggest that the user *must* visit *each* of the cards in sequence.

Whether or not tabs are used for canvas switching, one common error in using canvases comes from 'mixing levels'. Graphically, the use of tabs or similar mechanisms suggests to the user that the various canvases all have the same relationship to each other. For example, an application that I have worked on for student registration at universities presents basic information about the student in the top half of a window. In the bottom half, one of several sets of related records, such as course registrations, periods of attendance, addresses, next of kin and other contacts, and so on, are presented as tab cards. This works well: each set of details is, conceptually, a 'child' of the particular student record. Further personal details about the student, such as any special access requirements, dietary needs and so on, are presented on a secondary detail window, not as a tab card. These details are not at the same 'level' as the other tab cards.

A third design style that hides information effectively is the fold-out, a detail pane that is hidden entirely until required by the user. Figure 4.7 shows an example: everything below the (disabled) button labelled 'Define≫' is hidden until that button is clicked. The effect is that the user who only wants to examine an existing style is spared the complexity necessary for defining and modifying styles. Although the hidden detail could be shown on a separate window, the use of a fold-out pane avoids the inflexibility of a modal window. Fold-outs are also known as pull-outs, depending on the visual representation.

Window internal modes

It is common in transaction processing applications to encounter 'internal modes' within individual windows. For example, a single window may be used for both data entry and 'query by example'. There is a trade-off for the designer here between providing separate windows for different functions, and increasing the complexity and modes within each window. The economics of building separate data entry and 'query by example' windows are usually unappealing, with the result that windows must generally do double duty. When the designer finds herself in this position, it is important that she should apply the fundamental principles of visibility and feedback:

- Ensure that the user is aware that both modes exist.
- Make it clear to the user how he moves from one mode to the other.
- Make it *unmistakably* clear to the user which mode he is in at any time.
- Provide separate, distinct functions in each mode, not common functions that are interpreted differently.

Regarding this final point, I have seen certain transaction processing applications where a button or menu command labelled 'Exit' serves two purposes: in 'query' mode, it cancels the query and leaves the user in 'data entry' mode. In 'data entry' mode, it closes the application! Furthermore, the user is given only the most subtle of visual clues as to which mode he is in. This appalling design error is completely baffling unless you happen to know that, for obscure and bizarre historical reasons, the 4GL tool used to build these applications requires the programmer to use the same library function call to perform both actions.

Having described this example in one seminar, I happened to see the next application designed by one of the seminar participants. He had gone to considerable pains to eliminate this error: now on entering query mode, the label on the 'Exit' button was dynamically changed to 'Cancel Query'; on return, it was changed back to 'Exit'. I could not leave without explaining to him that this was not quite what I had in mind; that perhaps he should consider providing two completely separate buttons since, in the user's model, there was no discernible connection between these two actions.

Summary

The physical implementation of dialog design involves a number of complex interacting considerations, and the designer should expect that several iterations will be required before she arrives at a satisfactory design. The designer needs to:

- Identify distinct dialogs as document, tool, or detail style.
- Separate the information presented, both for input and output, within each dialog into frequently used and rarely used sets.
- Allocate frequently used information to the first window of the dialog, other information to secondary windows.
- When a window becomes overcomplicated, consider using canvases to reduce apparent complexity.
- Keep related fields together, but not to the detriment of the other goals above.

Message boxes

At first sight message boxes, or alerts, hardly seem worth mentioning. They are simple to design and, in most tools, trivial to implement. Even programming directly in C, they can be created with a single line of code. Despite this, they are the source of many errors of design at the detailed level. They are also one of the commonest forms of communication with the user, and so deserve specific attention. The following simple rules will enable the designer to avoid most common errors with message boxes:

- The message must be simple, and must make sense as an English sentence.
- The answers must make sense as English responses to the question.
- The answers must be easily distinguishable from each other.
- The message must be complete, and it must contain all relevant context.
- The message box must identify which application it came from.

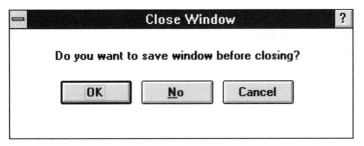

Figure 4.14. File Close confirmation from Lotus Freelance

Common message box mistakes

Remarkably, Fig. 4.14 manages to break every rule. First, the question makes no sense. The word 'the' is omitted, pointlessly, from the sentence, and the message refers to saving the 'window' when the user actually wants to save the file or document. I have seen even experienced users mistakenly believe that this box is offering the opportunity to save the size and shape of the document window, rather than the contents of the file. The question could so easily be 'Do you want to save the changes to the document?'

Second, the answers make no sense: in this message box, the opposite of 'OK' is not 'Cancel', but 'No'! The commonly offered choices of 'Yes', 'No' and 'Cancel' are not much better. Even then, many users have difficulty distinguishing between 'No' and 'Cancel'. The answers could be 'Yes', 'No' and 'Don't Close'.

Third, the message fails to identify which document is being saved. If you have several documents open in Freelance, and attempt to exit, how do you know which document is being referred to? The question should be 'Do you want to save the changes to the document CHAP4.PRE?'

This message box is by no means the only poorly designed message in a commercial application; but it is probably unique in compressing so many errors into one box.

Message box styles

Different window managers offer different styles of standard message box, but four styles are widely used. All four are illustrated on the disk accompanying this book.

The simplest form of message box is the *information message*. There is a tendency to overuse information messages; bear in mind that message boxes are strictly modal, so the user is obliged to acknowledge the message before being allowed to continue. An information message should only be used when it is essential that the user read and acknowledge the message, or would otherwise receive no feedback from an action. One appropriate example is found in MS-Windows File

Manager's 'Search...' function. If no matching files are found in the search, an information message box is presented informing the user of this result. Without this message box, the user would be silently returned to File Manager's base state, without any feedback as to why no 'Results' window had appeared.

As a general rule, an information message should have only one button, labelled 'OK'. If there is more than one button, the message is not information; it is a *question* of some kind. As noted above, the answers to a question should be easily distinguishable one from another, and should make sense as English responses to the question posed. One application that I have encountered frequently advises the user: 'Click OK for yes, Cancel for no'. Why did the designer not label the buttons 'Yes' and 'No'? The label 'Cancel' is also much overused. Despite common usage in computer interfaces, it is remarkable how few questions you can sensibly respond 'Cancel' to in real life. Let your yes be yes and your no be no.

Avoid using a series of questions to conduct a conversation with the user; if there are several questions to be answered, provide a single modal dialog and allow the user to answer them all at once. Finally, in any question, wherever possible there should be at least one choice that is completely safe for the user.

Whereas information messages are used to confirm to the user that an action has completed, *warning* messages can be used when an action cannot complete for some reason: for example, a file cannot be saved to a write-protected drive. A warning tells the user that the action did not succeed, but the problem may be correctable. Generally, a warning, like an information message, will have only one button, acknowledging the message.

The warning style is also sometimes used for questions that have serious or potentially damaging consequences: 'Are you sure you want to format this disk? All files will be lost!' It is a useful way to highlight questions that the user needs to answer particularly carefully, or to distinguish the normal case from the exceptional.

Finally, *stop* messages should only be used in the case of the severest errors: the database connection has been lost, or the building is on fire. It is rarely sufficient in a *stop* message merely to report the error. The message box should also explain the cause of the error, whether any consequential damage has occurred, and how the user can continue.

Wording messages

It is worth noting that users do not always read message boxes. Frequent users especially learn to expect and recognize a particular message box style, along with the size and shape of the message text, at particular dialog points. If the wording of a message text changes in a subtle way, the change may easily go unnoticed. It is advisable deliberately to use contrasting styles and layouts for otherwise easily confused messages. One application that I worked on in its first prototype version posed the questions 'Are you sure you want to commit. . .' and 'Are you sure you want to discard. . .' in response to the (adjacent) 'OK' and 'Cancel' commands respectively; and both messages used the warning style. The two message boxes looked almost identical, and users told us that they had to read very carefully to be sure that they had hit the right button. In the second version, we redesigned the two boxes so that 'OK' produced a question and 'Cancel' a warning; and changed the message texts so that the two messages had different lengths and shapes. The two messages were now distinguishable at a glance.

One seminar attendee asked whether it actually matters if the 'wrong' style is used. Do users actually know (or care) what the different styles are supposed to mean? In the absence of hard research to the contrary, I suspect that most users certainly recognize 'Stop' alerts as severe, but do not distinguish finely between the others. However, if the designer uses the styles consistently within her applications, it will provide an additional aid to recognition to the user, as in the example above.

Message boxes should always be carefully worded, but especially so in the case of error messages. The message should avoid placing the blame on the user when it is the system that is at fault. In this context, the word 'error' is to be avoided: it almost always implies that the user has done something wrong. The word 'failure' is a much better choice, implying that the fault lies with the system. Consider the difference between 'Format error: incorrect date entry, not saved' and 'OOE failed to save: Order Entry did not understand the date entered. Try another format'. The former is hostile and accusatory; the latter accepts the failure as a shortcoming of the application, and suggests a likely solution.

When the message informs the user of an error or failure, it is generally appropriate to give the user some explanation of how the problem can be corrected. In the example above, the message 'Press F1 to see acceptable formats' would be useful.

We will close this section with possibly the worst message box ever written. To save the designer from embarrassment, I will refrain from identifying the application in question:

> Warning: you must specify whether the selected objects are to be deleted from both the diagram and the dictionary or only from the diagram.
> Action: Invoke Yes to delete from the diagram and the dictionary. Invoke No to delete from the diagram only. Invoke Cancel to quit the operation.

Dialog design for common taskflows

In the previous chapter we introduced the two broad classifications of applications: task-oriented and subject-oriented. Certain basic forms of dialog flow, along with particular difficulties, arise commonly in each of these classes, so it is worth noting certain points that help to make the dialog flow successful in each class.

Task-oriented dialog design

Within a task-oriented application, the user generally begins with a list of tasks, from which each task is launched. As each task is completed, the user returns to the task list to choose the next. In highly sequential tasks, the user may automatically be presented with each task. It is essential that the user be able to keep track of the steps and her position within the process. In order to support this, the task list, however it may be represented, needs to be available to the user at all times. This can be done in a number of ways:

- The task list window and each task window are modeless, allowing the user to visit any window.
- Each task window is modal with respect to the task list window; the user can reveal the task list by moving the task to one side.
- The current process step and stack is summarized on each window.
- The task list and current task are presented in a single window; canvas switching is used to show different tasks as required.

The choice between, or indeed combination of, these different approaches will depend partly on how much space is required for both the task list and the task itself: can they be presented on a single window, or does the amount of information involved require separate overlapping windows? The choice may also be driven by the parallelism between the tasks themselves, which will determine the extent to which the user needs to be able to launch, view and switch between more than one simultaneous task.

An MDI-based approach is an interesting variant on the modeless approach. A pane at the left-hand edge of the application's main window is reserved for the task list or tree. The remainder of the window is an MDI client area; each open task is represented in a single MDI document window. Any parallelism or serialization of tasks is enforced in the task list window, by enabling and disabling the 'launch task' action. When more than one task can be in progress at a time, the user can minimize, maximize and arrange the task windows within the MDI area, just as in any other MDI application, but the task list always remains visible.

Subject-oriented dialog design

Within a subject-oriented dialog, the user selects a subject from a list, works on it in an appropriate editor, then returns to the list of subjects. Typically, the user can open as many documents as he feels he can manage (within the resource limits of the machine, of course). In addition, certain actions can be applied to documents directly in the list, such as 'Rename' or 'Discard' (delete), and some actions may be applicable to several documents at a time. For example, a supervisor may allocate several insurance claims to a particular assessor.

Generally, the subject-oriented dialog includes a filter that allows the user to limit the documents presented in the list, or order them in particular ways. Usually, the

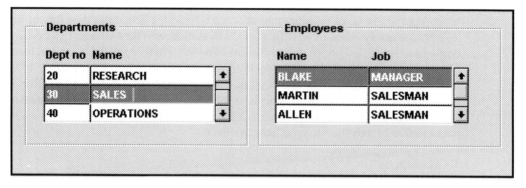

Figure 4.15. Employees organized by department

filter is defined on a separate window from the list of subjects; it is possible to present them on a single window, but this means that the amount of real estate available for the list will be reduced. The 'least effort' principle suggests that the filter dialog should be a window *below* the list, which the user invokes as required, rather than a window that precedes the list. The user should not be obliged to pass through the filtering process unless he wants to. MS-Windows' File Manager presents an example of the correct approach.

The subject list may be in a single part: for example, a list of all insurance claims in process. In many cases, the list may be in two or more parts, perhaps organized by category: burglary claims, flood damage, accidental damage, and so on. The list may also break down into geographic or other areas.

Figure 4.15 shows a simple subject list for employees in a selected department. Whenever the user is faced with a multi-part list like this, the designer should aim if at all possible to keep the entire selection process on a single window. I have seen implementations in which the user selects a department in one window, then must open a second window to select an employee. While this may be acceptable if the taskflow requires the user to work systematically through each employee in each department, it is highly inconvenient if the user needs to work in a less structured way. In other words, if the organization into categories does not correspond well to the organization of the user's work, the user wastes a lot of time closing and reopening the second window.

In effect, the categorization is a kind of filtering that is changed by the user at very frequent intervals. If other elements of the filtering are also changed frequently, they should also be made easily available. MS-Windows' File Manager, for example, makes common options for sorting and viewing available directly through menu commands, without requiring the user to invoke the 'View Options' window.

One important issue of visibility that affects a filtered list is that the user should be able to see easily what filter is in effect. MS-Windows' File Manager falls down badly here: the user cannot directly see in a file list whether the list is limited by a filter on the file type. This can lead to frustrating searches for invisible files (excluded from the filter). Worst of all, it leads to a particular catastrophic error. I have encountered many users who have accidentally deleted a directory mistakenly thinking it was empty, when in fact it contained many files, none of which happened to match the file type filter in effect.

To summarize:

- The filter should come below the list, not above it, in the dialog flow.
- The selection from the list should take place on a single window.
- The filter in effect should be visible.
- Frequently used filter options may appear directly on the list window.

A notation for dialog design

One significant obstacle when designing dialogs is the lack of a notation for expressing the design. Constructing a variety of proposed designs is expensive and time-consuming, particularly when all but one of them will ultimately be discarded. A notation that allows the designer to express in outline his designs, and share those ideas with other designers, will enable the designer to eliminate grosser errors, avoid blind alleys, and identify potentially the most efficient and effective dialog designs before committing resources to actual construction. Many paper-based techniques may be used, and I present here one simple technique suitable for business applications, both subject- and task-oriented.

Dialog flow diagrams

The notation presented here is not intended to be a formal notation. Like data flow diagrams, it is not the intention that an implementation could be generated mechanically from these diagrams. Rather, it is an informal notation that allows one designer to communicate his intentions to another. The notation is not intended to express precisely every detail of dialog flow; instead, the notation is intended to highlight those aspects of the user interface that most immediately affect the user, and allow the designer to answer questions such as:

- Where is the dialog flow constrained? Where is it free?
- How many windows must a user pass through to achieve a given task?
- How many modeless windows must the user open simultaneously to achieve a given task?
- Do similar tasks have similar flow?
- Are there similar dialogs that could become common dialogs?
- Where do points of closure or resolution occur?

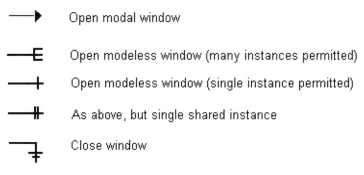

Figure 4.16. Basic transitions

Basic elements of the notation

As the notation is intended to support dialog design, rather than window design, the emphasis is placed on the relationships between windows, rather than the detailed contents of windows. The intention is to make explicit the transitions between windows, rather than events within windows. (Other techniques exist for that requirement.) Windows are represented by simple boxes, common sub-dialogs, such as Print/Print Setup, by a box with an additional vertical line (see Fig. 4.17), and possible paths between windows by various lines indicating different kinds of flow. Figure 4.16 shows the possible types of dialog flow, or transition, between windows; the transitions are explained below.

A modal window is, by definition, a single instance, so there is only one possible transition. In order to keep diagrams clear of duplicate flows, a window close is *not* indicated by a flow back to the previous window; instead the 'Close' transition (based on the electrical 'earth' symbol) is used. As well as eliminating many lines that add little or no information to the diagram, this approach also reflects more closely the reality of implementation. In MS-Windows, for example:

- When the user closes a modal dialog, control automatically returns to the invoking window.
- When the user closes a modeless (document) window, MS-Windows determines which window will receive control.
- If the designer wants anything other than this default behaviour, the programmer must implement it explicitly, so it is helpful to require this to be shown on the diagram.

For modeless windows, there are more possibilities. The commonest modeless transition is the first shown in Fig. 4.16: multiple instances of a window (usually a document) can be opened. This is the way that most subject-oriented applications, including word processors and spreadsheets, as well as nearly all other MDI

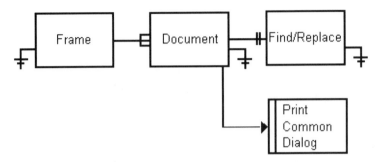

Figure 4.17. A dialog fragment for a word processor

applications, behave. In principle the number of open documents is unlimited; in practice, it will be limited by machine resources. There may be occasions where it is limited by design: for example, to limit the database resources that one user can lock or the number of database connections that he can tie up. Such limits can be explicitly noted on the diagram.

Tool windows are usually modeless, but limited to a single instance; Spell Checker and Find/Replace are typical examples in a word processor. A key design choice for tool windows is whether the tool is limited to one instance per document, or one for the whole application. For example, the designer may decide that the user can run a separate, independent spell check against each open document (using the single instance transition); or alternatively that the user can run only one spell check, which operates against whichever document window is active (the *shared* single instance transition). For simplicity of implementation, the shared single instance is the most common form in current applications, although it would probably be more useful to have an independent find/replace dialog in each open document, for example.

Examples of the notation

Figure 4.17 shows a simple fragment of a MS-Windows MDI-style word processor. The user begins from a frame window, from which she may open multiple documents. Each document may be closed. From any document window, a single modeless find/replace dialog can be opened; one instance of this tool is shared by all open documents. The find/replace tool can also be closed. Finally, each document may be printed using the Print modal common dialog.

Annotating the transitions

So far we have expressed the possible transitions within a dialog. In practice, the designer will want to specify many more details about a transition: the conditions under which it is possible, actions associated with the transition, and so on. As the notation is informal, the designer is free to annotate the diagram in any way she wishes; however, I have found it useful to restrict myself to a small, well-defined set of annotation elements. This set enhances consistency and conciseness, and also serves as a useful completeness check. The elements that I use, along with their abbreviations, are:

E The Event that causes the transition
P Any Pre-condition that must be satisfied for the transition to be possible
A Action associated with the event, assuming the pre-conditions are satisfied
F Action if the pre-conditions Fail to be satisfied

The transition should always be described from the user's point of view, rather than the system's; for example, 'E: Open document' not 'E: Click File/Open'. This is a matter both of principle and pragmatism. In principle, the flow should always be designed from the user's viewpoint. This is essential if the flow is to correspond to the way the user works rather than the way the system works. Pragmatically, there may be several different user actions that correspond to a single event: File/Open may be implemented as a menu item, a control key, and a button on the toolbar.

In Fig. 4.17, the designer might supply the following annotations. To close the frame:

E Application close
P No unsaved changes to open documents
F Resolve Save dialog for each changed document; continue Action
A Cleanup and exit

To open a document:

E Open existing document ...
P Document not already open
F Alert user; activate existing document window
A Create and activate document window; read in document

E Create new document
P None
F None
A Create and activate empty document window

Note that the designer has not overspecified detailed issues of implementation. For example, in resolving a Save dialog, the user may choose 'Cancel', thus cancelling the application close. This level of detail is not shown on the diagram in this case, but is left as an implementation choice to the programmer. Note also that a single transition can correspond to more than one event. Since both transitions in this example end up in the same place, it is more useful to show both events on a single transition.

Not every window is shown on this diagram: the action 'Open existing document...' may well involve passing through a dialog box (or sub-dialog) to specify the file. This can be indicated by the addition of '...' to the event, or can be described explicitly in the action.

Beyond these basic annotations, the designer is free to add any other notes she deems useful. Remember that this is not a formal specification language; rather it is a design tool to aid communication.

Annotating the windows

Although the focus of this technique is the transitions, it can also be useful to annotate some windows in more detail. These additions may become more detailed through iterations of design and testing. In particular, I often find it useful to note:

● That the window has maximize and minimize buttons
● That the window is resizeable
● The window's title, especially if it includes context such as the document name

As the design progresses, it is also often useful to indicate the overall layout or style of the window, for example a list of documents, a filter, or a detail window.

If the design process has begun with working prototypes, or has progressed to the point where detailed designs of some windows are available, there is no reason why screen snapshots of actual windows cannot be included in the diagrams. This is particularly useful when testing paper prototypes with users, who typically prefer to see actual window layouts rather than empty boxes. There is a danger in doing so, however, which is that the designer can become distracted by the detail of window design when she should be focusing on the dialog flow.

Summary

In this chapter, we have examined issues of practical implementation in making the transition from taskflow to dialog design. We began with the assertion that the job of dialog design is to support the taskflow identified in the previous chapter. Taskflow is essentially user-focused; dialog design is essentially implementation-focused. It is at this point of transition that many usability errors creep in, either through carelessness, a failure to specify requirements adequately, or an inappropriate regard for ease of implementation over ease of use (which a designer friend of mine calls an 'unhealthy respect for the computer'). We then introduced the idea of designing for minimum effort, through the use of dialog decision trees. This approach is a useful discipline in keeping the dialog design focused on user needs.

One significant aspect of dialog flow that was not addressed in this chapter is the question of error and exception handling. This issue combines issues of taskflow, dialog design and detailed design, as well as questions of online help and documentation. As this is such a broad-ranging issue, it is discussed in a chapter of its own, later in the book.

The second part of this chapter examined implementation issues, and provided some guidance in organizing windows. Various techniques for making best use of limited screen space, including canvases and fold-outs, are available to the designer, but must be used with care if they are to support, rather than confound, the conceptual model. We also highlighted the commonest forms of dialog flow, which support the two common forms of taskflow we introduced in the previous chapter.

The dialog design notation introduced in this chapter will be an important aid to the designer. Although it is an informal notation, it provides an effective technique for communicating with other designers and, when handled properly, with end users when testing paper prototypes.

In the next chapter we descend one level further into the design, and examine the detailed content of each window or dialog box. As we mentioned earlier, it is highly likely that decisions taken at that level will cause us to revisit choices made at this one.

5 Detailed design

'Have nothing in your houses that you do not know to be useful, or believe to be beautiful'

William Morris

Introduction

In this chapter we turn our attention to the aspect of user interface design that receives the most frequent attention, that of detailed design. Indeed, to the naïve observer detailed design is all that there is to user interface design. As we have seen in previous chapters, this is far from the case.

Detailed design is probably the most deceptive aspect of user interface design. Superficially, it is apparently something that anybody can do, yet examples of poor detailed design are all too common. This suggests that detailed design is rather more subtle than it may seem at first sight. One consequence of the apparent ease of detailed design is that it is also the most seductive aspect of design. It is very tempting to leap straight into window layout, and begin painting fields and buttons, in much the same way that a programmer may be tempted to jump straight into coding, without first conducting a proper design. Detailed design is not merely a question of cosmetic appearance; decisions at the detail level need to support the choice of conceptual model, the taskflow, and the dialog flow identified earlier.

We should beware of underestimating the importance of this stage of the design process. To the user, much of the immediate impact of the application is determined by visual design. If the conceptual model is compelling and natural, the taskflow has been well thought-out, and dialog flow has been smoothly implemented, users may never even notice these aspects. On the other hand, the graphical effectiveness of the screen designs will be judged by every user. Issues of detailed layout and field organization will also have a significant impact on the ergonomics for the user, and questions of visual design will strongly influence the comfort of the user over the medium to long term.

In this chapter, we shall discuss the use of basic, standard controls, and highlight some common errors in their use. We shall also look at the appropriate use of custom controls. We shall then go on to address issues of layout and organization of windows. Ergonomic aspects of graphical design, such as the readability of fonts and colours, will also be examined, as well as mainly cosmetic issues, including decoration. We shall also address less clear-cut issues such as the use of the mouse versus the keyboard, and the design of icons and iconic pushbuttons.

Cultural issues

It should be noted that the following discussion assumes a Eurocentric viewpoint; for example, that a page is normally read from top left to bottom right. If you are designing for a non-Western audience, you should be wary of cultural assumptions. Colour choices, layout, text fonts, icon and cursor shapes, and wording of messages all need to be sensitive to the cultural background of the users. Designing for an international audience has very broad implications, beyond the scope of this book. The safest path is to ensure that your designs are adequately reviewed by a sympathetic member of your target audience.

Controls

A control is any component of the display that the user or the program can interact with. Standard controls include pushbuttons and text entry fields. Most controls are used for both input and output (the user can both read and set the control's value) but some are output only (the application presents some system value that the user cannot alter). Controls are also known as widgets or, occasionally, interaction styles.

Programmers will be aware that, in implementation terms, windows and controls are both the same kind of object. From the designer's and the user's point of view, though, they serve very different functions in the user interface. Window styles were discussed in the previous chapter, and we shall restrict ourselves to other controls in this chapter.

Standard controls

Many readers will be familiar with the use of standard controls, but we shall review them briefly for the benefit of those less familiar with their use, and also to ensure that we are all using the same terminology. We shall also highlight some common oversights and misunderstandings.

Radio button groups

When the user must choose between a set of mutually exclusive settings, a *radio button group* is an excellent mapping. Only one item in the group can be selected at a time, and selecting any item automatically deselects all others. (Radio buttons are named after old-fashioned radios that had mechanical buttons for selecting a station or a waveband; these buttons operated in the same exclusive way.)

Radio buttons are appropriate when the possible values are static and are small in number. As well as selecting values, radio buttons can also be used for selecting between canvases, as seen in the previous chapter, although this usage is rapidly being obsoleted by the use of 'tabs'.

A radio button group can be laid out vertically (one above the other), horizontally (across the screen), or even a combination of both. Whichever layout is chosen, it is important that the buttons in the group be arranged to emphasize their relationship to the user. This is normally done with a group box, and the details of such 'decoration' will be discussed later in the chapter.

A large number of buttons in a group makes the screen look very cluttered and difficult to read. The number of buttons in a radio button group should therefore be restricted to a manageable size; six or seven choices is in general a reasonable limit. (It is tempting to associate this limit with the short-term memory limits discussed in Chapter 1; unfortunately there is no conclusive evidence of such a connection.) Beyond that number, other mechanisms such as lists are more appropriate.

Check boxes

When a field can have only two 'Boolean' values, Yes and No or On and Off, a check box is a good mapping. Depending on the platform, a check box may be represented by a box with a cross, X, in it; a box that is either filled or empty; or a box with a tick, $\sqrt{}$, in it. Of these possibilities, only the last is without problems.

The 'X' style of check box presents occasional problems of interpretation. In English-speaking countries other than the USA, the words 'check mark' and 'check box' may be unknown beyond the GUI screen. In British English, we 'tick' a box, we don't 'check' it. For many users and in many cultures, 'X' means 'wrong', and is used to cross something out, rather than to select it. For us as designers, the convention is so familiar that many of us have become blind to this difficulty. Many users by contrast have to be consciously aware of the altered convention on the computer screen.

The Motif style of filled and empty boxes also presents difficulties. It can be very hard for users to distinguish the checked and unchecked states on low resolution or grey-scale displays; and even when the two states can be distinguished, it can be difficult for the user to interpret which display represents filled and which represents empty.

Unfortunately, there is little we can do about a particular platform's representation of a check box, except to be aware of the difficulties and perhaps allow for them in other ways.

Check boxes should always be labelled with a positive statement, to avoid double negatives in interpreting the unchecked state. For example, if the label is 'Disable array processing', the user must interpret an unchecked box as 'Don't Disable array processing', which means 'Do Enable array processing'. Why not make the interpretation easier for the user, and simply label the box 'Enable array processing'? Such errors are all too common, as the following examples from popular desktop applications show:

☐ Print without Smartmaster background
☐ Suppress line numbers
☐ Omit return address
☐ Ignore remote requests
☐ Disable No Scroll

The last example must surely take the prize for the most confusing treble negative in a user interface.

Another common error to avoid is the assumption that a check box is automatically the correct choice for any field with exactly two values. A check box is only appropriate when the field is Boolean or on/off; in other words, the interpretation of the *negative* of the attribute is as obvious as the positive statement. Consider the following example from Microsoft Excel:

☐ Fast, but no graphics

What is the opposite of 'Fast, but no graphics'? Is it 'Slow, but no graphics'? 'Fast, with graphics'? 'Slow, with graphics'? If the value associated with the unchecked setting is not obvious, a radio button group with just two items is a much better choice than a check box.

Combo boxes and pop-down lists

Various kinds of pop-down list, or combo box, are useful for displaying dynamic choices (unlike radio button groups, which represent a static set of options). Pop-down lists are also appropriate when many choices are available to the user, where a large radio group would become unwieldy. The amount of real estate occupied by a list can be much reduced by displaying only a portion of the complete list at any one time, with a scrollbar to bring other choices into view.

Replacing simple data entry fields with lists promotes recognition over recall, and this is especially useful where the user may have difficulty providing an exact match. A typical example is the name of a customer: the correct spelling of a company in the customer database may be quite different from the way in which the company is commonly known.

A combo box consists of a simple field, with a pop-down list attached. The currently selected value is displayed in the simple field, and the other values available can be seen by popping down the list. There are three commonly implemented styles of combo boxes; we will compare the characteristics of each.

A *simple* combo box has the pop-down list permanently displayed. This style allows the user to see other choices, and is appropriate if availability of screen real estate is not a problem. The user can also enter a value directly into the simple field, if he knows the value he wants. The *drop-down* style is the most common; unlike the simple combo box, the list is only displayed on demand. This is more appropriate when the simple style would occupy too much space. The *drop-list* style can be used to force the user to select from the list; it is identical to the drop-down style, except that the user *cannot* type directly into the entry field, he can only select from the list. This style should be used with care: although it prevents entry errors, it is very blocking. An experienced user may be able to type a correct entry significantly faster than he can identify the required value and pick it from a long list.

The designer should also be aware that on certain platforms, the drop-down and drop-list styles appear almost identical (there is a subtle visual difference that very few ordinary users will be aware of). The designer may need to consider providing some additional information to the user to ensure that he understands the restriction on a drop list box.

List boxes

Like combo boxes, list boxes also allow a user to select one value from many, but are somewhat more sophisticated. A list box may have several columns, aligned to tab settings, and may be scrollable horizontally as well as vertically. For this reason, a list box is an excellent way of presenting a list of subjects (orders, invoices, etc.) to a user in a transaction processing application. The user can repeatedly select a subject and perform an appropriate action, returning to the list box after each action. List boxes may also be used to represent tasks and work queues. The only major drawback of list boxes is that they can occupy a large amount of real estate.

List boxes permit more sophisticated forms of selection than do combo boxes, allowing multiple entries to be selected and operated on at one time. Styles include *multiple* selection, which allows the user to select several entries in the list; and *extended* selection, which allows the user to select a range of entries by clicking the first and last while holding down the 'extend' key (usually the Shift key). These styles are particularly appropriate in a subject-oriented application, where the user may want to perform some task, such as 'Assign a case to somebody', to several subjects at once.

Pushbuttons

Pushbuttons, also known simply as buttons, are used for small numbers of commands or actions. Buttons should be used for actions that are specific to a particular dialog or context, whereas menus (discussed below) are preferred for commands that are widely applicable.

Pushbuttons are labelled either with a verb describing the action to be performed, for example 'Save', or a noun describing the result of the action, for example 'Options...'. Other ways of labelling a pushbutton can be ambiguous. One application I encountered featured a button labelled 'Required'; so naturally I pressed it! There was then a ten minute wait while the application verified my system privileges for a particular action that I did not even intend to carry out. The ambiguity, and resulting error, could have been avoided by labelling the button with a verb phrase, 'Check Privileges', or a noun phrase, 'Privileges Check'.

Buttons are often 'labelled' with an icon rather than a text; we shall discuss the merits and design of icons later in the chapter. In recent years, more and more functionality has migrated from menus to button bars and palettes, somewhat blurring the distinction between the purposes of the two. The advantages and disadvantages of button bars will also be discussed in more detail later.

One frequent ambiguity with buttons deserves special attention. Pairs of buttons labelled with arrows are often used for 'previous' and 'next' actions: 'next record', 'next date', 'next item in list' and 'next unread mail message' are common examples. Arrows are also often used for 'more' and 'less', or 'increase' and 'decrease', for example in setting text font size. A pair of buttons in the style of Fig. 5.1 is sometimes called a 'spin' control.

Arrows pointing Left and Right rarely cause a problem: Left always means 'previous' or 'less', and Right always means 'next' or 'more', according to context. On the other hand, Up and Down can sometimes lead to ambiguity. The problem occurs because Up can mean both 'previous' (in a list or sequence) or 'more' (of a quantity), and conversely Down can mean both 'next' and 'less'. If the user is unsure which interpretation is intended, ambiguity can occur. For example, in Fig. 5.1, does Up mean *increase* the date by one, or set the date to the *previous* day? Many people are adamant that there is no ambiguity here, that only one interpretation is possible. Unfortunately, about half of them insist that *increase* is the only possible interpretation, and the others insist that *previous* is the only

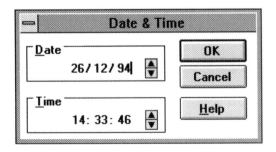

Figure 5.1. Control panel uses arrows to adjust time and date

possibility! The designer should avoid Up and Down arrows whenever there is a possible ambiguity of interpretation on the part of the user.

Menus

The most common mechanism for organizing a large number of commands or actions is in hierarchical menus. Generally, the menu appears as a set of categories at the top of the application's main window (depending on the platform); typical categories include 'File', 'Edit' and 'Help'. Each category can be clicked to open a list of specific commands or options, such as 'Save' or 'Print'. Specific implementation varies from platform to platform, but there is little practical difference between fixing the menu at the top of the screen; on the application's MDI frame; or placing a menu on every document window. The designer is best advised to follow the particular platform's standard presentation.

Menu items may contain sub-menus, also called pop-up, pull-down, or cascading menus. (Confusingly, 'pop-up' is also used for another type of menu, discussed below.) In theory, sub-menus could be nested to any depth, but in practice the designer should avoid more than two or three levels of menu below the main menu, as it then becomes difficult for the user to explore the extent of the menu structure, and to locate the command she needs. The designer may find that there is such a large number of commands to be implemented that she must choose either a shallow menu hierarchy that is very broad (i.e. many top-level categories) or one that has long menus with many items in each category. If this is the case, it is possible that she has placed too many commands on menus.

Remember that the menu is always available, so the commands on the menu should be those that are broadly applicable in many windows and in many modes. Commands that are specific to a particular tool or modal dialog are better implemented as buttons directly on the window in question. Menus can also be altered dynamically, so that a different set of menu commands can be presented according to context.

In theory, menus are worded using a 'Noun/Verb' model, which reflects the 'object/action' approach that is supposed to characterize GUI applications. In practice, even within a single application you will find all of the following:

- Noun/Verb, e.g. File/Save
- Noun/Adjective, e.g. File/New
- Verb/Verb, e.g. Edit/Cut
- Verb/Noun, e.g. Format/Character
- Noun/Noun, e.g. Tools/Spelling

In fact, users take little or no notice of these differences; it is far more important that the categories be well organized and well named, and that the items on the menu be clearly distinguished for easy recognition. Simplicity is the key.

There are various theories about the order that menu items should appear in: alphabetical, most frequently used, grouped by function, and so on. In practice, it seems to make little difference which scheme is used, providing some rationale is followed. Common current practice is to group by function, arranging functions with the most frequently used at the top. The most important consideration is stability: experienced users will rapidly learn the position of frequently used commands, such as Edit/Cut, in much the same way that a touch typist learns the position of keys on a typewriter. User productivity will suffer measurably if the designer is tempted to rearrange menus depending on mode or context, or to place 'most recently used' commands at the top, in a misguided attempt to help the user.

A similar consideration applies to the menu categories themselves. If you have many top-level categories, you may be tempted to 'scroll' the menu bar left and right to bring additional categories into view as required by the user. This is to be avoided at all costs. Research has demonstrated that the user's productivity will drop dramatically if she cannot rely on finding a given menu item in the same physical location at all times.

One common error in menu design befalls designers who move from the character mode world to the GUI interface. In character mode, a menu is typically used merely as a 'launch pad' for related applications or for modules within an application. The menu items tend to be names of modules, such as 'Invoice Entry', rather than user actions or tasks. In consequence, the menu itself is often only loosely integrated with the rest of the application: the user launches a module, then has no further use for the menu until it is time to launch the next module. By contrast, the menu items in a typical GUI application are closely integrated with the module and perform user tasks and actions against specific documents: formatting text, running tools such as spell checkers, and so on. The menu is a place to locate the user's actions, not the designer's modules.

Menus and options

As well as allowing a large number of commands to be presented in a very small space, menus can also be used to allow the user to choose between options. Simple on/off options can be represented by menu check items: when the option is selected or active, a check ($\sqrt{}$) appears next to the menu item. Otherwise, no symbol appears.

Large sets of options are good candidates for sub-menus (illustrated on the disk under 'Font Options'). Sub-menus are also a good place to put a long list of mutually exclusive options, such as line width or font size in a drawing package. Such options may appear as radio button items in the menu to emphasize the exclusivity.

Options can also be represented by changing the *wording* of the item when it is selected, e.g. from 'Lines Hidden' to 'Lines Shown', rather than placing a check next to the item. This is not recommended as it can be very confusing for the user: when the menu item reads 'Lines Hidden', does that mean that lines are *currently* hidden, or that clicking on the command will hide them? Wording the item as a verb phrase, such as 'Show Lines', is less ambiguous, but is still not ideal. Menu check items must be worded carefully for the same reasons.

For check items the use of adjectives, such as 'Bold', is normally clearer than using verbs, such as 'Embolden'. However, there may still be ambiguity for the new user, who may not be aware that the word 'Bold' appearing by itself (without a check mark) means 'No Bold'. Unlike a check box, there is no visual clue for the new user that a check mark might appear when he clicks the item; an unchecked menu check item is indistinguishable from an ordinary menu command.

Another disadvantage of using menus to represent check items and option choices is that the selections currently in force can only be seen when the menu is 'popped down'. In other words, the visibility is poor.

In summary, the visibility and the affordance of menu options can be poor, and the feedback can be ambiguous. On the other hand, the use of real estate is quite good. For these reasons, in modern applications button bars and tool bars often replace (or duplicate) such uses of menus.

Pop-up menus

In certain applications, a further kind of menu is available, usually called a pop-up menu. Such a menu is usually invoked by selecting an object, then clicking the right mouse button. Commonly required actions for that object are then available. While pop-up menus are attractive from the point of view of putting functionality close to the mouse position, they need to be carefully designed to be effective. For example, the menu shown in Fig. 5.2 uses the first three items for 'Cut', 'Copy' and 'Paste'. These commands can already be accessed in two clicks, under the 'Edit' menu; in one click on the toolbar; or from the keyboard as Ctrl-X, Ctrl-C and Ctrl-V respectively. It seems pointless to waste the first three pop-up items on repeating them yet again. The designer also should ensure that the first item, which is the one the user is most likely to activate by accident, by a slip of the finger, is harmless. My own preference is to put 'Help' at the top of every pop-up menu.

There is also a significant visibility issue with pop-up menus: how is the user to know when a menu is available, and how to invoke it? Using the right mouse button is a common, but by no means universal, means of invocation. If pop-ups are widely used, changing the cursor shape whenever the right button is active is one possible solution.

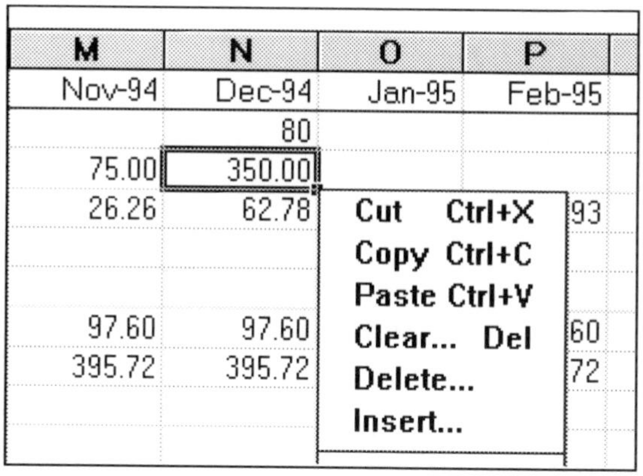

M	N	O	P
Nov-94	Dec-94	Jan-95	Feb-95
	80		
75.00	350.00		
26.26	62.78	Cut Ctrl+X	93
		Copy Ctrl+C	
		Paste Ctrl+V	
97.60	97.60	Clear... Del	60
395.72	395.72	Delete...	72
		Insert...	

Figure 5.2. Pop-up menu in Microsoft Excel

Custom and non-standard controls

Custom controls are currently very popular, partly because they are potentially more visually attractive (or at least more novel) than standard controls, but also because the popularity of Microsoft's Visual Basic product and the associated VBX standard have made the task of creating a custom control far easier than in the past.

This facility has led to some dubious or inappropriate uses of custom controls. The motivation behind some custom and non-standard controls seems to be visual novelty alone. Apparently, 'easy to use' and 'easy to learn' have taken a back seat to 'easy to sell'. On the other hand, a well-chosen custom control can greatly enhance ease of learning and ease of use of a specific feature.

Typical custom controls include various kinds of slider, rotating knobs, dials, and the 'tabs' we encountered in the previous chapter. As the 'tabs' illustrate, a well-designed, effective and appropriate custom control can rapidly move into the mainstream.

When is a custom control appropriate?

When we discussed mappings and cues in Chapter 1, we noted that a new control will nearly always give a weaker cue than a familiar one. We proposed this simple test for custom controls:

- Does the new control significantly improve the mapping, compared to a standard control?
- Does the new control give an adequate cue to the user?
- Does the gain offered by improving the mapping compensate for the unfamiliar cue?

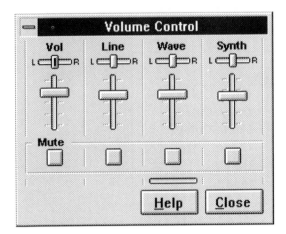

Figure 5.3. Slider controls

Of course, it is not always the case that an unfamiliar cue is a poor cue, especially if the new cue draws strongly on an effective real world metaphor. Sometimes a new control can be invented that replaces an inappropriate use of a standard control. The 'tab' for choosing between canvases, illustrated in the previous chapter, is an excellent example. Here, the cue is actually better than that offered by a radio button group, because of its real world associations. Similarly, a slider can be both visually more attractive and provide a better cue than the functionally equivalent scroll bar (Fig. 5.3).

It is often easier to design a custom control for output only, for example a thermometer to represent temperature, than for input. With an output-only control, the user only needs to figure out how to read the control, not how to set it.

A well-designed input can significantly contribute to the illusion of direct manipulation. The slider controls in Fig. 5.3 give a far more intuitive interface than would typing values into an entry field. One common danger in designing custom controls concerns the precision of the control. A rotating knob or a slider can give the user an impression that the control can be set to a very fine precision, as in Fig. 5.3. The reality may be that the underlying value may have a much coarser granularity. In such cases the designer may provide a scale showing the true granularity, or even 'snap' the control to the actual granularity, rather than allowing it to be varied continuously.

A design approach for custom controls

The first question that the designer should ask herself is whether a standard control will serve the purpose. If so, the designer should consider carefully what she expects to gain by using a custom control. If the answer is purely to make the

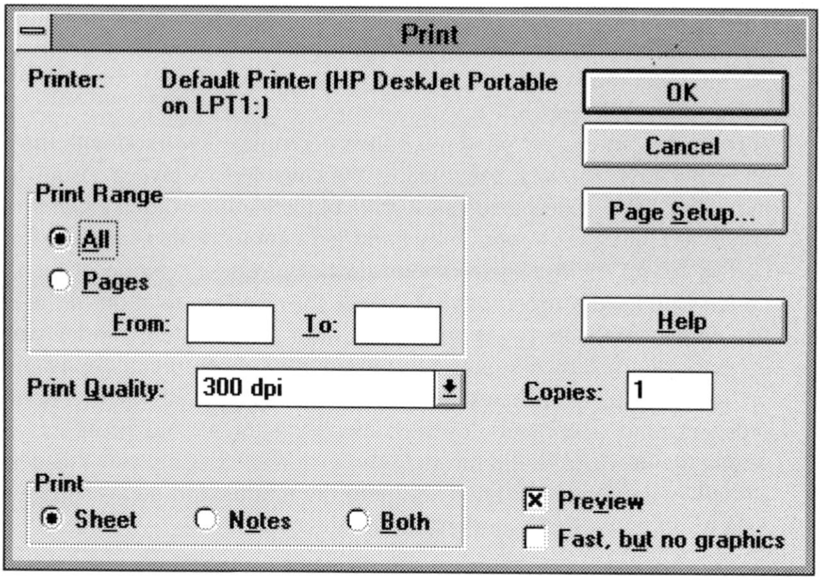

Figure 5.4. Three-dimensional versions of standard controls

control visually more attractive, she should base the behaviour and appearance as closely as possible on the standard control. The 'three-dimensional' style controls becoming widespread in MS-Windows applications (although standard for some time in Motif) are a good example of this approach; Fig. 5.4 as well as several of the other figures in this chapter illustrate this style. They differ from their normal counterparts only in the improved graphical appearance.

If there is no appropriate standard control, the design of a custom control becomes similar to the whole design process in miniature. First, the designer must choose a conceptual model or metaphor: index or tab cards; a thermometer; a knob that can be rotated; a slider; a pop-up calendar for setting dates; and so on. The metaphor that is chosen must make sense in the immediate context of its usage; but it must also make sense in terms of the application's own overall metaphor.

Next, the designer must decide how the user interacts with the control: by clicking, dragging, or through the keyboard; and also how the user reads the value of the control setting; in other words, the feedback, visibility, cues, and mapping of the control. The designer must be very objective in asking herself whether the usage of the control is self-evident. Again, the interactions should be consistent with the metaphor: in real life, you do not normally set a thermometer, you only read it. While it is true that user interface metaphors often 'stretch' literal real world meanings (most people do not keep a wastebasket on their desktop), a stretched metaphor may need a little additional explanation, either visual or literal.

Finally, the designer can fine-tune the visual appearance of the control. The visual behaviour may also be an important aspect of the feedback; for example, the thermometer may change colour from blue to red as the temperature rises.

A good custom control need not be very complex. I worked with the designers of an application to track sales leads; they wanted to give a visual 'at a glance' indication of the salesperson's estimate of the likelihood of a given prospect being converted into a customer. They had tried various designs, including traffic lights ('green for go') and a thermometer ('a hot prospect'). None of them was easily understood by the users, partly because they had no relation to the metaphor of the whole application. As the application's conceptual model was based on logging and tracking contacts, I proposed a simple graphical representation based on cartoons of telephones: a telephone ringing itself off the hook for a hot prospect; and a cobweb-covered telephone for a cold prospect. To alter the setting the user could 'flip through' the pictures. Not only was this design visually attractive, the metaphor fitted well into the model, and it was simple to interpret. As a result it was easily understood by the users.

Icons and cursors

Icons are used in a number of ways in GUI applications: an icon represents an application on the desktop or window manager; when a window or an application is minimized, it is represented by an icon together with the window title; and, most frequently, icons are used as pictorial buttons. These buttons usually come in two sizes: full size icons (typically 32×32 pixels), which are used on windows in place of ordinary labelled buttons; and miniature icons (typically 16×16 pixels), which are used on button bars to reduce space requirements.

Icons for minimized windows are a necessity in any application that has minimizable windows; the user needs to be able to distinguish different types of minimized windows at a glance. On the other hand, the decision to make use of iconic buttons on a button bar should not be taken purely out of a desire to follow fashion or brighten up the visual appearance of an application. Iconic buttons need to be thoughtfully designed and carefully implemented in order to be more effective than more traditional alternatives.

We shall not be discussing detailed graphical design issues as applied to icons: this is another specialized task best left to experts. However, it is perfectly possible for the average person to design adequate, competent, simple icons, in outlines or a few colours.

Principles of icon design

A picture is not always worth a thousand words; ideally an icon should be as easy, or easier, to interpret as a label on a button. A good icon is a 'sight bite': it instantly communicates its purpose to the user. A well-designed icon communicates as much as an entire phrase. If an icon needs an explanation it has failed in its major purpose of communication; it succeeds only as a space saver.

Generally, it is easier to depict a noun, such as a disk or a printer, than it is to depict a verb, such as 'Save'. When choosing an image to depict, begin with the object being touched: the printer, for example. If this is not an adequate explication of the command, consider the result of the action: a clean sheet for the 'New' command, for example. If neither of these is appropriate, try to find a simple method of depicting the action in question. Icons that attempt to depict a complex action risk ending up as miniature cartoon strips, completely unfathomable to the user. Consider the second group of four icons in Fig. 5.5. They all apply formatting to paragraphs in a document. The first produces a numbered list, the second a bulleted list, and the third and fourth decrease and increase the level of indent. Notice how the first two, by depicting the result of the action, are much simpler and more easily interpreted than the last two, which attempt to depict the action itself. It is significant that from the user's point of view, it is the result, not the act itself, that is important.

Figure 5.5. Example icons

As well as being easily interpreted individually, icons must be easily distinguished from each other. Remember that icons are supposed to support recognition. Consider the third group of icons in Fig. 5.5, taken from Microsoft Visual C++. They are used to rebuild an executable from a set of project files, and perform the actions 'Compile the current file', 'Compile files affected by changes', and 'Compile all files'. Which is which? Not only are they individually meaningless, the second and third are so similar that only the most dedicated of frequent users will ever learn to distinguish them.

In addition to being clear in themselves, the images chosen for icons should support the overall metaphor of the application, otherwise it will be difficult for the user to interpret them. Avoid icons that, although attractive in themselves, have no ready interpretation within the conceptual model. Worst of all are 'visual puns' which the user must interpret; for example, one designer is fond of images such as a hangman for 'Execute'. Unless the user puts the right word to the picture, she will not understand the pun and so will not see the point of the icon. Such puns are particularly dangerous in an international application. For example, although in English we might 'run' an application, in French they 'launch' it.

Visual language

Iconic buttons frequently form part of a set of related actions. When designing such a set of icons, the designer may try to find a consistent set of simple elements that can be combined in different ways, such as a document with or without writing on it. This is much the way pictographic languages work: the pictogram for 'sun' behind the pictogram for 'tree' becomes a new pictogram meaning 'sunrise'.

To exploit this approach, a group of icons uses consistent visual language derived from a common pictorial vocabulary. Compare the first group of icons in Fig. 5.5: the first represents the 'New document' command, the second represents 'Open existing document'. The former depicts the thing that will result from pressing the button: a clean sheet. The second shows a folder with an arrow, presumably the action of opening the folder. Yet, elsewhere in MS-Windows this folder image represents a directory, not a file. It would be far simpler for the user, as well as more consistent, if the second icon were replaced by a document like the first, but with lines of writing; or perhaps with several pages depicted, one behind another.

By contrast, Fig. 5.6 shows some icons from an editor for remote (stored) procedures and triggers in a relational database server. The icons are all composed from a small set of elements:

- A stylized PC represents the client
- A drum represents the database server
- A small rectangle represents a code module

The four icons are then interpreted as:

- A PC connected to a database, meaning 'choose a database connection'
- A PC connected to code modules, meaning 'remote procedures'
- A database connected to code modules, meaning 'database triggers'
- A code module connected to other code modules, meaning 'show code cross-references'

When a large number of icons are presented on a tool bar, a pictographic language such as this is not only easier for the user to learn and interpret, but is also easier for the designer than trying to invent an individually stunning and original design for each button.

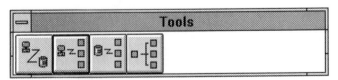

Figure 5.6. Icons from a database code editor

Cursors

On most platforms, different cursor shapes are used to provide feedback to the user. An 'I Beam' indicates a text field, an hourglass indicates when the user must wait for an action to complete. The designer can make effective use of the same idea to provide strong feedback to the user. Changing the cursor shape has the great advantage that it cannot be overlooked by the user; the visual indication appears exactly where the user's attention is focused. The principles of cursor design are similar to those of icon design; it is even more important that different cursors are easily distinguished.

Some of the uses that the designer might make of different cursors include:

- Indicate modes, such as query, by adding a question mark to the tail of the cursor in query mode
- Indicate invalid fields by putting a cross on the cursor when the user points to a missing or bad field
- Indicate that the cut buffer contains material that can be pasted

There are many other ways that the cursor can be used to provide feedback; I particularly favour the use of different cursors to make modes visible.

Colour and perspective

The 'amateur' icon designer should beware of overusing colours in icon designs. Choose a small set of colours, no more than three or four in addition to shades of grey, that are strongly distinguished from each other. Use the colours to support the pictorial language: a given element should always appear in the same colour. Use strong contrasts between elements and black borders around the outside of the icon. Remember that the final image is going to appear very small, and must be recognizable at a glance. Ensure that icons are still distinguishable without the benefit of colour: never use colour alone to distinguish icons, but incorporate changes in brightness and position as well.

Many icons, especially the icons representing the application on the desktop or window manager, are designed to have a three-dimensional look. The universally observed rule in depicting perspective on the screen is that the object should appear to be lit from over the user's left shoulder. In other words, the light comes from the top left of the screen. Look at an ordinary pushbutton: the top and left edges appear 'lit', the bottom and right edges appear 'in shadow'. The eye interprets this lighting as the button being raised out of the surface. Conventionally, icons are presented either as if seen 'head on', like buttons; or as if seen from slightly above and to the right, like the icons in the Program Manager of MS-Windows.

The strange effects of incorrect shadows can be seen in Fig. 5.7. Here, the designer appears to have used the same arrow twice, simply inverting 'Up' to

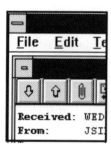

Figure 5.7. Incorrect shading

create 'Down'. The result is that the 'Down' arrow appears to be lit from the bottom of the screen, and the eye interprets it as being strangely twisted, like an Escher etching.

Icon hints and tips

The human eye is eager to be fooled; it will gladly 'see' three dimensions and curves where none exist. Sometimes, the eye may perceive fewer colours or shades than are actually present: it may 'integrate' a speckled (dithered) pattern of small colour areas to an intermediate colour. In other cases, the eye may perceive more shades than are really used: the perceived colour depends on the colours that surround it. Certain visual tricks are especially effective at the small scale of icons. The following hints may be of use to the icon designer; many of them are illustrated by the example icons on the disk accompanying this book.

Use white lines for lit edges, and dark grey (rather than black) for shadow. Showing the top and left edges as lit gives a raised effect, the bottom and right gives a lowered effect. This can readily be seen in the three-dimensional versions of standard controls used in many applications. Lines need not necessarily be the same width; in particular, diagonal lines appear thinner than vertical and horizontal lines, and may need to be made wider. Nor need lines be a single colour; the apparent thickness of a diagonal line can be subtly adjusted by a mixture of single and double thickness, and black, dark grey, and light grey pixels.

Pay particular attention to the corners where lines meet, especially lines that are differently lit. The designer may need to experiment with setting the intersection pixel lit or unlit to achieve the best effect. Interior and exterior corners may also need to be lit differently. Omitting the intersection pixel entirely can give a slightly rounded effect, especially on small icons. Very small circles can be satisfactorily represented by drawing a 4x4 square with the corners omitted; larger circles use short diagonal segments, two or three pixels long, at different angles. More complex curves are difficult to achieve, and should be approached with care.

Three-dimensional shapes, especially curves such as bands or ribbons, can be enhanced by judicious use of lighting effects, for example by using a light and a dark shade of a single colour. If the parts that face the imaginary light source are drawn in the lighter shade, and the parts that face away in the darker shade, the eye may easily interpret the effect as a three-dimensional object. Particular care is required to get the shadow line in the correct place. In a full-size icon, there may be sufficient detail to add a white highlight, or specular reflection, at the point of the curve that directly faces the imaginary light source.

Icon design is by no means easy; ideas that work well in a drawing may fail when reduced to a 16×16 or 32×32 grid. The designer must take into account subtle effects that occur at such small scales. The best ways to learn are by experiment and by examining other designer's icons. Many icon editors are able to extract icons from executables, and examining closely such icons is an excellent way of learning the tricks of icon design. Finally, the designer should not get discouraged too easily: early attempts may well appear clumsy, but it is only with practice and experience that the icon designer will learn what works and what does not.

Animated icons and cursors

Icons and cursors are increasingly being used in animations, for example as progress indicators. Norton Desktop uses an animated 'stack of files' to indicate the progress of a file search; Microsoft Word Version 6.0 uses paper sheets feeding through a printer to indicate a background print in progress; and the Mac has the famous 'jumping dog' wait indicator.

The actual value of animations, as opposed to visual cuteness, is often questionable. Motion is highly attention grabbing: drawing the user's attention to a *background* print seems somewhat contrary. Animations as progress indicators are most useful when an action will take an unpredictable amount of time (ruling out conventional indicators such as a flood fill or a countdown), and the user must wait for completion. It is not unknown for a MS-Windows application to become (or at least appear) hung while showing the 'hourglass' cursor, especially when network connections are involved. Norton's file search is a good example of an appropriate use of an animation.

Control combinations

Mapping simple values or actions to single controls is straightforward enough, even though some application designers seem determined to use standard controls in 'interesting' ways. The task becomes more complex when we need to represent some more complex value or action that does not map to a standard control in an obvious way. Typical examples include:

- *A control can take exactly one of three values*   A database could be online, offline but available, or unavailable due to error or offline backup.

- *A control's value usually takes one of a few common values, but potentially may take any value* Line spacing in a document is usually single or double, but can potentially be set to any custom spacing.
- *A control depends conditionally on some other control* This is very common in filters: I might want to show all documents, or only those for a particular company. The applicability of the 'Company Name' field depends condition-ally on the 'Select By Company Name/Select All Documents' choice.

It is hard to generalize about such requirements as they are so varied, but a few principles will help the designer avoid the worst errors:

- *Consider the suitability and value of a custom control* A well-designed custom control may often be more appropriate than a complex combination of simple controls. Tognazzini (1992) has an excellent discussion of the creation, iterative testing, and refinement of a custom control for a 'one or more' control.
- *Map one concept to one control, wherever possible* In Fig. 5.8, the zoom level is represented by a radio button, the 'Custom' entry field with a spin control, and two pushbuttons. How do the different mechanisms interact with each other? This particular control could have been a simple combo box, list-ing all of the preset values, as well as allowing a custom value to be typed directly into the simple field, as in Fig. 5.9.
- *Use visual cues to emphasize grouped controls* Where separate controls combine to set or represent a single value, group boxes, lines and indentation can emphasize the relationships and dependencies.
- *Respect fundamental principles of visibility, feedback, mappings and cues* A simple test of any complex control is to show it to somebody else; how much narrative explanation do you need to give him of how to operate it, and how the components of the control interact? If nobody else is available, draft a help page for the control. Ask yourself, objectively, how complex the explanation is.

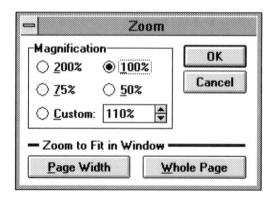

Figure 5.8. Zoom setting (before)

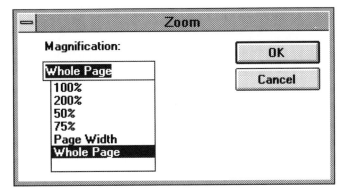

Figure 5.9. Zoom setting (after)

Tool bars and palettes

Most modern applications feature some form of tool bar or palette; indeed, in some applications, if all the available tool bars are enabled, more screen space may be devoted to tool bars than to the actual document. Tool bars and palettes serve essentially the same purpose, the major difference being that a tool bar is fixed either to the frame window, or to a document window (depending on the platform in question), and may be either vertical or horizontal. A palette is usually an independent floating window. As tool bars and palettes are functionally very similar, we will refer to both simply as tool bars for the purposes of this section. The distinction between them is chiefly a matter of how the designer wants to make use of screen real estate.

The purpose of tool bars is to provide one-click access to a range of commonly used actions; typical examples include File Open and File Save; Cut, Copy, and Paste; and Print. For this reason, tool bars mainly contain pushbuttons. To cram as many functions as possible onto the tool bar, these buttons are usually small and iconic.

The tool bar may also feature a kind of 'iconic check box': this looks like a button, but when clicked it remains down, in the 'checked' or 'selected' state. Clicked again, it becomes 'deselected'. In Fig. 5.10, the buttons labelled **B**, *I* and <u>u</u>, which set the text style to bold, italic, and underline respectively, act

Figure 5.10. Part of the tool bars from Microsoft Word Version 2.0

in this way. There may also be 'iconic radio buttons': the group of four buttons to the right in Fig. 5.10 set the paragraph alignment to one of the four paragraph styles left aligned, right aligned, centred, or justified. Just as with a radio button group, clicking one automatically deselects the previous selection.

Tool bars serve three major purposes:

- *They make global, frequently used functions quickly available* Widely used functions such as 'Cut' can be made easy to reach. Tool bars are an excellent way of fulfilling the goals of least effort dialog design, discussed in the previous chapter. For example, the 'Print' iconic button may allow the user to print the document using exactly the same settings as last time, with only a single click.
- *They can make important functions easy to find* In a complex application, the number of menu choices may be overwhelmingly large. Providing tool bars or palettes for specific tasks or document types is an effective way of bringing the most useful functions in each mode readily to hand. A mail application that I use provides different tool bars depending on whether I am working on messages, folders, or distribution lists.
- *They can be visually very attractive* Provided that the graphic design is done well, icons can add a splash of colour to an otherwise bland screen. However, this should be seen as secondary to the other two purposes.

There are certain risks and dangers with tool bars, also:

- *Too many tool bars can clutter the screen* Certain applications seem determined to get every available action onto a button, regardless of how obscure or arcane it might be. Some applications have actions available from several tool bars along the top of the window, a palette at the left edge, and an 'active' status bar at the bottom! This overload defeats entirely the original purpose of the tool bar, which was to make the most useful functions most easily available.
- *Tool bar functions that merely duplicate menu commands are pointless or even confusing* The Print icon should immediately print the document, using whatever settings are currently in effect. A Print icon that merely invokes the same dialog box as the readily available File/Print menu command is a waste of space. The icon bar should provide some kind of shortcut or other advantage over the menu.
- *Poorly designed icons can be difficult to decipher* If icons are badly designed, the user will be unable to figure out their purpose, and so will not use them, thus defeating the purpose. A form of help known variously as 'bubble help', 'balloon help' or 'micro help' can be useful here: if the user positions the cursor over an iconic button and does not move it for around two seconds, a small 'balloon' pops up under the button with a one- or two-word description of the button's function.

Issues in database applications

When we try to apply these principles to transaction processing applications running against a database, specific issues of mapping and interpretation need to be addressed. While GUI controls such as radio buttons and check boxes are excellent for presenting information to the user, and are useful for data entry, problems arise when using GUI controls in *query-by-example* (QBE) forms. Particular difficulties arise as many transaction processing applications use a single window in two modes, for both data entry and QBE. Recall the discussion in Chapter 2 of input and output transformations: a control that is appropriate for output may not work so well for specifying a query.

One application that I have used for support call tracking categorizes calls as 'Pricing', 'Availability', 'Technical', and so on. In order to enforce the correct categorization, the designer obliges the user to choose the call category from a drop list combo box. This is fine for entering new calls, but when using the same screen to query existing calls, I can only query one category at a time. There is no mechanism that allows me to ask for both 'Technical' and 'Availability' calls at the same time, for example.

Query by example and Don't Care states

Radio button groups present a similar problem; if the designer uses a standard implementation, the user can, indeed must, only choose one value. How does the user specify 'Don't Care' for the radio button group, a very common requirement? In fact, 'Don't Care' in QBE is a problem with controls of all kinds.

There is a form of check box, sometimes known as a 'three-state check box', that does allow a 'Don't Care' or 'Don't Know' state. In MS-Windows this state is represented by filling the check box with grey hatching (Fig. 5.11), and this state could be used for indicating 'Don't Care' in a query. Strangely, few GUI design tools make this state available to the designer or the user.

One design tool implements the following bizarre protocol for check boxes. When the user enters Query mode, the check box is blank, representing 'Don't Care'; one click sets it, representing 'Checked'; a second click clears it again, only now representing 'Unchecked'. There is, apparently, no visible way for the user to set the state back to 'Don't Care' once it has been changed, and the clear state represents either 'Unchecked' or 'Don't Care' depending on whether the check box has been changed!

Query by example and null values

Difficulties of presentation and visibility are further compounded by the possibility of NULL values. (For those unfamiliar with database NULLs, a NULL repre-

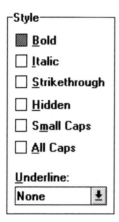

Figure 5.11. 'Don't Care' check box state

sents a value that is 'missing' or not applicable. For example, an invoice that has not yet been paid would have a NULL value for the column 'Date Paid'. By definition, NULL is different from any other representable value, including an empty string.) It is very common in QBE for the user to want to specify all records with NULL in a particular field. Such queries frequently have the most interesting interpretation from a business point of view, as they represent 'exceptional' records: all support calls with no engineer assigned, all unshipped orders, or all unpaid invoices, for example.

There is no easy resolution to these problems. Within a query screen, the user may need to be able to distinguish between fields that are explicitly blank, explicitly NULL, or 'Don't Care'. Visually, this is possible: for example, 'Don't Care' can be represented by extending the three-state check box style to other types of control. However, there is little help from design tools to support such requirements.

In some cases, the best solution may be to avoid use of GUI controls other than simple text entry fields in a form that will be used for QBE. Drop-down lists may be used where the user is obliged to choose one from a number of reference values. In such cases, using a single screen for data capture and QBE may be inappropriate, and separate query and entry screens may be a better, if more expensive, design.

Window layout and graphic design

'In matters of grave importance, style, not sincerity, is the vital thing'

Oscar Wilde, *The Importance of Being Earnest*

In the previous chapter, we examined the organization of dialogs into windows. In this section we turn our attention to the details of size and layout of particular windows, including 'merely' cosmetic aspects of graphical design.

The principles of layout as applied to a window are not very different from those that apply to other forms of graphic design, although of course the specifics will be quite different in our domain. If you are not trained in graphic design, it is well worthwhile investing in a little knowledge of the fundamentals of layout. If your team includes a dedicated graphic designer, you will find it easier to understand his vocabulary and concerns if you have read a graphic design primer such as Siebert and Ballard (1992). If you have no graphic design professional on your team, such a primer is even more useful as it will help you to avoid some of the grosser errors committed by untrained designers.

The purposes of layout

Siebert and Ballard (1992) suggests that a good layout serves three basic criteria: it works, it organizes, and it attracts. These certainly sound like criteria that the GUI designer should be concerned with. Unsurprisingly, these criteria are not completely independent of each other: a well-organized window layout will be more attractive, and will work better for the user. These three criteria are a useful reminder that 'look and feel' are only part of user interface design; to get the full picture, we need to consider 'look and feel and operation'.

The layout works

A good layout, whether it be a poster or a window, communicates a particular message to a particular audience. From our point of view as designers of a user interface, this is usually both the most important and the most difficult aspect of layout. Whereas a traditional graphic medium such as a poster or an advertisement is inherently static, and must passively await the reader's response, a user interface is dynamic and interactive, and so has an entirely new dimension not normally considered in pure graphic design. The user interface designer must consider not only how the interface should look, but how it will behave.

Many graphic elements, such as fonts, size, position and colour, will interact to determine how well a layout works; but so will active software elements such as when validation is carried out (immediately or deferred?) and how errors are handled (prevent or react?). We have already addressed some of these issues in Chapter 4. The graphic elements are considered below; the 'operational' aspects of how the layout works will be discussed later in this chapter; and errors will be discussed in Chapter 6.

The layout organizes

The layout of a window maps out a visual path for the user to follow. Elements such as position, colour, font size, use of white space and 'decoration' such as lines, boxes and arrows, serve to lead the user into, through, and out of the window. Where should the user begin? How should she proceed? How does she continue to the next window, task, or subject? In other words, the layout seeks to answer that universal user's question: 'What do I do now?':

Layout organization is important to comfort of use, in that it can either support or interfere with natural taskflow. It also has a dramatic influence on productivity, if it enables the user to work in a continuous, natural flow. Finally, layout organization can contribute to accuracy, by helping to ensure that every element on the interface receives the appropriate amount of attention from the user.

The layout attracts

The attractiveness of a layout is more than cosmetic. Certain choices of font or combinations of colour will be easier to read than others, some may be hard on the eye for the constant user. An attractive layout has a balance and flow that supports the other two objectives. The attractiveness of the interface may have a strong influence on 'soft' issues such as the motivation and satisfaction of the user. From a purely practical point of view, the attractiveness will also have a dramatic impact on your ability to sell the application, whether this be commercially to external buyers, or to internal users.

Unlike most kinds of graphic design, the user interface designer is not usually aiming for high impact. Generally, a good user interface is understated. Bear in mind that the user may have to sit in front of this application for many hours a day. A design that at first seems bright and exciting will quickly become brash and tiresome. You would not want the control panel on your video recorder to be more visually exciting than the film on the screen; nor does the user want the interface itself to attract more attention than the information with which she is working.

Pragmatically, the amateur graphic designer will make fewer blunders if he is under-ambitious rather than over-ambitious. Accordingly, the advice that follows errs on the side of caution rather than boldness.

Windows and layout

In designing windows, we need to consider their size, position, shape and style. Size and shape will depend strongly on the fields allocated to the window, but the use of multiple canvases or tabs within a window gives the designer considerable freedom.

Size and shape

Renaissance painters held that a particular proportion of height to width known as the 'Golden Ratio' was the 'perfect' rectangular shape. Unfortunately there is no evidence that, for our purposes, it is any better or worse than any other shape for a window. Nor is there any conclusive evidence that windows should be deep rather than wide, or even square. Other than avoiding extremely narrow or very flat shapes, the designer is at liberty to use whatever shape best suits the organization of the fields.

Wherever possible, the window should be designed to show all controls without scrolling. If that is not feasible, all *essential* controls should be shown without scrolling. In particular, the controls that resolve a dialog (such as the 'OK' button) should be visible at all times. Windows that are resizeable should retain the size that the user sets; if the user closes and reopens a window, the window should return at the same size that he set it to, not the default size set by the designer.

Consistency should be a significant factor in window size and shape; the designer can reinforce the relationship of similar types of window by the use of a consistent style. For example, the 'Find' dialog and the 'Find and Replace' dialog have the same size and shape, although 'Find' has fewer fields and substantially more white space.

Position

When a window or dialog is first created, the designer needs to position it in the most appropriate place for the user. The designer needs to consider two aims:

- *Put the window close to the point of activation*   Forcing the user to track the mouse right across the screen from the point at which a dialog box is invoked to the dialog box itself rapidly leads to frustration.
- *Do not obscure fields that the user needs to see*   The user will be equally frustrated if she must move the window as soon as it is opened because it overlays some critical piece of information on the previous window.

When a stack of modal dialogs is opened, it is often appropriate to cascade the dialog boxes from top left to bottom right, with a constant offset for each new window, provided that this does not obscure critical information in the previous dialog box. For a sequence of dialog boxes implementing a series of steps, each dialog box replaces the previous one. Each new window should appear in the same place as the previous one. If the windows are of different sizes, the designer may keep the top left corner fixed, or centre all the windows over the same spot.

Modal dialogs that are frequently closed and reopened should respect the user's positioning. If the user moves a modal dialog box, it is usually for a very good reason, and it is extremely annoying for the user if the next time she visits the dialog, the designer has put it back in the original incorrect position.

Canvases and visual stability

With the use of multiple canvases on a single window, it is important that the designer maintain the apparent stability of the window. If the canvas changes size and shape as each new canvas is presented, the user will lose the sense of integrity that was implied by the use of canvases. The window will appear as an unrelated set of overlays, rather than as an integral whole.

If the 'tab' implementation of canvas switching is used, the designer will automatically have visual stability as each 'tab card' is the same size. If the canvas switching is implemented by some other mechanism, it is the designer's responsibility to ensure that each canvas has the same size, shape and position, even if this means that some of the canvases have a lot of white space.

MDI and other subject windows

For MDI style applications, it is conventional to cascade each new window relative to the original position of the previous document. This ensures that the new document does not completely obscure the previous one. As the windows approach the bottom right corner, to remain within the application's frame the stack begins again at the top left of the frame.

A similar approach is often suitable in subject-oriented applications, when many subjects can be opened at the same time. If the subject windows are not resizeable, when the bottom right of the application frame is reached the designer must choose between clipping the window to the frame, overlapping the document beyond the frame, or returning to the top left corner. The appropriate choice will usually be to follow the convention for the platform in question.

The title of an MDI document or other subject window must identify the particular document or subject. One MDI application that I have used gives every subject window the same title. In consequence, they all appear on the 'Window' menu as 'Application X', and when minimized they are all indistinguishable, having the same icon and title!

Controls and layout

In positioning text fields, buttons, and other controls on each window, the designer needs to consider issues of ergonomics, such as spacing; taskflow, such as the order of fields; and cosmetic issues such as alignment and size. Other design issues, such as choice of colour and font, are dealt with separately below.

Position

All other things being equal, the user's attention will normally begin at the top left of a window. It is then normal to work down towards the bottom right, as the user would if reading a page in a book. This gives the designer two choices for leading the user through the window: across then down, or down then across. The former approach lays out fields across the window before the moving down, like a page in a book. However, in my experience many users

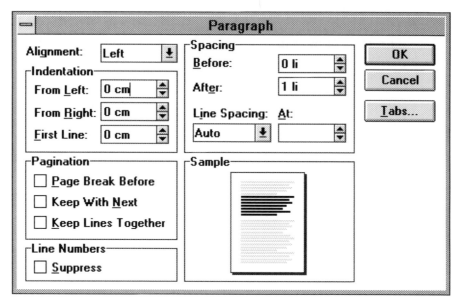

Figure 5.12. 'Newspaper width' columns

find it easier if the window is divided into a number of columns, like a newspaper, as in Fig. 5.12. It is easier for the eye to take in the entire width of a single column than the whole page. Note that this normal direction of reading can very easily be disrupted by graphical and layout elements: a splash of colour, an icon, or even a larger than normal font, can all catch the eye. Consider carefully where you want the user to look first.

Consistency is again an issue in laying out controls. Most windows contain common panes, or functional areas, and the designer should attempt to keep these panes in a consistent position. One common example is the buttons that appear on most dialog boxes; these are typically grouped in the same place, either in a column on the right of the window or in a row at the bottom. Other examples of common panes include:

- System information, such as system time and date
- Context information, which identifies the object (database record) being edited

When a window is resized, the designer must decide what to do about field layout. I have seen applications that attempt to adjust the window layout to take account of the new geometry, but this is rarely successful or useful. For most form filling applications, the window is not normally resizeable. If it is resizeable, the designer may either clip the displayed controls to the window edge, or provide scroll bars.

Size and alignment of fields

In order to give an impression of order, the window layout is normally arranged to present as many vertical and horizontal straight lines as possible. Newspaper width columns are the first step in that process, and the effect is further enhanced through the judicious sizing and alignment of controls.

Within each column, it is normal to align the left edge of controls. This gives a sense of visual integrity to the window, and makes it easier for the user to read through the controls. It can also be attractive to adjust the sizes of fields so that the right edges also align, rather than being ragged. A single height is also normally used for all fields.

Field prompts may be left aligned, as in Fig. 5.12, or right aligned; in other words, a constant separation between prompt and field. When prompts are left aligned, it is normal to terminate the prompt with a ':' character. With right aligned prompts, this is optional: the left edge of the field itself acts visually as a terminator to the prompt. The choice between left or right aligned prompts is largely one of personal taste; either is acceptable, provided the designer chooses one and uses it consistently.

Size and alignment of buttons

Buttons are normally arranged across the bottom of the window, or down the right-hand edge; the convention varies from platform to platform. To maintain the orderly appearance, buttons are also arranged to present as many straight lines as possible.

Buttons across the bottom of a window are all given the same height, and are aligned top and bottom. The width of the buttons may vary, but it is a good idea to keep to one, two, or at most three different standard widths of button. The buttons are mostly regularly spaced, although some sets of buttons may be offset slightly to separate them into functional groups. Again, the designer should restrict himself to no more than two different separations.

Similar considerations apply when buttons are arranged in a column. The buttons have the same width, and are aligned left and right. The buttons will be mostly the same height, though some double-height buttons may also be used. It is also sometimes useful to split a button into two half-width buttons, for example a pair of buttons for 'previous' and 'next' actions.

Grouping and decoration

Controls should be organized into groups that are related in the user's perception of the task; Fig. 5.12 is again a good example. It is not necessary, or indeed helpful, to group all controls of a given type together (for example, all checkboxes) or to group required fields first, followed by optional fields. The organization of controls on windows should primarily support the user's perception of the task, not the designer's implementation choices, nor the data integrity required by the data model.

As Fig. 5.12 shows, the ease of navigation for the user is considerably enhanced if the designer uses lines, frames and boxes to communicate the intended navigation sequence and relationship of controls. The sizing of the boxes further enhances the horizontal and vertical lines of the design. Figure 5.13, from the same application, shows the difficulty that occurs when the designer neglects to provide such cues. In this window it is unclear where in the tab sequence the 'Points' field occurs: logically it should fall immediately after the 'Font' field, but the layout suggests that the 'Style' group follows the 'Font' field. Similarly the two fields labelled 'By' appear to fall after the buttons; in fact they come immediately before the buttons.

When we discussed custom controls above, we mentioned the attractiveness of the three-dimensional look and feel. The same approach can be applied to group boxes: by appropriate use of lighting cues, the eye can be fooled into perceiving areas of the window as being raised, lowered or surrounded by an inset line (Fig. 5.14), and this is an attractive complement to the use of three-dimensional controls. The designer should be careful not to use too many layers as this stretches the credulity of the viewer. In this respect, the inset line is preferable to raised or lowered panels.

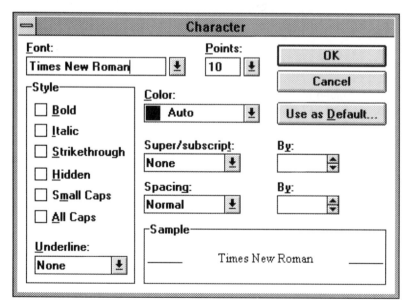

Figure 5.13. Lack of grouping makes navigation more difficult

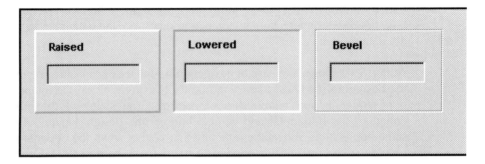

Figure 5.14. Raised, lowered, and inset line effects

Window density

Although there is no simple rule regarding the number of controls that may be allocated to a single window, there is a simple rule for density. Experiment shows that user performance suffers markedly when less than 25 per cent of the screen is given over to white space; ideally as much as 50 per cent of a textual screen could be left as white space. This requirement can conflict with the desire to keep related fields on a single window; if so, multiple canvases are often a good solution.

Controls should not be placed too closely together; a gap of one third to one half of the height of a normal field is appropriate in most cases. A similar gap between a group of controls and the surrounding frames, and a larger gap between group frames, also help the eye.

Text fonts

As the first step in selecting a font, the designer must choose a typeface, such as Swiss or Times Roman. He must then select the weight, for example bold; style variations, or effects, such as italic; and the size. Modern type management technology gives the designer an almost unrestricted choice of font, weight, effect and size combinations; this flexibility may not necessarily be a benefit.

In choosing fonts the designer must consider readability and clarity as well as visual appeal. An application can be given a subtly different look that appears more modern and more professional simply by choosing a font that differs slightly from the standard for the platform. This should be balanced against the conventions of the platform in question; it may be more attractive to your users if your application looks the same than if it looks different.

A full typographical discussion of the characteristics of fonts, and their representation on different physical devices, is well beyond the scope of this book. In this section, we just present sufficient information for the average designer who needs only to lay out windows and design dialog boxes in a readable and manageable form.

If your application requires sophisticated font management, for example if you need to print professional quality documents that are accurately aligned, spaced and justified, you should either purchase an appropriate off-the-shelf application or construction tool; or engage the services of an experienced graphic designer who understands the complexities of typesetting. You will also need a good understanding of the implementation of font management on your particular platform. This is itself rarely a simple task.

Font terminology

There is a degree of ambiguity in the terminology used to describe fonts, partly because the way in which fonts are managed and presented on computers does not correspond completely with the way in which they have traditionally been handled in the world of typography. For example, is Times Roman Italic a variant of the Times Roman typeface, or a typeface in its own right? Nor is there a consistent use of terminology across different platforms. For the purposes of this book, we will adopt the following simplified definitions, which correspond most closely to software conventions, rather than to typographical conventions:

- Typeface: a particular representation of the character set, for example Times Roman or Helvetica
- Font family: a given typeface in all its different sizes, weights and variants
- Font: a specific member of a font family; a given typeface in a specific weight, size and variant

We shall follow the established computer convention of treating an italic typeface as a style variant of the basic typeface. For example, the typeface Helvetica gives rise to a font family including bold and italic forms. The combination 'Helvetica bold 8 point' is an example of one font from this Helvetica font family. Note that this definition of font family is by no means universal. For example, the Software Development Kit for MS-Windows uses the term 'font family' to describe a collection of related typefaces, except when it is discussing 'True Type' fonts, in which case it uses the term in the way it is defined here.

Font size

Font size is usually described by giving the height in points; for software purposes, a point is 1/72 of an inch. This may seem a strange choice, but (like many non-metric measures) it has the advantage that it has many integer divisors, which simplifies the typesetter's calculations: 72 is evenly divisible by 36, 24, 18, 12, 9, 8, 6, 4, 3 and 2. Of course, this is of little direct relevance in our metric and computerized world, but the tradition is firmly established. The stated font size generally refers to the height of the 'character cell', a bounding box which surrounds the tallest character within the character set. Most characters will be smaller than this maximum height.

The designer should note that a font will rarely appear in the actual size specified: a 12 point font is unlikely to be 1/6 of an inch high. In the first place, the font size you request is a purely nominal size; the system must map the size to physical pixels in order to display it. Depending on the platform, the physical size of a pixel may vary. For example, VGA resolution on a 14-inch desktop monitor produces significantly larger pixels than the same resolution on a laptop's 9-inch screen. The operating system may or may not take account of such differences. The software point is thus 1/72 of a 'logical inch' that may be larger or smaller than a physical inch.

To make life even more complicated, MS-Windows adjusts upwards the display size of fonts by around 30 per cent. Even if you have a monitor on which a physical inch equals a logical inch, a 10-point font will not be 10 points high. The rationale offered by Microsoft is that the combination of typical screen resolution and normal viewing distance means that a 10-point font is difficult to read.

In all, the best advice for the designer is simply to choose font sizes pragmatically: try it out on all of the platforms that you intend to implement on, and see how it looks.

Choosing a font

Although many studies have been done on the readability of different fonts, most of these studies are unfortunately not relevant to human computer interfaces. Most studies have been based on written or printed material, and the screen is not like paper in certain very important ways. In particular, the resolution of a typical screen is substantially lower than most printed material.

One of the most important choices is between a serif or sans serif font. Serif fonts such as Times Roman are those with strokes and other embellishments on letters; they are used almost universally in books, newspapers, and other extended pieces of text. Sans serif fonts such as Arial are much plainer; they are used on most computer screens and typically for very short pieces of text such as signs and notices. Most studies have shown that serif fonts are generally easier to read than sans serif, but this is by no means universal. For example, road signs use a sans serif font in Britain as a result of extensive readability tests; in Australia, road signs apparently use a serif font for exactly the same reason.

Probably the most significant issue for the user interface designer is the simple fact of the relatively poor resolution of a typical screen. This means that serif fonts generally look 'dirty' and jagged, whereas sans serif fonts, which lack fine detail, look cleaner and smoother. For the same reason, italic fonts, whether with or without serif, should be avoided. Bold fonts are attractive for three reasons. First, the thicker strokes mean that it is possible to make the characters appear even smoother. Second, a bold font is easier to read against the kind of soft grey window backgrounds that are now fashionable under MS-Windows. Third, bold has the advantage that it is still clearly legible when a control is disabled and the text is 'greyed out'. For these reasons, bold is particularly appropriate for push-buttons.

A second important choice is between a proportionally spaced and a monospace font. In a proportional font, the width of each character varies: for example, a 'W' is much wider than an 'I'. In a monospace font, each character occupies a fixed width character cell. Monospace fonts are considerably less attractive than proportional fonts, but are appropriate when it is important that each letter of the text lines up accurately in columns.

One issue with proportional fonts and form filling database applications concerns the size of text entry fields based on database columns. For example, if a field such as 'Company Name' is based on a 60 character column, the designer must make a difficult decision about the field width. If he makes the field wide enough to hold the longest name with the widest characters, a name composed of narrow characters such as 'i' or 'l' will reach the 60 character limit long before the field appears filled to the user. On the other hand, if he makes the field narrower, perhaps the width of 60 average characters, a very long and wide name may need to be scrolled to be seen in full. This can be a considerable problem when the most significant part of the field is at the end, and is invisible without scrolling the field. It is by no means uncommon for the most significant part of a field to be rightmost: for example, typical customer names might include 'Oracle Corporation Limited (Bracknell)', 'Oracle Corporation Limited (City)', and so on.

How many fonts?

Finally, there is the question of how many fonts to use. Unless you are a trained graphic designer, the best advice is to keep it simple. Use only one font family; stick to plain and bold variants of the typeface, and avoid italic unless your users have sufficiently high resolution screens to display it cleanly. Choose one or two font sizes, and use them consistently; for example, all pushbuttons should use a single font size. Different variants and sizes may be used to express different kinds of fields, such as required and optional fields, provided users understand the convention. A second font may be used for purely cosmetic purposes, such as a company or application logo, or other decoration, but should not be used extensively.

Legal issues

Fonts are artistic creations that are protected by intellectual property laws. Generally, fonts are licensed to a particular computer and are installed on that machine. When an application is run on another machine, the developer is responsible for ensuring that the required fonts are available and licensed on that machine. In general, a font cannot simply be copied from machine to machine without violating the font vendor's proprietary rights. Not only may the particular computer implementation of a font be protected; the actual graphical design itself will often be owned by the originator. Even if you design your own font that closely resembles an existing one, you may still be in breach of copyright.

On certain platforms, a font can be 'embedded' in a document, allowing it to be moved to another computer along with the document itself. Embedding guarantees that the font specified in a document will be available on the computer receiving the document. This is extremely useful if an application allows a user to dynamically select a font for a document; otherwise, every font needs to be present on every machine. The designer is responsible for respecting the licence requirements when embedding a font. Some fonts may only legally be embedded in 'read only' documents, and some may not legally be embedded at all.

Whether the font is installed directly on the machine, distributed with an application, or distributed with a document, the designer must treat the licence restrictions for fonts just as seriously as the licence agreement for any other piece of software or intellectual property. For this reason, many designers find it simplest to restrict themselves to the core fonts distributed with the operating system or window manager.

Colour

Colour in all its fullness is an immensely complex subject, involving aspects of physics, physiology and perception. As with fonts, extensive use of colour requires the services of a professional. There is a vast body of research on how colours are perceived and how finely they can be distinguished. Fortunately, a very small amount of pragmatic knowledge is adequate for the designer of mainstream applications.

Probably more design errors are committed with colours than with any other single aspect of graphical user interface design. Colour is not just a cosmetic issue: it has many subtle and interrelated effects on the user. Colour is also a matter of taste; it is difficult for a designer to accept criticism of her personal colour preferences. The designer needs to consider at least four related aspects of colour:

- *Colour is meaningful* Consciously or subconsciously, people associate all kinds of meanings and implications with colour. Such issues must be handled with great caution: red may mean 'Urgent' to one user, and 'Error' to another. Colours are associated with literal meanings (green for go), metaphorical meanings (green for envy), and cultural meanings (green for ecology). Conversely, the designer may deliberately try to convey additional information to the user through colour associations.

- *Colour is ergonomic*   The eye is drawn to a splash of colour on an otherwise monochrome screen, potentially disrupting the natural flow of the screen. Some colours are easy to read, others are difficult. Some colours are tiring on the eye, others are restful.
- *Colour is operational*   Users expect colour differences to be semantic. Colour changes are interpreted as conveying meaning: fields in an incorrect format, required fields, and so on. The designer should support, not contradict, this assumption.
- *Colour is cosmetic*   Cosmetic and decorative uses of colour are an important part of the attractiveness of a layout. They also have a role to play in 'branding' a suite of tools or applications, and emphasizing the relationship of components.

We shall examine each of these aspects of colour in more detail below; but before we do so, we review the vocabulary and fundamentals of colour.

Colour fundamentals

To completely describe a colour requires three values, or 'dimensions', which is why designers sometimes talk about a 'colour space'. The *red–green–blue* (RGB) model is perhaps the best known, and corresponds most closely to the way that common display technology works, but it is not necessarily the easiest to work with. The problem with RGB is that it does not easily map to normal descriptions of colours. For example, if I describe a colour as 10 per cent red, 15 per cent green, and 40 per cent blue, this gives you very little intuitive sense of how the colour will appear. For this reason another model, the *hue–saturation–value* (HSV) model, is more useful to the designer. Artists use yet another model: they will talk about tints, shades and tones of a pure pigment.

Hue is the basic 'colour', in conventional terms: red, green, yellow and so on. In perceptual terms, hue corresponds to most people's intuitive idea of colour. Sky blue, royal blue, pale blue, and dark blue are all intuitively recognized as the same 'colour', or more strictly hue.

Saturation describes the purity or strength of the colour; low saturation gives a pastel colour, and zero saturation gives a colour on the black–grey–white axis, depending on the *value* of the colour. Value is a measure of the intensity of a colour: a value of zero and saturation of zero gives black, regardless of the hue. Increasing the value, while maintaining zero saturation, gives colours along the scale of grey; a value of 100 per cent gives pure white.

When value and saturation are both 100 per cent, hue corresponds to the artist's idea of a pure pigment. Adding black pigment to create a shade corresponds to decreasing value without altering saturation. Adding white pigment to create a tint corresponds to decreasing saturation without altering value. A tone, created by adding both black and white pigment, corresponds to decreasing both value and saturation. One of the benefits of the HSV model is this strong correspondence between the artist's and the designer's models.

The accompanying disk includes a 'Colour Map' dialog, which allows the user to experiment directly with a colour space; to develop a feel for the correspondence between the HSV values and appearance; and to map between HSV and RGB values. (RGB values are often required when setting colours programmatically.) Note that the dialog box uses the Microsoft terminology of *luminosity* in place of value. This is not generally recommended as the term luminosity has a very precise meaning in colour technology, which could lead to confusion.

Cultural aspects of colour

Most designers are aware that people attach associations to colours, and nearly all are aware that different cultures have different colour associations. Many of us have read amusing anecdotes about how white means 'Peace' in one country, but 'Death' in another, and the resulting disastrous or embarrassing design error. Once you start to work in colour, you are not in Kansas any more. However, the often-presented tables of countries, colours, and associated meanings are not very useful in practice, for two important and related reasons:

- *A single colour has many meanings*   Red may mean hot, anger, stop, danger, or communist, depending on the person seeing it and the context in which it is encountered.
- *Colour is rarely presented independently of some supporting context*   A red traffic light and a red flag are unlikely to be confused or misinterpreted.

The context of presentation, including the conceptual model, helps to reinforce the particular meaning that the designer wants to convey; but colours do not, in general, convey a consistent meaning without context.

It is rather more useful to turn the question around: given some metaphor or concept to be presented, what colour represents it in different cultures? Table 5.1 shows the colours that different countries associate with three useful metaphors.

	UK	USA	France
Mail box	Red	Blue	Yellow
Motorway signs	Blue	Yellow	Green
First aid box	Red or green	Red	Green

Table 5.1

Even if your user population is not multinational, you may still need to consider colour associations carefully. Meanings depend not only on geography but also on history. People of my generation expect telephone boxes to be red; someone who grew up in the 1980s and 1990s may never have seen a red telephone box; indeed, he may never have seen a traditional telephone box of any colour. 'The past is a foreign country; they do things differently there', as L.P. Hartley reminds us. Geography and history are just two examples of context; many other factors may also affect cultural interpretations of colour.

Ergonomic aspects of colour

The ergonomic issues of colour centre mainly on the readability and comfort of the display, especially where it will be used constantly throughout the working day. (Some applications are not designed for continuous use; for example, information booths in tourist locations. Such designs need to attract attention and have very different goals from the typical business applications with which we are concerned here.)

For the background of the window, it is important that the colour chosen be restful rather than tiring. This was rarely a problem with character mode applications and their white on black or green on black terminals; however crowded the display, the majority of the screen remained unlit. On the other hand, many of the first generation of MS-Windows applications presented a bright white background, perhaps based on the mistaken analogy of black text on white paper. (An important difference is that a screen emits light, whereas paper reflects it.)

Various studies have failed to come to a unanimous verdict on the best colour for background. In practice, the best choices seem to be a low or zero level of saturation and a moderate to high value; in other words, medium to light shades of grey. In the MS-Windows world the current fashion is for a soft grey (the same colour that is used for the face of pushbuttons), and this seems to work well.

As for background, there is no unanimity on the best colours for controls, prompts, and other boilerplate text. Controls must be easily readable, so blues should be avoided: the human eye is least receptive to blues. A strong contrast between foreground and background will also help. This can be achieved by choosing colours with strongly different values; for example, black on light grey.

In many applications, the situation may be complicated by the use of different colours for field backgrounds, field foregrounds, and the overall window background. Control values may be presented using a field foreground colour of black, on a field background of white, bevelled into a canvas of soft grey. This gives the user a strong contrast between the field foreground and background, a lower contrast between prompts and the canvas, an overall low brightness, with bright areas containing the control values that will attract the eye. This is often a satisfactory scheme for the designer who does not want to work too hard on visual novelty.

Prompts do not necessarily need to stand out: one designer deliberately used blue prompts on a grey background for an application that would be in constant daily use. He reasoned that the users would rapidly learn the meanings and positions of fields, and he did not want to distract the users' attention from the fields to the prompts. The validity of this hypothesis remains to be proven!

Operational aspects of colour

Colour is widely used for semantic purposes. 'Greying out' is used universally as a visual cue to distinguish between enabled and disabled fields. Most users have been exposed to the idea of highlighting, and so will expect colours to be used consistently, not arbitrarily. If prompts suddenly change colour, the user will attempt to associate the change with some interpretation.

As well as disabled controls, colour coding may be provided for required values, read-only (display) fields, fields where a lookup or value list is available, and many other uses. If the designer does choose to use colour in this way, he needs to ensure that the coding scheme is communicated to the user. He also needs to be cautious that his choices do not conflict with cultural associations. For example, highlighting an erroneous field in red is probably a more meaningful choice than green.

The designer also needs to consider how dynamic the colour changes should be: should a required field always appear in red, or only when the user attempts to resolve the dialog without providing the missing value? This issue is discussed in more detail in the next chapter, when validation is addressed.

Cosmetic aspects of colour

As we have suggested already in this chapter, unless you are a trained graphic designer it is better to be too conservative than too radical. Just because a workstation supports 16 million colours, you do not have to use them all.

Colour may be used for decoration, such as a company logo, and as a way of branding a set of applications or tools, but the designer should not overuse decorative colour. Taking into account icons, windows, decoration and fields, the conservative designer should expect to use no more than a dozen or so colours within windows. Those colours should be chosen carefully so as to support, not to contradict, other colour issues such as culture and semantics. The skills of a graphic designer will be of great value in this area.

Communicating with colour

The golden rule of colour is that the designer must never rely on colour alone; in other words, colour must always be a redundant cue. Not only are a significant number of people colour blind, a great many still have to use grey scale monitors. Others have portables with flat panel displays, which often have low brightness and saturation, and poorer colour differentiation than desktop monitors.

If the designer plans to use colour to communicate meaning, it is essential that she test her colour choices on all the technologies that she intends it to be used on. The design must always be tested by a colour-impaired user, or failing that on a monochrome display to ensure that it will be usable by the colour blind.

Some applications allow the user to customize the colours. This facility is not necessarily worthwhile, and may even be damaging. If the colours have been carefully chosen for their ergonomic, cultural and semantic value, customization may significantly damage the effectiveness of the design. Required and optional fields may become indistinguishable, and other visual cues may be lost. If customizability is genuinely considered valuable, it may be more appropriate to give users a choice between a small predefined set of 'palettes', each of which ensures that important colour differences are maintained.

Portability

Many design tools claim to build portable applications. While this may be true in the strictly literal sense — that is that the tool will generate a working application for different platforms — the designer needs to be aware of more subtle portability issues, for example:

- *Fonts* The conventional fonts used on the Mac, Motif, and MS-Windows platforms differ markedly.
- *Colours* Again, different platforms have different standard colour conventions.
- *Layout* Should the OK button be to the left or right of Cancel?
- *Screen size* The different aspect ratio and larger size of monitors typically used with Motif are reflected in window size and shape, and the number of windows that can comfortably be open simultaneously.
- *Screen resolution* Graphic elements such as icons that are easily distinguished on one display may become cramped squiggles on another.

If these cosmetic issues are not taken into consideration, the application will not have the 'style', or look and feel, that the users of that platform will expect. Furthermore, issues of screen size and resolution may mean that an application designed on Motif, for example, becomes unusable on MS-Windows. The designer should be more than a little sceptical of tools vendors' claims of portability.

A key question for the designer concerns user populations. Will a given user use the application exclusively on a single platform, alongside other applications? If so, the user will expect the application to conform closely to the conventions of that platform. Or will a given user use the application on different platforms? In this case, the user might be happier for the application to be identical on each platform, and ignore the local conventions.

Application design

Having looked at detailed design as it affects individual controls and windows, we now turn to detailed issues that are applicable across the entire application. These issues include the use of language, the importance of consistency, and some broad-ranging issues in the use of the keyboard and the mouse.

Language

We have already discussed some issues in the use of language as it affects the labels on buttons, menu items, and the prompts for check boxes. In the previous chapter we discussed the wording of the questions and answers in message boxes. These examples illustrate a general principle: the language used should be direct and clear. Active statements, for example 'check the box', are clearer than passive ones, for example 'the box is checked'. The latter begs the question: who does the checking?

The vocabulary used in the user interface should be drawn from the user's domain, not the designer's. Unless you are a book or newspaper editor, how many times in real life have you 'deleted' something, other than when sat at a computer screen?

Table 5.2 illustrates some common examples of system terms that are meaningless to the average user. General alternatives are hard to find: by definition, the correct term depends on the domain of the task in question. However, some alternatives are suggested. Unfortunately, some useful words, most notably 'Cancel', have passed so firmly into general computer usage that they are probably irredeemable for normal use. Much as we would like to 'cancel' an appointment or an order, a confirmatory dialog such as that shown in Fig. 5.15 would be more than a little confusing to anyone who has used any other MS-Windows application.

Consistency

'A foolish consistency is the hobgoblin of small minds', said Ralph Waldo Emerson. Although in general consistency is a goal worth striving for, it is not worth being obsessive about. Consistency should not be allowed to become an obstacle to other usability goals. For example, the designer may have decided to place all buttons on the right-hand side of dialog boxes. If a particular dialog box consequently becomes too wide to be seen without scrolling, it is better to break the consistency and put the buttons at the bottom of the window.

Consistency is extremely important at the levels of the conceptual model and taskflow, less so at the detailed level. Indeed, at the detailed level we might go so far as to say that consistency is the guideline of last resort: when there is no strong usability reason to override consistency, the designer should be consistent. The consistency that matters most is consistency with the user's expectations.

System domain	User domain
Record	Line item, Order header, Order Detail, Employment record...
Transaction	Order placement, Order entry, Booking, Reservation...
Commit	Save, Confirm, Validate, Book, Reserve
Post	No equivalent
Rollback	Discard, Cancel (but see below), Revert, Back Out
Default	Standard, Normal, Preset
Null	Any, None, Missing, Unspecified
Kill, Abort	Interrupt
Invalid	Incorrect, Wrong (format), Out of range, Not understood
Delete	Erase, Discard, Remove, Eject, Reject, Dismiss, Destroy, Shred
Key, Unique, Key, Primary Key	Locator, Identifier, Reference, Serial number, Issue number...

Table 5.2

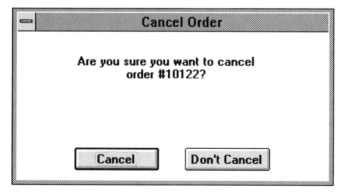

Figure 5.15. Cancel the order

The mouse

Extensive use of the mouse can be very effective in supporting the illusion of direct manipulation. Judicious use of drag and drop can be particularly effective: drag and drop is a very 'soft' mode that the user can slip into and out of very easily. Compare picking and dragging a piece of text with the sequence select, cut, move, and paste.

There are certain dangers, in particular that the mouse can become overloaded. If the mouse can be used to click, double click, click and drag, click and drag with the Shift key, click the right button, and so on, it becomes easy for the user to make a mistake. Mouse actions risk becoming abstract invisible functions, no better than magic control key combinations.

The danger can be reduced by providing strong visual cues to the user when mouse actions are available, perhaps by changing the cursor, and by implementing mouse actions consistently.

The mouse and the keyboard

Research has shown that when simple tasks such as hitting a menu command are compared, users are consistently faster when they use the mouse, for example to click 'File/Save', than when using the keyboard to type 'Alt-F-S'. At the same time, test subjects consistently reported that using the keyboard *felt* faster. This seems to apply regardless of the level of experience of the user. Tognazzini (1992) discusses this odd result in some depth.

This presents something of a dilemma for the designer: should he insist that users use the faster mouse, or allow them to use the keyboard? In other words, should the designer provide keyboard equivalents for every menu item? My own preference is to provide keyboard equivalents for the commonest commands, but not to adjust the names of menu items merely to provide 'better' shortcut keys. It is far more important that menu items be clear and easily distinguished to the menu user than that the keyboard accelerator be 'memorable' or 'obvious'.

There is an important exception to this rule. The keyboard commands for Cut, Copy and Paste are often faster than the menu equivalents. This is partly because they are used so frequently that the user develops a 'muscle memory' for their locations, much like a touch typist who can find any key on the keyboard without consciously being able to draw the keyboard layout. The same advantage may accrue to any other command that is used consistently across the entire system. Note that the benefit of muscle memory is completely lost if the key usage is even slightly inconsistent across applications; all advantage is lost if the user ever has to stop and ask herself: which keys does this application use?

The efficiency of Cut, Copy and Paste is enhanced by the fact that the user can make use of both hands simultaneously. Apple deliberately chose Cmd-X, Cmd-C and Cmd-V to allow the user to select and point with the mouse in the right hand, while cutting and pasting with the left. Microsoft apparently overlooked this subtlety when they originally nominated Shift-Del, Ctrl-Ins and Shift-Ins for the same commands. You would need to be a concert pianist to hit any of these commands with your left hand while keeping your right on the mouse. Microsoft has belatedly moved to the more sensible Apple layout, but as long as some older applications still use the original key set, MS-Windows users forfeit the benefit of muscle memory.

Fitt's Law

One well-established piece of research, known as Fitt's Law, tells us how quickly a user can accurately click on a target, such as a button, with the mouse. The research shows that, for a target of constant width, the time to hit a target depends on the logarithm of the ratio (distance:depth), where depth represents the size of the target in the direction of motion. This confirms our intuitive expectations: the further the target, the longer it takes to reach, and the larger the target, the less accurately the user has to decelerate to avoid overshooting. The logarithmic nature of the relationship suggests that a large screen and large distances make less difference than intuition might suggest. The user can move the mouse right across the screen very rapidly, providing he does not have to worry too much about where he stops!

From this law we can deduce how effective we might expect different implementations of buttons and menus might be, starting from the easiest to hit:

- *Large, nearby, vertically arranged buttons*   Buttons are usually wider than they are deep, so putting them at the side of the window gives a larger target in the direction of mouse motion.
- *Macintosh style menu bar*   The Mac menu bar is hard up against the top of the screen, so it is impossible to overshoot. For the purposes of Fitt's Law, the menu bar is effectively infinitely deep.
- *Floating tool palette*   The palette can be positioned very close by, or hard up against the edge of the screen like the Mac menu bar.
- *Pop-up menu*   Although invisible and abstract, a pop-up menu at least has the virtue of being nearby.
- *Microsoft or Motif style menu bar on application frame*   Unlike the Mac, even when the application is maximized there is space above the menu bar for the user to overshoot.
- *Tool bar fixed below menu bar*   There is even more room to overshoot than with the menu, plus iconic buttons are usually small in both depth and width.
- *Microsoft or Motif style menu bar on document window*   Putting a menu on the document window allows plenty of scope to overshoot, and is only slightly quicker to reach than a menu bar at the top of the screen.

It is important to emphasize that Fitt's Law only refers to the physical movement of the mouse; it tells us nothing about the time taken to choose and identify the target. An iconic pushbutton might well be recognized much more rapidly than the location of a menu item can be recalled, compensating for the relative difficulty in hitting the target.

Summary

In this chapter we have addressed a great number of issues that relate to detailed design: controls, windows, application-wide issues and the interactions between them. We have surveyed the cosmetic as well as the ergonomic issues involved. The most important point to bear in mind throughout this chapter is that detailed design is not independent or separate from the rest of design: it is the final stage in a process that began with a conceptual model, and as such it must support the conceptual model, the taskflow, and the dialog design. Furthermore, the fundamental principles of design that we identified in Chapter 1 apply every bit as strongly at this level of design.

6 Errors and help

'Whether 'tis nobler in the mind to suffer the slings and arrows of outrageous fortune; Or to take arms against a sea of troubles, and by opposing end them?'

Hamlet, III.i

Introduction

We have postponed to this final chapter two extremely important topics that cannot be ignored if the user interface design is to be regarded as thorough and complete. These two topics are validation and error handling, on the one hand; and online help and documentation, on the other. These topics have been held back this far for three related reasons:

- *Error handling is intertwined with all levels of the interface* Error handling touches significantly on issues of taskflow, dialog design and detailed design, so it has seemed appropriate to hold back a discussion of this area until all three of those topics have been explored.
- *Online help and documentation should reflect the whole of the rest of the design* Online help should be closely integrated with every level of the application; online documentation should stand as an integral whole in its own right, while at the same time reflecting the conceptual model. Help and documentation need to support each other closely: a user who begins by seeking help may need to continue by exploring the documentation.
- *Errors and help are inseparable aspects of the design* Decisions taken about error handling will intimately affect both the necessity for, and effectiveness of, the online help.

Errors and mistakes

It is useful for the designer to distinguish between errors and mistakes; both are explored in some detail in this chapter. The term 'error' covers a very broad range of disagreements between the user and the interface. All these various types of error are characterized by a refusal on the part of the interface to accept the user's input. More strictly, errors fail *validation* in some form, which implies that the designer, in the guise of the application, has an opportunity to detect and respond to them. As we shall see, one of the key decisions for the designer is whether to respond proactively or reactively. Validation and errors are two sides of a single coin, so naturally they are discussed together.

Mistakes are situations in which the user chooses an action that is perfectly valid from the application's or business' point of view, but is unwanted, unintended, or damaging from the user's point of view. Mistakes may occur simply through 'finger trouble'. More dangerously, they may occur because the user has an incomplete or incorrect understanding of the consequences of their actions, either within the application or outwith the application, in the broader context of the business. By definition, the designer cannot explicitly respond to mistakes; it is inherent in their nature that the interface cannot determine when they occur. A key question for the designer is this: how tolerant is the application of mistakes?

Help and documentation

Throughout this book, we have tried to bear in mind Dr Norman's maxim: when simple things need instructions, the design has failed. In an important sense, the user interface should 'explain itself'. A visionary friend of mine working in both documentation and design believes that once user interfaces become sufficiently good, documentors will be unnecessary (or rather, documentors will all become designers).

In the meantime, while we anticipate the arrival of this utopia, it is important to acknowledge the differences as well as the connections between design and documentation. As we noted in the introduction, some documentors may become excellent user interface designers, bringing to the design process a trained and experienced ability to explain, as well as a user-centred viewpoint. A documentor may well make a valuable team member, and not merely to write the documents after the design decisions have been taken, but also as an evaluator of the design: if something is hard to explain, it is almost certainly harder to use. However, not every documentor automatically qualifies as a user interface designer, in the same way that not every art critic is an artist. (Of course, the same is even more true in the case of technical people!)

Let us now turn our attention to a detailed examination of errors. We shall examine closely categories of error, and address techniques and responses in validation. We then look at mistakes, and elaborate an approach of tolerance and appropriate response. Finally, we discuss the topics of help and documentation.

Designing for error

Accounting for error is most influential on the three lowest levels of design: task-flow, dialog flow, and detailed design. We shall deal with the principles of error design with respect to all three levels in this section, which will involve something of a review of some topics in detailed design. We shall also address specific visual and ergonomic issues of error handling, validation, and the presentation of errors.

In practice this is an area where decisions at the three levels affect each other so closely that the designer will often find himself iterating between these three levels in search of an effective balance.

Classes of error

The designer can usefully draw a distinction between *user errors*, in which the user tries to do something that is clearly incorrect, and could be seen to be incorrect at the time of design; and *exception errors*, or more simply exceptions, which occur when circumstances combine to make a particular action temporarily inappropriate. User errors are relatively static, whereas exceptions are dynamic. Let us define these distinctions more precisely:

- User error is a situation in which the user interface designer deliberately misleads the user into making a mistake for the pleasure of correcting him. User errors are often associated with humiliating messages pointing out the user's stupidity and emphasizing the damage he might have caused were it not for the alertness of the programmer. A loud 'bleep' can also be used to draw the attention of colleagues to the error. Rarely, user error refers to a situation in which the user ignores the copious guidance and obvious clues provided by the designer and insists on attempting something dumb.
- Exception are situations in which the user has entered data or performed an action that is invalid in the current system state, or which would prevent the user from proceeding to closure. In an exceptional situation, certain actions or values, which might otherwise be valid, become invalid. Exceptions may also be associated with situations in which two actions may be performed in either order, depending on data values or other context.

Whereas errors are relatively predictable beforehand, exceptions are highly dependent on state, context, and history. To understand why an exception has occurred, the user needs to be able to answer three questions: Where am I? What am I doing? How did I get here?

Some user errors can be eliminated from our applications by relatively simple improvements in visibility, feedback, or mappings; in other cases the effort involved is simply too great to be worthwhile, or may even be counter-productive. Most exceptions cannot be prevented; there are simply too many combinations of circumstances to code for them all. Nor should all exceptions be regarded as errors: the example of the warehouse receiving clerk and the missing supplier from Chapter 4 will be revisited below. In the detailed discussion that follows, we shall explore mechanisms for addressing various types of error and exception.

Data errors

A typical example of user error is the user who attempts to enter a date as '29/11/66' when the application requires '29-NOV-66'. This kind of error usually occurs because the user does not know the required format, and rarely occurs because the user ignores information indicating the correct format. Whose error is this, the designer's or the user's?

We could eliminate, or at least reduce, this error by, not surprisingly, appealing once again to basic principles:

- *Improve the visibility*   If the format were visible in the first place, the user would stand a better chance of entering the information correctly. For example, instead of presenting the user with a blank field to type in, we fill the field with a mask, such as 'DD-MON-YY', which the user then overtypes. This is precisely how many electronic personal organizers operate, yet seems to be beyond the capabilities of many GUI tools.
- *Improve the feedback*   If the user enters a date in an unrecognized format, the error message should explain the correct format. One 4GL tool that I worked with generated applications which always produced the error 'Invalid data format' for bad input, the designer having no control over this aspect of error handling. After some weeks of frustration, one of the tool's developers told me that there was an undocumented 'magic key' that caused a field to display its format mask!
- *Improve the mapping*   In a previous chapter we suggested a flexible 'input mapping' as one solution to the date problem; in other words, the field accepts many different entry formats. Another solution is illustrated by a number of personal organizer applications, including Lotus Organizer. If the user chooses a date by clicking on an image of a calendar or year planner, rather than by typing, we can dispense with the question of format entirely, and the possibility of user error (although not of mistakes, of course) is completely eliminated. Unfortunately, not all inputs are so easily mapped to an error-free 'decision space'.

Certain categories of error deserve close attention, as they constitute the vast majority of specific user errors. We shall consider set errors, format errors, range errors, and reference errors in turn.

Small sets and set errors

If an item can take values from a small restricted set, it is relatively easy to prevent errors. The user can be forced to choose from a radio group, or from a drop-down list, for example. (The relative advantages of different controls were explored in the previous chapter.) Such mechanisms have high visibility — the user can easily determine all possible values — and provide a good mapping: the user may recognize the correct choice, even if she does not know the exact value. Choosing a font in a word processor from a list of available fonts is an excellent example of this kind of error prevention.

If a user is restricted to a small set of choices, and those choices can all be seen easily by the user, the visibility will be very high. All too often, however, the user is restricted to a set of choices but has no way of determining what those choices are. One application that I use regularly requires the user to supply the name of an operating system; legal values are 'MS-DOS', 'WINDOWS' and 'OS/2', spelt, capitalized and punctuated *precisely* as shown. Nothing in the user interface gives any clue as to the correct values. Even when an incorrect value is entered, the user is still not told the legal values. To add insult to injury, the field is mandatory. A user who does not know the magic words can become completely trapped in this field, unable either to leave the field blank or to supply a valid value!

Format errors

Most GUI design tools allow more or less complex format rules to be specified for fields. Format rules are appropriate where the set of values is too large for simple set validation, but the format is simple enough to be validated at reasonable cost. There are two simple rules to follow in designing format rules:

- *Make the accepted format or formats clearly visible to the user* There are many mechanisms for making the format visible, both before and after an error occurs. Some of these mechanisms will be discussed below, under validation and presentation. When the user persists in entering data in an incorrect format, the designer must ensure that the feedback clearly identifies the acceptable formats.
- *Where possible, accept as many common formats as possible* It is strange that numbers can almost universally be entered in multiple formats (for example, 2 or 2.0 or 2.00 all represent the same numeric value) but dates, which are much more likely to be entered erroneously, cannot.

Some applications attempt to enforce format rules keystroke by keystroke. For simple formats this may be useful, but for complex formats there are considerable dangers of a loss of visibility, which are discussed below. In particular, a key may be illegal at a particular point because the user made a mistake much earlier in his input. It is very hard for the application to either prevent or react sensibly to such errors. We return to this issue below, when we discuss keystroke restriction.

Large sets and complex formats

If the set of acceptable values is large or the format is very complex, the approaches outlined above begin to encounter difficulties. It becomes impossible to present the user with all the available choices; there may be so many choices that the user cannot easily find the one he wants, or choices may become difficult to distinguish, eliminating the benefits of recognition. A better solution may then be to allow the user to enter any value (free format or perhaps to a restricted format), and validate against a list, such as a database lookup table or codes table.

For example, consider a data item in which the user enters a United Kingdom postcode (the British equivalent of the USA's ZIP code). United Kingdom postcodes are among the most difficult formats of data to validate; a postcode is composed of a mixture of letters and numbers in a wide range of forms. A postcode begins with one or two letters, followed by one or two numbers, possibly another single letter, a space, one or two numbers, and one or two more letters. Readers are invited to design a format validation routine or state machine for such codes!

If validation alone is the objective, we could accept any format and check the value entered directly against a table of all valid postcodes in the UK. Such lists are readily available for purchase and if the correct entry of postcodes is valuable to the organization, this option is worth consideration, provided that other issues such as the performance of the lookup can be resolved satisfactorily. For example, I recently bought a new cooker on credit. The assistant taking my details asked for the street number of my house and the postcode. He entered these two items, and the application then produced my full address from its postcode database. This was very impressive, apart from the fact that it took so long to perform the lookup that it would have been quicker to type the address in full. There is a balance to be found between performance and accuracy.

Keystroke restriction

A more restrictive approach, if error prevention is desired, is to validate the user's input keystroke by keystroke. At each stroke, the application determines which further keystrokes are acceptable as valid. For example, if a postcode begins with two letters, the next keystroke must be a digit.

Unfortunately, a visibility problem can also occur with this approach. If the user cannot see the list or range of possible acceptable values being reduced as each keystroke is entered, she may find herself unable to continue: the key she wants to press is not acceptable, but she has no way of knowing which keys are acceptable, nor of telling where in her typing she began to go wrong.

For example, imagine a user trying to select the name of the company 'Schweppes' from a long list of customers or suppliers. She begins by typing 'S', then 'H', erring almost as soon as she has begun. Plenty of companies match those two letters, so the interface allows the user to continue. Now the user attempts to type 'W'. Nothing in the list matches 'SHW', so the application bleeps at the user and ignores her 'W'. Maybe she mistyped it, she wonders? She types 'W' again, and gets the same useless feedback. The application cannot help her because it has already missed her real error, the missing 'C'.

Such problems are typical of keystroke restriction. For reasons such as these, I would not recommend keystroke restriction except in those cases where the user can clearly see the set of possible matches being reduced before her eyes, as for example in Windows Help 'Search' windows (Fig. 6.1).

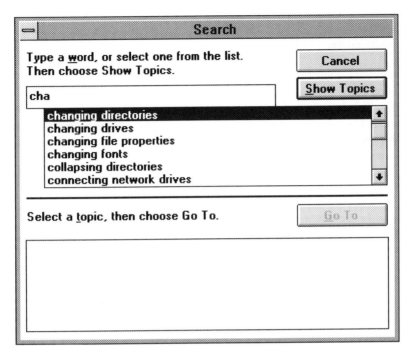

Figure 6.1. Keystroke restriction in Windows Help

Range errors

If a value must lie within a particular range, or a small set of ranges, there are two approaches that I would recommend that the designer consider.

Ideally, the designer can provide the user with a control that can only be set to legal values; in other words a better mapping. For example, if a temperature setting must lie in the range 10° to 40°, the designer can provide the user with a slide bar representing that range.

Such a mapping is an excellent method of preventing errors. For example, in my word processor I can set margins either by directly manipulating an image of the page, or by entering exact measurements into a dialog box. The direct manipulation implementation prevents me from setting meaningless margins, such as overlapping left and right margins. The dialog box lets me enter anything, however meaningless, and only checks when I attempt to resolve the dialog box.

Such direct manipulation solutions can be expensive to implement, although simple custom controls such as a thermometer are today relatively cheap to construct, as we noted in Chapter 5. If such a mapping is not possible or practical, range-restricted values can realistically only be validated after entry. It would be

extremely difficult even in principle to force a user *a priori* to type a value
between 10 and 40: it is only when the user finishes typing that the application
can judge the validity of her error.

Exceptions

The case study from the beginning of Chapter 4 shows a typical exception. Taking
a user-centric viewpoint, the user is attempting a perfectly reasonable action:
entering the delivery information as shown on the paperwork. Unfortunately this
data violates a data integrity rule: it contains a reference to an unknown catalog
number. The key question then is: whose side is the application on, the data's or
the user's?

Reality check

Any time your application has to interface with the outside world, you are dealing
with circumstances beyond your immediate control, and therefore you are dealing with a strong possibility of unpredictable and unavoidable exceptions. Dealing with the file system (or a database, for that matter) is a rich source of
exceptional circumstances. Figure 6.2 shows a typical *Save As* dialog. As it
happens, the disk in the drive is write-protected: it is my backup disk. (A similar
exception occurs if I pick a protected network drive.) When I attempt to save, my
word processor is unable to cope (Fig. 6.3).

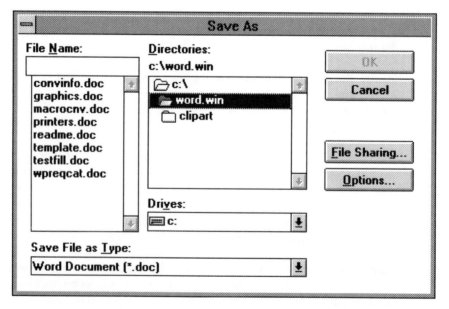

Figure 6.2. Save As... dialog

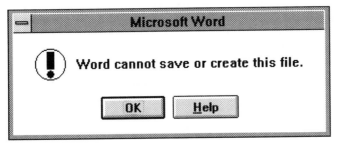

Figure 6.3. Microsoft Word is baffled

Microsoft Word is a highly sophisticated package that has been around for years. It is even built by the same company that built the offending file system. Is this really the most informative feedback that they can deliver? Once again, fundamental principles have been broken:

- *The visibility is poor* The *Save As* dialog box could indicate beforehand that the disk is write-protected at the moment the user selects the drive.
- *The feedback is all but non-existent* It would be hard to conceive of a less helpful message. The message implies that the problem lies with Microsoft Word: perhaps some other application *could* save the file? In fact, the problem is with the disk.
- *The dialog design is poor* Having acknowledged the message, the user is immediately returned to editing the document, not to the Save As dialog. This failure to resolve the dialog leaves the user with a frustrating sense of lack of closure, experienced as a feeling of uncertainty as to what state his document is in, saved or unsaved.

There is no way that we as designers can prevent this exceptional situation. It depends entirely on the disk that the user inserts at the moment of save. However, it is very easy to present a much more informative message (Fig. 6.4), as Microsoft knows perfectly well.

Reference errors and cross-field validation

Exceptional situations frequently occur when a field depends on lookup values, in other words *reference errors*; or depend on other fields, in other words *cross-field validation*. These situations involve validation against other values that are themselves dynamic or variable, implying that the designer must look beyond prevention to helpful response.

References typically involve lookups in tables of codes or values, or foreign key references to other tables. A classic example is the postal abbreviations for the states in the USA, which will normally be held in a lookup table referenced from many places. Another common example is the parts catalogue, which may be referenced by the use of item numbers in many places.

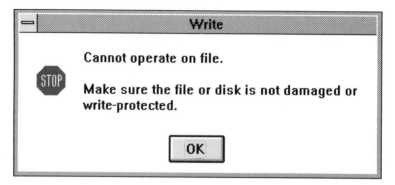

Figure 6.4. Microsoft Write knows what is wrong

In principle, the application should provide the user with the ability to choose a value from the list of all valid values, and the application could prevent errors by forcing the user to pick from that list. At the very least, the application should validate input against the list. In practice, a number of issues arise.

If a field is frequently used, such as the abbreviation for the states, experienced users may be more productive if the application allows them to type the value rather than pick it from the list. Once the application permits this, prevention becomes impossible as we immediately open ourselves to the possibility of typing errors, which must then be trapped after the event.

If the list of values is long, such as a customer base, it may be harder for an experienced user to find the name he wants than to type the name of a customer he knows. Fetching the entire list to display it to the user may also have unacceptable implementation costs. A certain amount of cleverness in the implementation may be required to deliver both adequate performance and adequate validation.

This is another example of a design issue in which the needs of expert and frequent users conflict directly with those of new or infrequent users. In many cases, where the list is small or static, the choice is relatively simple, but the designer should be careful not to assume automatically that picking from a list is always a good way to prevent error; potentially, she is trading off accuracy against productivity.

The classic example of cross-field validation is the date range; for example, specifying a search that must lie between two dates. The difficulty here is that when two fields conflict, the application cannot possibly decide which of the two is wrong. Efforts to prevent the user from entering a 'To' date that is inconsistent with the 'From' date risk, once again, a problem of visibility: the user must somehow deduce that the problem is not with the field that he is entering, but with another field elsewhere on the window. The designer must consider carefully the visibility of the fields in error in any error prevention involving cross-field validations.

Prevent or react?

As we noted in Chapter 4, and have illustrated above, it is a gross over-simplification to assume that it is always better to prevent errors than to react to them. In fact, the choice between these two strategies will depend on particular circumstances. This choice can be guided by consideration of the nature of the error. If an action, choice, or entry is never valid, it may be disallowed, perhaps by providing a mapping that entirely eliminates the erroneous action from the user's 'decision space'. If it cannot reasonably be disallowed, the application should provide enough visibility to help the user to distinguish between situations where the action is valid and those where it is invalid.

Some errors occur under such complex combinations of circumstances that they can never be eliminated. If the user falls into such an error, the application must provide sufficient feedback to allow him to correct the error. A little later in this section we shall explore specific mechanisms for providing feedback to the user in exception and error situations.

Having chosen to react to a particular error, we need to determine how to handle it. Will the application deal with the error immediately and interactively; postpone handling it to later; redirect the user to corrective action; or re-route the item in error to another place in the system or to another user? As we have illustrated in Chapter 4, this kind of choice should be driven very strongly by the business rules, which will determine the appropriateness of immediate action, and is closely associated with the authority of the user to deal with exceptional data, as discussed in Chapter 3.

Validation and presentation

There are many possible approaches to the issue of validation, in terms of when it is performed, how it is handled, and how it is presented visually. These decisions will strongly affect the character of the interface, and will influence how constrained the interface feels; how much guidance or obstruction the user perceives; whether the user receives too little, too much or just enough feedback; and whether the interface feels visually stable or unstable, among other issues.

In order to give a concrete example, the discussion is cast around the issue of required or mandatory fields; the principles dealt with in these considerations apply equally to other forms of field validation. We can look at validation issues of required fields from three aspects: *Look*, or the visual distinction of required fields; *Feel*, or how each field reacts to user actions; and *Behaviour*, or how the application deals with fields that fail validation. Another way to look at this is to consider the three questions:

- *How* are required fields distinguished?
- *When* are required fields distinguished?
- *What happens* when required fields are not supplied?

Clearly, these three aspects are not disjoint; each has a bearing on the others, as we will see.

Visual distinction (Look)

The first question that the designer must address is the visual appearance of required fields. In order to provide adequate feedback, the interface may need to provide the user with a visual distinction between required fields and optional fields. Possible approaches include:

- *Change field background colours* A different field background is a strong cue, but has the disadvantage that it may be distracting for the eye: colour tends to attract attention. If frequent users quickly learn which fields are required, the different colour may be merely a nuisance. Note that the colours should be chosen to differ strongly even when seen without the benefit of a colour display.
- *Change field text colour or font* Less distracting, but the user does not see any cue if there are no characters in the field. The different font style only becomes apparent when the user begins to type. Since the error we are trying to avoid is that of failing to supply a value, this is somewhat self-defeating.
- *Change prompt text or background colours* This may have the same disadvantages as changing the field background colour, but if the colours are chosen so that prompts have less emphasis than fields (for example, they use a medium rather than bold weight), then changing the prompt colours is potentially less distracting than changing the fields.
- *Change prompt font style* This can be effective, providing fonts are carefully chosen, for example using bold for required fields and medium for optional fields. Using different typefaces can look messy, and different sizes of font may be too subtle to distinguish.
- *Change the cursor or pointer* Potentially very effective, this gives good feedback without being unnecessarily distracting. It is especially helpful if the cursor changes as it passes over the field, so that the user does not have to click in the field to see the feedback. However, a required field is not distinguished when the cursor is not over it. This may be preferred by experienced users, but difficult for new users.
- *Do not distinguish at all* In certain cases designers have decided that the distraction is more trouble than it is worth. For example, the vast majority of users may be frequent and experienced. In such cases, the needs of experienced users may dominate over those of new users. If this approach is adopted, the designer should ensure that status line hints clearly identify required fields.

Timing of distinction (Feel)

The next question for the designer is when to present the visual feedback: is it static, and always present in the interface, or only dependent on certain conditions? Possible approaches include:

- *Always distinguish required fields*   This may be helpful for novice users but distracting for experienced users, as discussed above. It does ensure that visually the display is relatively stable.
- *Distinguish on demand*   The designer may provide the user with a method such as a control key or 'help pointer' that turns the distinction on and off. Naturally, each user's preference should be retained and restored across sessions. This has the advantage of devolving control to the user, who may choose to use the distinction initially, turn it off as he becomes more experienced, and perhaps turn it back on again when he returns from a significant break from using the application.
- *Distinguish based on role or level of expertise*   A data entry clerk may simply be transferring information that he has received on paper into the system; if a required field is missing from the paperwork there is not a lot that he can do about it. A manager who makes occasional use of the system, on the other hand, may appreciate the feedback. Users may also 'graduate' through levels of expertise, each of which provides less visual clutter, but correspondingly less feedback. Ideally, the user will be allowed to nominate his own level of expertise.
- *Distinguish only when validation fails*   With this approach, required fields are not distinguished in normal use. However, if the user attempts to leave the field or resolve the dialog (depending on the strategy chosen), the missing fields are highlighted to remind him. This approach is unobtrusive until the user actually makes a mistake and so is helpful to the experienced user but provides no visibility to the novice or infrequent user.

Behaviour

The third aspect of required field validation concerns the question of what to do when a field is found to be missing:

- *Forbid field exit until value supplied*   The interface traps the error when the user attempts to leave the field, without supplying a value. This gives instant feedback, but can be very constraining: suppose the user wants to fill in some other fields, then come back to this one? Also, there is a danger that there may not be enough feedback to the user to explain the cause of the error. If the user does not know a valid value for the field, she may be completely trapped; she must at least be able to reach the 'Cancel' button (or equivalent) to escape.
- *As above, plus display explanatory message box*   This gives the user an explicit explanation of the error, but is extremely modal, and so can be very irritating for experienced users.
- *Disable the positive resolution command in the dialog*   The OK, Save, or other button may remain disabled until all required fields are supplied. The

dynamic enabling of the button provides good feedback. This is effective in simple cases (for example the 'Logon' button remains disabled until the user name and password fields are completed), but for complex situations with many required fields, it lacks visibility. A disabled button prompts the question 'What must I do to enable the button?'; in complex cases it may be difficult for the user to deduce what combination of fields will enable the command.

- *Show alert on attempted positive resolution*   In this version the OK or other button remains permanently enabled. If the user attempts to use it without supplying all required fields, she will receive an error message, and required fields will become distinguished, if they are not already distinguished. This gives strong feedback as well as an explicit explanation to inexperienced users without obstructing or distracting experienced users until they make a mistake. This is at the loss of the dynamic, pre-emptive feedback provided by enabling the button when all required fields are supplied.

Validation summary

As can be seen from this discussion, there is no simple right or wrong answer to questions of validation. On the one hand, pre-coding the field might help the user to avoid the error; on the other hand, the different colours may be distracting, especially to an experienced user who already knows which fields are required. Changing the colour dynamically may be distracting; but a pre-coded colour may be missed or misunderstood by a new user. These are classic conflicts of ease of use versus ease of learning.

A good solution depends on the designer's understanding of the needs of the user population; but it is almost certainly a bad idea to use inconsistent approaches within a single application.

Summary

Every check, validation, and error prevention has a performance cost. Many such costs are trivial and can be disregarded. Others are far from insignificant, and must be carefully considered. It is pointless for the designer to insist that every foreign key reference will be cross-checked and every product code will be looked up as soon as it is entered, if the result is a crippling increase in network traffic or a discernible pause as the user tabs between fields. The designer must assess the benefits and the cost, and ask the users: is this particular validation so valuable to you that you are willing to pay this price for it?

In an earlier chapter we mentioned the danger of visibility becoming overload and guidance becoming blockage. Prevention versus reaction in the handling of errors is one of the ways in which the designer finds the balance between too much and too little intervention. Confirmation of potential mistakes, discussed below, is another.

The great advantage of reacting to errors is that the designer has an ideal opportunity to present strong, precise, contextual feedback, in other words online help, to the user. For example, the designer can show the user the correct format for a field, or explain how he can invoke a list of valid values. The response can also be tailored to be specific to the particular error. The *Save As* example above is one instance of this.

Over-zealous attempts to prevent data entry errors are fraught with dangers, in particular of over-obstruction. Prevention is often useful, but it may also be difficult, impossible, or unhelpful. Where possible, errors are best prevented by improving the mapping. Attempting to prevent errors in other ways risks a dramatic deterioration in visibility or feedback. Consequently, many data entry errors are best handled by reacting rather than preventing.

Mistakes and tolerance

'If there is a wrong way to do something, then someone will do it'

Edward A. Murphy, *Murphy's Law*

As a designer, you certainly want users to make use of all of the features that you have so carefully designed and crafted. If you want them to learn, to become skilled, fluent users of your application, you must help them to explore the system. Exploration is encouraged or discouraged to a great extent by the fundamentals of visibility, mappings and feedback; in particular, explorability is strongly determined by the way in which the application handles mistakes.

Data-centric design disregards mistakes entirely, providing only that the data is valid. Process-centric design regards mistakes as the user's fault and misfortune. User-centric design tries to anticipate likely mistakes, and so help the user to avert them. Mistakes can never be prevented entirely; by definition, the user is pursuing a legal course of action within the terms of the application. By good design we can reduce both the likelihood of, and the damage caused by, mistaken actions.

Explorable systems

It is sometimes said that users are like scientists, conducting experiments against the system to determine what it does and how it behaves. A scientist is not merely looking at the visible phenomena, but searching for the underlying rules *behind* phenomena. You can see this process in action anytime a developer encounters a bug in another developer's application. She will immediately say something like 'It looks like he forgot to clear the buffer'. The user is *hypothesizing* about the system based on external behaviour. She may, if she is particularly motivated, conduct further experiments to attempt to confirm or deny her hypothesis.

While this scientific approach is certainly true of a certain class of users, notably those who are technically competent and confident in their own abilities, many users do not take such an approach. As we observed in Chapter 1, most users are not like us. For this reason I prefer to think of users as explorers. Unlike a scientist, an explorer does not necessarily have any clear idea of what he expects to find. An explorer is interested in phenomena for their own sake, observing and collecting, but rarely attempting to explain. A scientist's environment is under her control, whereas an explorer is always on the edge of the unknown. A scientist expects her environment to be rational, explicable and predictable; an explorer expects his environment to be dangerous and unpredictable. Exploration is much riskier than science and, for many users, learning an application feels like exploration, not science.

Users will only explore with confidence if:

- Actions are clearly visible and freely available
- Effects are easily interpreted through timely feedback
- Exploration is harmless or reversible

We have already examined the first two of these points in considerable depth in earlier chapters; the third is the subject of this section.

When users feel confident that they can explore without causing unintended damage, or that mistakes can be corrected without undue cost, they are far more likely to become expert or fluent users of the system. It is not hard to find users of poorly designed applications who literally flinch when they perform certain tasks, as if the user interface were about to blow up, so afraid are they of the dangers of unanticipated consequences. Three principles can guide the designer:

- The Principle of Forgiveness: make it easy to reverse unwanted operations
- The Principle of Confirmation: make it hard to do irreversible damage
- The Principle of Failsafe: make the default or easiest action harmless

The Principle of Forgiveness

Users always make mistakes, often mistakes that they recognize and immediately want to correct. Whether it is simply 'finger trouble', such as hitting the wrong key or deleting the wrong file, or a misunderstanding, such as expecting the 'Enter' key to move the focus to the next field rather than fire the *OK* button, mistakes are everywhere. A well-designed application forgives as many mistakes as possible. However, designing in forgiveness can involve substantial costs, and the designer needs to take a careful view as to when these costs are worthwhile. This decision will depend on his judgement both of the likely frequency and of the cost of the mistake.

The commonest form of forgiveness is the concept of an 'Undo' command. Wherever a command can reasonably be reversed, make it reversible. Some modern applications, such as Lotus Freelance and Microsoft Word Version 6.0, allow multiple commands to be backed out. This is an admirable goal in certain applications, but the designer should not be obsessive about it. For example, Lotus Freelance allows the user to undo the completely harmless 'Next Slide' and 'Previous Slide' actions. In consequence, it is possible for the user to make a change to her presentation, browse through some other slides, then decide she wants to undo the change, only to discover that the change has fallen off the bottom of the undo stack because of all the 'change slide' commands.

The major consideration in implementing any form of 'Undo' is consistency. There is little worse for the user than discovering that Undo is available every-where except when it is really needed. This is particularly frustrating as the user will invariably only find this out when she least wants to hear it. One of the most baffling lapses in Microsoft Word version 2.0 is the implementation of undo. If Word is in 'Insert' mode, characters that the user types are added into the document. If the user makes a mistake, she can very easily backspace or delete the erroneous characters; Undo is of little value, other than as a minor time saver. On the other hand, if Word is in 'Overtype' mode, characters overwrite the existing text as the user types. In this situation, the user may unintentionally overtype something that she wanted to keep. In this case, Undo would be valuable as it would restore the overwritten text. Strangely, in 'Insert' mode Undo of the most recent typing is available, whereas in 'Overtype' mode, when Undo could be extremely useful, it is not available.

One common problem in providing an Undo capability is that if 'Undo' cannot itself be undone ('Redo', in other words), 'Undo' then becomes an irreversible, destructive action. It is very easy for the user casually to undo more than was intended, especially when multiple levels of 'Undo' are available. Microsoft Word Version 6.0 has an excellent implementation of multiple Undo and Redo: not only are several levels available, but the user can see explicitly the Undo and Redo stacks.

Forgiveness and transaction processing

In a transaction processing application, forgiveness implies not committing data-base changes until absolutely necessary. This applies especially to record deletes. One application that I use postpones commit until the user explicitly asks for it, *except* in the case of delete. The only irreversible mistake that the user can make with a single wrong keystroke is to remove an entire record. Just to compound the difficulty, the keystroke in question performs a highly useful and frequently required function in another mode of the application, thus guaranteeing the maximum number of destructive, unrecoverable mistakes.

Transactional integrity requirements can make it difficult to postpone commits or provide multiple levels of Undo. If the ability to undo is considered to be of high value, the designer can consider the use of temporary or shadow tables for 'physical' commits, avoiding the need for 'logical' commits to the real tables until the user requires or expects it. It is worth noting that a user-centric approach to saving partial work, discussed in an earlier chapter, and postponing commits can often be supported by the same mechanism of temporary tables.

In support of multiple levels of Undo, many relational databases provide 'save-points', markers within a transaction that allow the user or application to roll back part of a transaction to a known point, without losing all uncommitted changes. For those databases that do not provide such capabilities, temporary tables can provide equivalent capabilities, provided that the development team is able to put in the effort to build the more complex code required. Otherwise, the implementor will need to consider providing multiple levels of Undo within the client code. This is inevitably a complex task, and the designer must carefully balance the value to the user. Remember that in a limited development budget, the decision to include complex multiple Undo is inevitably at the cost of some other feature.

The Principle of Confirmation

Actions should not all be equally easy to carry out. If an action is destructive, the application should aim to make the action more difficult to perform by mistake. In its simplest form, as most designers are aware, this means asking the user to confirm any destructive action. In principle, where a command cannot be reversed, the designer must make it clear to the user with appropriate visibility that he is about to perform an irreversible change.

On closer inspection, it is apparent that actions do not divide neatly into 'destructive' and 'non-destructive', or 'reversible' and 'non-reversible'. In fact, there is a continuous spectrum of difficulty or cost of reversing an action, from trivial to very expensive. Consider the following actions against a large word processing document:

- View the document, without changing it, then close it
- Make some additions, then save and close the document
- Make some additions, then close without saving
- Delete a few sentences, then close without saving
- Delete the most recent version of the document (undelete available)
- Delete the most recent version of the document (backup copy available)
- Format the disk

Some of these changes would be easy for the user to correct. The second change involves merely reopening the document and removing the changes. The third and fourth changes involve some retyping. The last change involves a huge loss of work: every change to everything since the last full disk backup. In general, confirmation is not a simple yes or no decision: the degree of confirmation should be proportionate to the damage caused.

The availability of Undo in effect reduces the damage caused by any command. However, even if Undo is universally available, it may still be necessary to confirm destructive commands. For example, if only the single most recent change can be reversed, a major change followed by a minor change causes the major change to become irreversible. I have frequently made this mistake in my word processor. I 'cut' a large piece of text, intending to move it elsewhere. I then notice a minor typing error, which I immediately correct by cutting the offending text. At this point I have invisibly lost the large text I cut a moment earlier.

One particular danger when designing confirmation is that asking the user for an immediate confirmation almost invariably gets a 'Yes'. The problem occurs because at the point where the application asks for confirmation, the user is still sure that he is doing the right thing (except in the rare case where he knows that he has accidentally hit the wrong command or key). For example, if the user is asked to confirm a deletion, he will mentally confirm the *action*, 'delete', rather than the particular *file*, and so will almost always confirm without thinking further. This is one of the advantages of the Mac's Wastebasket: discarded files remain in the wastebasket until it is explicitly emptied.

When a confirmation is postponed, the user is automatically forced to think harder about the action. The tradeoff is that by disrupting the user's mental flow, to force her consciously to consider the consequences of the action, the designer risks damaging the user's productivity. Hence the designer must not only consider the cost of the mistake, but must also balance the cost of demanding confirmation.

Confirmation and transaction processing

In transaction processing, changes generally become expensive to correct at the point of commit. Up to that point, it is equally easy for the application to rollback the changes as to commit them. It is therefore normal to ask the user to confirm at that point. The designer should try to ensure that such points of confirmation correspond to the user's expectation of closure, as we have noted before. Otherwise, the user may not appreciate the significance of the confirmation that she is being asked to give.

It is interesting to contrast the confirmations offered to a user working with documents in a file system, and those offered to a user entering orders into a database. In the file system, I am asked to confirm when I delete a document; this is generally irretrievable and destructive. I am not usually asked to confirm when I open, change and save an existing document, although this is destructive in a more subtle manner: it loses the previous version of the document. I am only asked to confirm when I try to save the document not under its original name, but as a replacement for another existing document. In this case the cost is the loss of the whole of the replaced document. In the case of confirming updates to a document, the designer must balance the cost of occasional accidental damage against the cost of continually asking the user to confirm a change, given that the change is nearly always what the user intended. In the case of creating a new document, I am never asked to confirm. The cost of saving a document that I intended to discard is almost nil, since I can simply delete it. Finally, I am always asked to confirm when I attempt to discard changes, since discarded changes are irretrievable without retyping, assuming I can even remember what changes I made.

By contrast, in a typical transaction processing application the user is asked to confirm indiscriminately every database commit, regardless of whether it is an insert, an update, or a delete. There is often no equivalent to the file system's 'rename' or 'save as': attempting to save a record with the same key as an existing record usually produces an unintelligible message that complains to the user about non-unique primary keys. Designers should perhaps rethink this approach: asking for confirmation of trivial changes not only irritates the user, it also dilutes the effectiveness of the confirmation of significant changes.

Before stretching the analogy too far, the designer should bear in mind one significant difference between the two situations. When a document is saved, it does not usually have any immediate consequences, so any errors can potentially be corrected after the event, for a period. In this sense, the change may not be totally unrecoverable, although it may well require significant effort to correct. At worst, though, the cost is generally limited to the cost of rework.

By contrast, when data in a transaction processing application is committed to a database it is often totally irrevocable. If a travel agent enters a flight booking, the ticket may only be changeable on payment of a fee. In some cases, the ticket may not be changeable at all; it may only be cancelled, forfeiting the entire ticket price. In other situations, data entered by one user may be acted on immediately by other users. For example, if the warehouse supervisor records a stock delivery, other agents may immediately begin accepting orders against that stock. If there was an error in the stock data entry, the organization may find itself accepting orders that it cannot fulfil. In an online, interactive, multi-user, *shared information* environment, a mistake will frequently have *business costs* that far exceed the cost of rework. The implication is that the designer should be more cautious and more discriminate in the transaction processing environment.

In summary, the aim of confirmation is to make the difficulty of the user in making a mistake proportionate both to its likelihood and to its business cost, but without obstructing correct actions unnecessarily. This is a very subtle balance for the designer to achieve.

The Principle of Failsafe

This principle says that the default action must always be safe. When I present this principle at seminars, some people protest that the *commonest* action should be the default. I agree — *except* at the point of an irretrievable and expensive change. Users may forgive you for putting the commonest action one key click further away than absolutely necessary; they will rarely forgive you for putting a destructive mistake at their fingertips.

If the user accepts the default action without properly understanding the consequences, the result should, wherever possible, be harmless. Frequently, the user may not have read a confirmatory dialog properly, or at all. One common cause of this is that (through poor design) many message boxes look similar, even though they present very different messages. We cannot assume that the user will dutifully read and digest every detail of every message box that the application throws up on the screen.

Another cause of incorrect choices is that the design causes the user to misunderstand the controls. One common example concerns dialog boxes that contain both a default button (typically 'OK') and a multi-line edit box (Fig. 6.5). In some dialogs, hitting 'Enter' gives a new line in the edit box; in other cases, 'Enter' fires the 'OK' (default) button. A subtle visual clue, the thicker border on the 'OK' button, distinguishes the latter case. In this particular example, the problem is no more than irritating as I can simply reopen the dialog and continue, but it is an error I make very frequently. A similar problem occurs in more expensive circumstances in many other applications. Some people have suggested that the user will be safe if she always hits 'Shift+Enter' rather than 'Enter'. I would reply that the *application* ought to failsafe if the user makes the highly probable mistake of hitting 'Enter'.

A third cause of incorrect choices is simple finger trouble; it is not unknown for a user to 'double bounce' the 'Enter' key, thus both launching and confirming an action quite unintentionally. In such a case, very few people will be sympathetic to a designer's claim that the user got the commonest action, which is probably what he wanted anyway.

Figure 6.6 illustrates one common oversight in designing for failsafe. The default reply is yes, save the changes. Unfortunately, this is not safe: it saves the work in memory, but loses the previous version from the disk. On a PC, this will come as an unwelcome surprise to a user who is used to minicomputer or mainframe

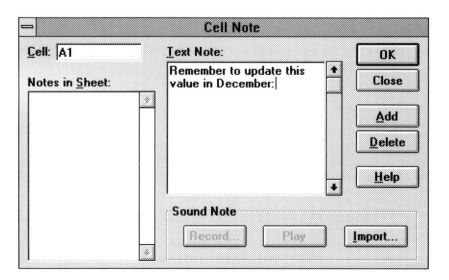

Figure 6.5. The 'Enter' Trap in Microsoft Excel

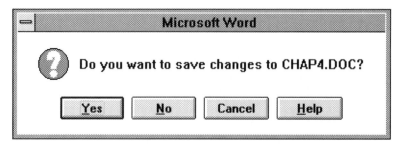

Figure 6.6. Which is the safe choice?

operating systems that automatically create a previous version of the file. Only 'Cancel', which returns the user to the previous state, is truly safe. Most of us have become so immune to this design error that it is present in almost every application I encounter. In a transaction processing application the same consideration applies: neither commit nor rollback is truly safe. The former loses the previous version of a record, the latter loses the current changes.

Summary

So far in this chapter we have examined ways in which errors and mistakes arise, and what can be done to minimize both their likelihood and effect. Good design, in the form of visibility, feedback, strong mappings and consistent cues, can go a long way to reducing the amount of error handling that the application must perform.

As we discovered, some errors, many exceptions and most mistakes cannot be designed out. What can be designed out, however, is our usual approach to error handling. Errors can be an opportunity to provide specific and timely feedback, increasing visibility at just the moment that the user demonstrates that the visibility is insufficient, instead of being taken as an opportunity to punish and intimidate the user. Exceptions may be an opportunity to follow the user's taskflow, rather than our own preconceived taskflow. Exceptions are also an opportunity to give the user an explicit and detailed explanation of the state of the system, and what she needs to do to get the system into the desired state. Mistakes can be treated with tolerance and forgiveness, not punished without mercy.

Help and documentation

Realistically, no matter how good the interface there comes a point at which the user needs more help than the interface itself can directly deliver. This is the point at which help comes into play. Help in turn may prove insufficient in more complex situations; at this point documentation becomes relevant.

The designer may find it useful to think of a pyramid of information: at the apex of the pyramid is 'point help', highly specific to the context of error or request for help; at the base are the broadest explanations of the conceptual basis of the application. The levels of this pyramid include:

- The interface itself, designed to be easily understood
- Instant hints and micro help ('inline help')
- Field and window level contextual help ('online help')
- Task level contextual help and documentation
- Conceptual documentation

The distinctions between help and documentation are not entirely rigid; the differences are more to do with the kind of question that the user is asking rather than the information contained in the system. In addition to the areas mentioned above, there is usually also a need for detailed reference documentation. The relationships between inline help and online help, contextual and conceptual documentation, and between help and reference documentation, are the subject of this second part of the chapter.

Let me emphasize very firmly that I am not recommending that designers or programmers can or should write documentation. This chapter will make no attempt to teach amateurs to write full-length user documentation: this area is so important and so complex that it has an extensive literature of its own, not to mention a wealth of training courses leading to academic and professional qualifications. On the other hand, it is important that the designer should appreciate the relationship between the interface and its documentation. Remedial help is not a cure for a bad design. The world is already too full of difficult, obscure applications where a poor interface is 'fixed up' by the efforts of technical writers.

Different questions, different help

Abigail Sellen and Anne Nicol, in their excellent essay 'Building User-Centered On-line Help' (Laurel, 1990), describe how online help, in the narrow sense, is inadequate for many users. They describe five types of question that users ask:

- Goal-oriented: 'What kind of things can I do with this program?'
- Descriptive: 'What is this? What does it do?'
- Procedural: 'How do I do this?'
- Interpretive: 'Why did that happen? What does this mean?'
- Navigational: 'Where am I?'

Standard online help only addresses the second of these questions. The help index may contain some procedural, or task-oriented, help, but it is often difficult to find. One cause is that the help is often expressed in terms of system tasks rather than user tasks. Sellen and Nicol cite the problem of trying to place a box around some text, and eventually discovering that the word processor in question unexpectedly considers this to be part of the task 'Format a paragraph'.

Each of these types of question is best answered by a particular organization of information, corresponding to the types of help we identified earlier (Table 6.1).

Question type	Help or documentation style
Goal-oriented	Conceptual documentation
Descriptive	Inline and online help
Procedural	Task-oriented documentation
Interpretive	Troubleshooting and common problems
Navigational	The interface itself

Table 6.1

We shall discuss each of these help and documentation styles in turn, beginning at the apex of the pyramid and working our way down to the base.

Inline help

Help at the precise point of work is often the simplest to implement and the most tightly integrated within the application itself. There are a number of mechanisms that can be used to present inline help to the user, most commonly:

- Micro help, one or two word explanations that pop up under iconic buttons when the pointer is held over them
- One line hints, a 10- to 20-word explanation of a control that appears in a fixed position, such as a status bar
- Bubble or balloon help, similar in length to one-line hints, but the help appears adjacent to the control like micro help

As inline help is so tightly integrated into the application, it is the level of help most likely to be written by the designer himself. The first question that the designer should ask of any inline help is: why is this necessary? In other words, there may be something wrong with the detailed design, if the interface is not sufficiently self-explanatory. This is perfectly illustrated by micro help: if iconic buttons are so intuitive, they should not need words; and if they do need words, why not display the words permanently?

Of course, this is deliberately unfair: even the best-designed iconic buttons may not be instantly recognizable, but once the user has become familiar with the iconic language, the icons may become more easily understood and eventually may be learned. Micro help that pops up only after the pointer is held over the button for a second or two may well be a useful tool in this learning process, and this leads to one of the major motivations for inline help. The designer may use inline help to distinguish between experienced and inexperienced users. The interface alone, with its short field prompts and unlabelled iconic buttons, may be crafted to be easily and rapidly used by the frequent or experienced user; the inline help may be designed to provide the information missing from the interface, but required by the infrequent or inexperienced user.

Inline help may appear instantly, after a delay, or on demand. If it is only provided on demand, the mechanism for invoking help must be so obvious that even if the user discovers nothing else about the interface, he can discover how to get help. I have encountered several applications in which help is invoked with the right mouse button; this is far from obvious to the average user.

There are two key requirements of inline help. The first requirement, particularly important when inline help is used as the bridge between inexperience and experience, is that it should disrupt the user's flow as little as possible. If help appears automatically, without an explicit request from the user, it must be unobtrusive. Help that appears automatically must disappear equally freely; it is not acceptable to force the user to dismiss help that she did not ask for.

The second requirement is that the help must actually be useful. This may seem too obvious for words, but I am sure that we have all encountered applications where the field prompt reads 'Reference' and the inline help explains 'Enter the value for Reference'. Microsoft Word Version 6.0 includes an iconic button labelled with the symbol ¶, and the pop-up micro help reads 'Show/Hide ¶'. This is not very enlightening for the user who does not already know what ¶ means.

Online help

When inline help is inadequate, the user may turn to online help. Unlike inline help, online help is not normally displayed automatically, but only on demand. Whereas inline help provides a few words of explanation, online help provides a few lines. Inline help is available instantly and unobtrusively; online help typically takes some seconds to appear, and usually must be explicitly dismissed, or at least moved aside.

Online help may be invoked in a number of ways. Typically, there will be a 'magic' key, such as F1, that invokes the help system, as well as possibly a help menu. Either mechanism brings the user into a paragraph of explanatory text specific to the context. However, such keyboard mechanisms are inadequate in many modern applications. Consider the user new to MS-Windows, who does not know what the system menu box in the top left corner is for: how does she ask for an explanation of this object? Buttons, especially iconic buttons, present a similar problem: if the user cannot navigate to a button without executing it, it becomes impossible to invoke contextual help for that control through the keyboard.

Recall the type of question that online help is intended to answer: 'What is this? What does it do?' Very often, the user cannot name the thing that she needs help on. Ideally, the user should be able to point at the thing in question and ask: 'What is it?' One mechanism to implement this is the provision of a 'help tool' on the toolbar. Clicking on this tool puts the user into 'help mode'; she can then click on any object on the interface to invoke help for that object. It is a helpful idea to change the cursor during this process to affirm to the user that she is in help mode.

Depending on the complexity of the context, online help may describe a single control, or it may describe the entire window, with just one or two lines describing each control. It is important to note that online help differs markedly in this respect from online reference: contextual help should be self-contained as presented to the user. That is, for an average user the help should stand by itself. By contrast, a paragraph of reference documentation describing the same field or window may make sense only when the surrounding context is also read. Reading a paragraph of reference documentation in isolation is like opening a book at random and reading the first paragraph you find. On the other hand, a paragraph of online help is more like a dictionary entry; wherever you open the dictionary, the definition of any word makes sense without reference to the immediately surrounding words.

Online help is often implemented using 'hypertext' style links that connect each entry upwards, from the control or field to the window or task level; downwards, from the window to the control level; and sideways, to related definitions. This allows the user to follow a reference to related topics that may complete her understanding of the topic in question. Hypertext needs to be implemented with care if the user is not to become hopelessly lost in a maze of twisty little passages.

Online documentation

As we move through help into documentation, we are passing out of the domain of the designer into that of the professional documentor. (In an ideal world, Help is written by professional documentors, not designers; in practice it may require close collaboration between the two.) The two disciplines do not stand independently, of course; the documentor cannot clearly describe the conceptual documentation, which answers goal-oriented questions, if the designer has failed to incorporate a clear conceptual model in the application.

The creation of both procedural- and goal-oriented documentation is itself a useful check on the design: if tasks and concepts cannot easily be described, it is unlikely that they will easily be understood by users.

As with online help, online documentation must be explicitly designed for online use, especially when technologies such as hyperlinking or full text search are implemented. It is not adequate simply to make an electronic version of the reference documents available.

The delivery mechanism for documentation need not be the same as that for help, as the needs are quite different. Help needs to be delivered rapidly, read quickly, then dismissed easily; documentation by contrast may be browsed, searched, or read from start to finish. Documentation benefits from user annotations, bookmarks (to allow the user to leave the document and pick it up again, or mark frequently used packages), summaries, and indexing as found in paper books. If the delivery of such sophistication means longer load and access times, this may be acceptable for documentation whereas it would make help frustrating and time-consuming.

Task documentation

Task documentation may be contextual ('What tasks can I perform here?') or general ('How do I perform that task?'); both these needs must be addressed in the way that the documentation is organized. In designing the index and other access paths for task-oriented documentation, the documentor also needs to consider that the user may not express the task description in the same way as the designer; indeed, the user may have difficulty describing the task at all.

Task-oriented documentation may not need to be invoked as often or as rapidly as online help, but once invoked the user may need to keep the documentation online alongside the application as he works through a sequence of steps that make up a complex task. One highly frustrating feature of some online documentation implementations is that the window in which the document is presented always sits above the application's windows, thus obscuring the application itself. In consequence, the user is required constantly to move the documentation to see his work. While it is often beneficial to have the document float on top, this must be under the user's control.

Conceptual documentation

Conceptual documentation may be rarely used directly in response to a question that arises in the user's mind while using the application. It is more likely to be accessed only a few times, when the user first begins to work with the application. For this reason, conceptual documentation is primarily designed to be read through in a structured and organized way, as opposed to the 'sound bite' approach of online help. At the same time, it is possible that a user who begins with the question 'How do I do this?' may finish with the question 'What can I do?'; conceptual documentation needs to be integrated with, and supportive of, other elements of the documentation.

It may seem surprising that the user of an application should need to ask what the application does, but experience has shown that this is often the case. This is illustrated in particular by the documentation example below. Furthermore, conceptual documentation is an excellent method of making explicit the conceptual model underlying the application. This can avoid the problems associated with a user independently forming a false conceptual model.

Case study: Oracle Designer/2000

One of the best examples of online documentation that I have encountered recently is that for Oracle Corporation's new CASE product set, known as Designer/2000. The new product set represents a radical change from previous versions of the product:

- A character-based, dictionary-oriented approach is replaced with a highly graphical interface.
- A small number of diagramming tools for the analyst are superseded by a complete set covering the whole development life-cycle (Fig. 6.7).
- The new diagrammers use a new naming convention that reflects their purpose more accurately than did the old one.
- A completely new tool for business process modelling is added; this supports a technique potentially unfamiliar to many analysts.
- The user interface of almost every feature has been redesigned or replaced completely.

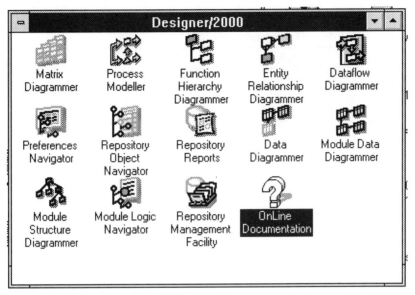

Figure 6.7. The new Oracle CASE product set

Clearly, with so many new facilities and features, good documentation is essential to the successful uptake of this product set. An early decision was taken to provide all documentation online, and documentation professionals designed a documentation set that provides conceptual, task, reference, and troubleshooting documentation for each tool in the set (Fig. 6.8).

- *Concepts* provides an overview of the entire product set; an overview of the particular tool itself and its role in the product; and a brief description of the techniques associated with the tool. This is particularly useful for the tools that are completely new or renamed.
- *Tasks* describes procedures and actions within the particular tool, both from a 'What can I do?' and a 'How do I do that?' point of view. This reflects the fact that many tasks have been redesigned compared to the previous version.
- *Reference* is, as the name suggests, a complete online reference of every menu item, field and button in the application. In addition, there are descriptions of each menu, window and dialog box. Entries are cross-linked to each other, and, where appropriate, linked back to tasks associated with the particular item. For example, in the Matrix Diagrammer section, the 'New diagram' iconic button is linked back to the task 'Create a new matrix'.

The organization of the help is illustrated in more detail on the disk (Chapter 6) using a Lotus Screencam recording of the system in use.

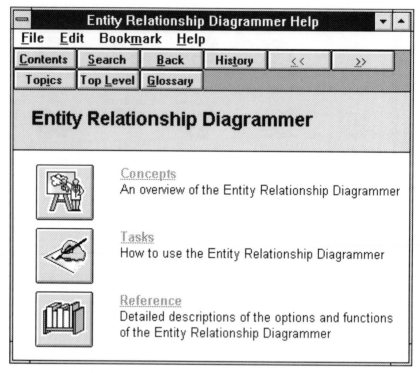

Figure 6.8. Help available for each tool

Summary

Much of the difference between the user's perception of good and bad user interface design lies in the handling of errors and exceptional situations. It is precisely when the user is in doubt or in error that he most notices the interface; when the user is making no mistakes, the interface should be so unobtrusive as to almost disappear. The quality of the help and documentation available makes a dramatic difference to the user's productivity, satisfaction and overall effectiveness.

Designing for error is neither an option nor a luxury: errors, exceptions and mistakes are a constant part of any ordinary user's experience. Any fool can design a user interface for infallible users.

Appendix A Choosing a design tool

There are many criteria to be considered in choosing a tool for developing GUI applications. There are questions of productivity, capability, and ease of maintenance. Important issues include speed of development; ease of learning of the tool itself; support for large projects; team working; version control; client/server partitioning; control of network traffic; platform portability and interoperability; server, network and database support; transaction processing support, etc. All of these are relevant to tool selection.

Your tool selection process must begin with an identification of the issues that matter most to you, and of the kind of tool you are looking for: are you planning to build prototypes only? tactical, departmental level applications? strategic or mission critical applications? or an enterprise wide infrastructure? The characteristics of tools for all of these needs are very different, and it is unlikely that any one tool will satisfy all of them.

Having said that, the subject of this book is the user interface, not the entire client/server process. The points suggested here particularly impact on the capability and usability of the user interface. These are points that will make the difference between a tool that merely allows you to paint windows, and one which actively supports you in building good user interfaces.

Incidentally, some people assert that the 'only' way to build a GUI is with object-oriented (OO) tools and methods. While the OO approach does have certain strengths in this area, it also has its share of weaknesses. Most notably, an OO approach represents a major shift in development style and mental model for most developers. This can significantly impact their learning time and early productivity with the new tools. Serious thought should be given to the cost of moving to GUI and adopting object orientation simultaneously. The advocates of using OO techniques for user interface design say that this is the appropriate tool for the job and that it is easier to make the conceptual leap in one go. Other opinions suggest that it is better to come to grips with the requirements of GUI design in a familiar, 3GL or 4GL procedural environment, before embarking on OO. I have included in the list below features which are I believe of direct and practical benefit to the designer or the end users of the application, rather than more abstract features (such as inheritance) which may or may not better support these requirements.

237

Many of these questions will not have a simple yes or no answer. You may find it useful to allocate a weighting factor to each statement, then to score the various tools that you are evaluating, to arrive at an overall score for each tool. A warning: do not simply copy this list and send it off to your prospective tool suppliers as a 'request for information' or as a means of shortlisting suppliers by number of 'yes' answers! No pre-sales support person appreciates devoting considerable effort to responding to questions that the customer does not even care about — I speak from experience. Of course, there may be questions that you cannot answer from your own investigations, and your supplier's pre-sales engineers should then be able to help. You might also usefully ask yourself (and them) why the answer to the question was not easy to find in using the tool.

The list is by no means complete and universal. Consider it a starting point for your own tool evaluation process.

Evaluation criteria

Application development can be divided horizontally between a team (one developer produces controls, visual styles and other low-level elements, another defines dialogs and windows, another defines callback code, etc.).
Application development can be divided vertically between a team (each developer is responsible for one area of the application, from top to bottom).
Application components developed by different team members can be integrated easily.
Application development supports version and configuration management.
Applications can be reused as sub-modules within other applications without change.
Applications based on task-oriented metaphors can be built.
Applications based on subject- (document-) oriented metaphors can be built.
Applications can include navigator trees.
Applications can include task lists.
Buttons can be enabled and disabled under program control.
Buttons: iconic buttons can be displayed.
Context sensitive help can be displayed for fields, windows, and tasks.
Controls: all standard controls can be created.
Controls: lists can be populated dynamically.
Controls: 3D style controls can be created.
Controls: custom controls can be created.
Controls: industry standard custom controls (VBX, OCX, etc.) can be used.
Cursor shape can be set under program control.
Cursor position can be set under program control to anywhere on display.
Cursor position can be set by setting focus to any enabled control.
Data fields: application can respond when field entered.
Data fields: application can respond when field exited.

Data fields: application can respond when field modified, immediately upon modification.

Data fields: application can respond when field modified, but only on field exit.

Dialog flow can be designed and viewed graphically in the tool (i.e. dialog flow is not 'hidden' in code but is explicitly visible).

Dialog flow can be modified at runtime.

Dialogs can be reused across multiple applications.

Direct manipulation interfaces can be implemented.

Drag and drop events available to application through high-level interface (drag event, drop event).

Drag and drop events available to application through low-level interface (mouse down, mouse move, mouse up).

External functions in DLLs can alter the application's display (control and window handles available).

External functions in DLLs can be called, passing parameters and returning results.

External functions in DLLs can display their own dialogs.

Graphical appearance (fonts, colours, etc.) can be applied at design time without coding.

Graphical appearance and associated simple functionality can be set consistently across an application (e.g. all required fields have red background).

Graphical appearance and associated complex functionality can be set consistently across an application (e.g. when displayed data has been modified and must be saved, a visual indicator appears).

Graphical appearance (style) can be set consistently across an application.

Graphical appearance (style) can be changed easily across an application.

Graphical appearance can be changed under program control.

Graphical objects can be displayed.

Graphical objects can present dynamic (run-time) data.

Graphical objects are interactive and can be manipulated by the user.

Hints can be displayed as balloon (bubble) help.

Menu commands can be enabled and disabled under program control.

Menu commands can implement any code that buttons can implement, and vice versa.

Menus support cascading menus, separators, menu check items, graphical menu items, separators, etc.

Menus can be altered or replaced under program control.

Message boxes (alerts) can be displayed easily (does not require window painting).

Message box icon (style) can be set at runtime.

Message box text can be set at runtime (context specific alert messages).

Message box title can be set at runtime.

Modal windows can be displayed.

Modeless windows can be displayed.

Modeless windows: multiple instances of a modeless (document) window can be opened.

Modeless windows: particular instances of a modeless window can be activated under program control.

Modeless windows: Particular instances of a modeless window can be closed under program control.

MDI functionality (Cascade & Tile windows, etc.) is available without coding.

Mouse position available to application as high-level description (control or window at time of event).

Mouse position available to application as low-level description (coordinates).

Mouse: application can respond to mouse button click.

Mouse: application can respond to mouse button down.

Mouse: application can respond to mouse button up.

Mouse: application can respond to mouse double click.

Mouse: application can respond to mouse move.

Mouse: key state (Shift, Alt, Ctrl) during mouse events available to application.

Objects (controls plus associated events) can be reused within an application.

Objects can be reused across different applications.

Objects can be sub-classed.

OLE and DDE client support (another application's data can be embedded as an object).

OLE and DDE server support (the application's data can be embedded as an object in another application).

Status messages can be produced automatically (database commits, runtime errors, etc.).

Status messages can be replaced with designer-provided messages.

Status messages can be suppressed.

Style guide can be enforced within an application.

Style guide can be enforced across applications.

Style guide is represented explicitly in the design tool.

Toolbars can be displayed on individual windows.

Toolbars can be displayed on the application frame.

VBX and OCX control methods can be invoked.

VBX and OCX control properties can be retrieved and set.

VBX and OCX controls can be embedded, including VBXs that display bitmaps or dialogs.

Appendix B   The demonstration disk

Installation

The demonstration application requires MS-Windows 3.1 or above, 8 MB of RAM, and 1 MB of free disk space to install. A colour VGA display is recommended, but not required. The application can be run directly from the Program Manager's File/Run command, but you may prefer to create a program icon under MS-Windows that runs the program.

To install the application, perform the following steps from the DOS prompt:

- Create a directory to hold the demonstration files.
- Copy the contents of the disk to that directory.

For example,

C:\> **mkdir c:\bookdemo**
C:\> **copy a:*.* c:\bookdemo**

The MS-Windows command line to run the program is:
 c:\bookdemo\bookdemo.exe

Contents

Bookdemo application

The disk contains an application that includes simple demonstrations appropriate to each chapter of the book, as follows:

Chapter 1

Feedback: A font selection tool that demonstrates the use of a previewer. This allows the user to experiment with font settings, and see immediately how each change will affect the font.

Chapter 2

Metaphors   A simple example of three icons representing common actions, namely 'Create New File', 'Open Existing File', and 'Save Work (to disk)'. The first set uses a mixed metaphor, referring to paper, a file and a physical disk. The second set uses a consistent metaphor based on the paper document.

Chapter 3

Taskflow: Using Lotus Screencam, a simple task list based application is illustrated. Note how the application adds new tasks to the list as each set of tasks is completed. The check marks against each task enable the user to track his progress through the task.

Chapter 4

Alerts: An example of the correct use of the common styles of alert.

Chapter 5

Colour map: A tool that allows the designer to understand the hue–saturation–value (HSV) and its relationship to the red–green–blue (RGB) model. Note that in MS-Windows, Value is referred to as Luminosity.

Options: An example of the use of check mark options on a menu.

Chapter 6

Documentation: Using Lotus Screencam, the user is taken through a guided tour of a model online documentation system.

Icons

The disk contains a set of sample icons, sized for use on toolbar buttons, for the common subject- (document-) oriented and task-oriented models described in the book. As well as illustrating the principle of pictorial language, the icons also illustrate various useful tricks in icon design. Permission is granted to the purchaser of the book to copy, use and distribute the icons without payment of royalties or other legal obligation, provided only that the source of the designs is acknowledged in any commercial or for-profit usage. All copyright is reserved.

Tables B.1 to B.3 lists the icons, their descriptions, and their suggested interpretations.

Files	Document-oriented icons	Suggested interpretations
zsdocdel.ico	Document torn halfway through	Destroy (delete) entire document
zsdocdup.ico	Standard document with a copy behind	Duplicate the document
zsdocera.ico	Document with eraser	Undo changes
zsdocfnd.ico	Stack of documents, one highlighted in yellow	Find or filter documents
zsdocget.ico	Hand grasping document, palm upwards	'Get' a document or set of documents; fetch a set, acquire locks, etc.
zsdocinf.ico	Standard document with the 'i' icon on top	Document information or status
zsdoclck.ico	Standard document with a key on top	Lock the document
zsdocnew.ico	Blank document (standard 'New' icon)	Create a new document
zsdocopn.ico	Document with lines (standard document icon)	Open an existing document
zsdocput.ico	Hand grasping document, palm downwards	'Put' a document; release documents fetched with 'Get', release locks, etc..
zsdocrvt.ico	Standard document with red 'X' on top	Discard changes since last Save; revert
zsdocsav.ico	Standard document with green tick on top	Save or commit changes

Table B.1

Files	Task-oriented icons	Suggested interpretations
zstskcol.ico	Task with green '+' on top	Expand task hierarchy; show sub-tasks
zstskexp.ico	Task with yellow '−' on top	Collapse task hierarchy; hide sub-tasks
zstskgrn.ico	Task with traffic lights, green lit	Close task, set status to Complete
zstskinc.ico	Task with upper half solid, lower half in outline (incomplete task)	Begin or continue to perform a task
zstskman.ico	Task with stick person on top	Assign task to somebody
zstskred.ico	Task with traffic lights, red lit	Close task, undo changes
zstskstd.ico	Standard task (curved arrows end to end)	Standard task symbol; Show all tasks (in list); or Mark task as non-urgent (in single task)
zstsktri.ico	Task with traffic lights, all lit	Show/hide task status
zstskurg.ico	Task coloured red with yellow '!' on top	Urgent task symbol; Show only Urgent tasks (in list); or Mark task as urgent (in single task)
zstskyel.ico	Task with traffic lights, yellow lit	Close task, set status to Pending or in Progress

Table B.2

Files	Standard icons	Suggested interpretations
zsxcopy.ico	Standard copy icon	Copy
zsxcut.ico	Standard cut icon (Scissors)	Cut
zsxflopy.ico	Floppy disk	Save
zsxfoldr.ico	Standard directory icon (Folder with arrow)	Open folder; Find document
zsxhelp.ico	Question mark	Help
zsxnew.ico	Standard new icon (Blank page)	Create new document
zsxpaste.ico	Standard paste icon	Paste
zsxprint.ico	Two-dimensional printer	Print

Table B.3

References and further reading

Hix, D. and Hartson, H.R. (1993). *Developing User Interfaces: Ensuring Usability Through Product and Process.* John Wiley and Sons, ISBN 0-471-57813-4. A widely referenced and well-respected discussion of the process of interface design, this book also includes a notation for describing detailed, low-level user interface interaction.

Laurel, B. (ed.) (1990). *The Art of Human Computer Interface Design.* Addison-Wesley, ISBN 0-201-51797-3. This collection of essays combines the pragmatic with the visionary. Contributions from a variety of authors will give the reader plenty to think about. Much of the material is beyond the scope of 'ordinary' business applications, but nonetheless this is a fascinating book.

Norman, D.A. (1988). *The Psychology of Everyday Things.* Basic Books Inc., ISBN 0-456-06709-3. Widely read, widely quoted, this book has become a popular classic. Required reading for anybody with pretensions to designing anything that will be used by other people. If you only read one book on design, it should be this one. Also published in paperback as *The Design of Everyday Things.*

Siebert, L. and Ballard, L. (1992). *Making a Good Layout.* North Light Books, ISBN 0-89134-423-3. A useful primer on the basics of layout and graphic design. Although not specifically aimed at the user interface designer, an excellent way to become acquainted with what graphical issues are all about, and the relationship between attractiveness and effectiveness in design.

Sitton, S. and Chmelir, G. (1984). 'The Intuitive Computer Programmer'. *Datamation,* 15 October. Cited in the text, follow up this reference if you are interested in further detail.

Thimbleby, H. (1990). *User Interface Design.* Addison-Wesley, ISBN 0-201-41618-2. By turns fascinating and infuriating, this book examines many aspects of the theory and principles underlying interaction. Thimbleby touches on many issues of science, mathematics, philosophy, and psychology. More thought-provoking than directly practical.

Tognazzini, B. (1992). *Tog on Interface.* Addison-Wesley, ISBN 0-201-60842-1. A tremendously enjoyable collection of writings from one of Apple's user interface gurus. Tognazzini presents practical solutions to specific issues raised by practitioners of interface design. The shorter pieces are interleaved with frequent anecdotes and occasional essays. Although nominally about the Macintosh, Tog's ideas may be appreciated by all designers, whatever their platform.

Platform-specific standards

The Windows Interface: An Application Design Guide, Microsoft Press, ISBN 1-55615-439-9.

Macintosh Human Interface Guidelines, Addison-Wesley, ISBN 0-201-62216-5.

Index

abstraction, 60
acceptability, 5
affordances, 30, 32–33
  and character terminals, 56
  of custom controls, 32
alerts, *see* message boxes

burden of interpretation, 53, 57
  see also input gap; output gap
burden of evaluation, *see* output gap
burden of execution, *see* input gap
buttons, 166–168
  and recognition, 41

check box, 164–165
  versus radio button group, 165
closure, 87, 93–101, 104, 124
  and dialog flow, 141
  and modal dialogs, 144
  and resolution, 126
  and task lists, 117
  and task oriented applications, 121
  serial and hierarchical, 99
cognitive psychology, 11, 38
cognitive science, 37
colour, 196–201
  as redundant cue, 200
  associations, 198
  ergonomics, 199
  for decoration, 200
  semantic, 200
  terminology, 197
combo box, 165–166
  see also pop-down list
command interpreters, 41, 44
  and input transformations, 81
  and visibility, 70
  as abstract expression, 69
conceptual model, 8, 52, 53, 58–85, 100
  centre of, 61–62
  domain of expression, 62
consistency, 2, 32
  in detailed design, 202
  myth of, 2
controls, 163–184

alignment, 190
  and layout, 188
  and query-by-example, 183
  and visibility, 23
  custom, 32, 171
  grouping, 190
  in combination, 179
  position, 188
  see also buttons; check box; combo box; list
    box; pop down list; radio button group
cues
  and modes, 110
  see also affordances
cursors, 177
custom controls, *see* controls
customization, 119–120
  see also macro languages

data flow diagrams, 87–88
data-centric dialog flow, 129
  see also process-centric; user-centric
data-entry applications, 135
degrees of freedom, 101–102, 124
dependencies, in task flow, 105, 124
detailed design, 54, 162–206
  and dialog design, 127
  and modes, 110
dialog, 154
  defined, 126
dialog boxes, 142–143
  and visibility, 23
  as forcing technique, 115
  see also window layout; window style
dialog design, 126–161
  and detailed design, 127
  and windows, 136
dialog flow, 52, 54, 127, 153–154
  and closure, 138
  and modes, 110
  defined, 126
dialog flow diagrams, 156–160
dialog resolution, defined, 126
direct manipulation, 7, 58, 73, 204
  in File Manager, 77
documentation, 207, 208, 229–236

documentation (*contd*)
  authors as designers, 12
  conceptual, 234
  procedural, 233
documentors, 208
  see also documentation
documents (window style), 142–143
  see also subject-oriented applications
drag-and-drop, *see* direct manipulation
drop-down menus, and recognition, 41

ease of learning, 5, 8, 21
  and design conflicts, 110
ease of use, 4, 8, 21
  and design conflicts, 110
  myth of, 1
effectiveness, 5, 57
errors, 207–221
  and feedback, 210
  and mapping, 210
  and visibility, 210
  format rules, 211
  large sets, 211
  ranges, 213
  references, 215
  small sets, 210
  see also exceptions; mistakes
exceptions, 209, 214
  and dialog design, 215
  and feedback, 215
  and visibility, 215
  see also errors; mistakes
exploration, 221, 222
expressions, 68–78
  abstract, 69–71
  concrete, 69, 72–74, 100
  symbolic, 69, 71–72

fax (as case study), 69, 74–75
  and taskflow, 123
feedback, 24–27, 32, 33, 36, 57, 149
  and character terminals, 56
  and closure, 96
  and design conflicts, 111
  and modes, 110
  and task lists, 117
  in file selection, 76
  in Microsoft Word, 49
File Manager, 34, 35, 45, 68, 72, 77, 155, 156
  and navigation trees, 118
  mixed metaphors, 77
file systems
  and conceptual models, 65–68
  and symbolic expressions, 71

Fitt's Law, 205
fonts, 192–196
  licensing, 195
  serif and sans serif, 194
  size, 193
  terminology, 193
forcing techniques, 115–116
  see also guidance

graphic design, 10
  see also detailed design; icons
guidance, 101
  and design conflicts, 110, 111
  and working styles, 91
  mechanisms, 113

help, 229–231
  iconic buttons, 231
  inline, 230, 231
  online, 232, 233
hypertext, 233

iconic buttons, 174
icons, 174–179
  and visual language, 176
  animated, 179
  design principles, 174, 177
incomplete work, 100–101
input gap, 34–35, 53, 57
  see also output gap
input transformation, 80
interpretation, burden of, 26, 33–36
  see also input gap; output gap

Jackson structure diagrams, 112

Kay, Alan, 3

language, in detailed design, 202
learning, 11, 37, 40, 42, 57
  see also long-term memory; memory; short-term memory
list box, 166
  and subject-oriented applications, 166
locks, 114–115
  see also guidance
long-term memory, 37, 39, 40–41, 57
  see also learning; memory; short-term memory
Lotus 1-2-3, 147
Lotus Ami Pro, 22, 23, 24, 30
Lotus Freelance, 28, 102, 113, 150, 151, 223
Lotus Organizer, 59, 62, 77
  and concrete expressions, 73

macro languages, 119
  see also customization

mail merge, as design example, 34, 122
mappings, 27–33, 35, 57
    and abstract expressions, 69, 70
    and character terminals, 56
    and modes, 110
    and recognition, 41
    in Microsoft Word, 49
    of custom controls, 32
MDI, *see* multiple document interface
memory, 11, 37, 40, 42, 57
    and closure, 93–94, 99
    and task lists, 117
    see also learning; long-term memory; short-term
        memory
menu options 169
    visibility, 170
menus, 168–170
    and recognition, 41
message boxes, 150–153
    styles, 151
    wording, 152
    worst ever written, 153
metaphors, 47, 58–68, 147
    and symbolic expression, 69
    see also conceptual models; expressions; trans-
        formations
Microsoft Application Studio, 28
Microsoft Excel, 30, 140, 145, 170
Microsoft Powerpoint, 28
Microsoft Word, 22, 23, 25, 30, 34, 49, 122, 145,
    215, 223
minimum effort design, 131–132
mistakes, 207, 208, 221–228
    and confirmation, 224
    and failsafe, 227
    and forgiveness, 222–223
    see also errors; exceptions
modal dialog
    and message box, 152–153
    defined, 141
modal window
    defined, 141
    sequences, 138
    stacked, 138
modeless window, defined, 141
modes, 105–109
    and granularity, 106, 109
    defined, 107, 109
    supporting taskflow, 109
    within windows, 149
mouse, 204
    versus keyboard, 204
    see also direct manipulation
multiple document interface, 106, 142–143, 154

    and window layout, 188
    defined, 141

navigators, 118
Norman, Donald, 17, 18, 21
    see also burden of interpretation; feedback;
        mappings; visibility

one-to-one transformation, 81
    see also transformations
online help, 207, 230
    see also help; documentation
Oracle Designer/2000 (as case study), 234
Oracle Forms
    and navigation trees, 118
output gap, 34–35, 53, 57
    see also input gap; burden of interpretation

palettes, *see* tool bars
partial work, 99, 124, 224
    and task lists, 117
personality types, 47–49, 87, 91
    and design conflicts, 110
    see also working styles
pop down list, 165
    and recognition, 165
    see also combo box
pop up menu, 170
portability issues, 201
Print Manager, 18, 45, 68
Print Setup, 60
privilege, 89–90
    and authority, 90
    and responsibility, 90
process-centric dialog flow, 130
    see also data-centric; user-centric
productivity, 5, 6, 11, 37, 39, 44, 57, 91
    influence of graphic design, 10
Program Manager, 68
prototyping, 8
    see also usability testing

radio button group, 163
recall, 40–42, 57
    see also memory
recognition, 40-42, 57
    see also memory
representative user testing, *see* usability testing
required fields, as forcing technique, 115
resolution
    of dialog, 126
    see also closure

satisfaction, 5, 6, 11, 37, 57, 91

short-term memory, 37–39, 41, 57
  see also long-term memory; memory
spreadsheet
  and closure, 93, 99
  and guidance, 101
state diagrams, unsuitability of, 112
style guides, 55
subject-oriented applications, 121
  and window layout, 188
  dialog design, 154
  see also task-oriented applications
system centred design, 11
systems analyst, role of, 11, 12

tabbed dialogs, 147–149
task lists, 116
task-oriented applications, 121
  dialog design, 154
  see also subject-oriented applications
taskflow, 52, 53, 103, 104, 86–125
  and automation, 91
  and dialog design, 126
  and dialog flow, 127
telephone, as design example, 21, 24
text editors, 52
  and symbolic expressions, 71
tool bars, 180
transformations, 69, 78
  see also conceptual models; expressions;
    metaphors

undo, 223, 225
  and transaction processing, 224
usability testing, 9–10, 30
  and design conflicts, 110
  and taskflow, 125
  risks, 8
user-centred design, 11
user-centric dialog flow, 130

validation, 185, 207, 208, 217–220
  and visual appearance, 218
  behaviour, 219
  timing, 219
visibility, 21–24, 27, 32, 33, 35, 36, 57, 105,
    149–150
  and abstract expressions, 70
  and character terminals, 56
  and design conflicts, 110, 111
  and modes, 110
  and recognition, 41
  and working styles, 48
  in file selection, 76
  in Microsoft Word, 49

wastebasket, as metaphor, 45, 58, 59, 72
weather forecasts, as design example, 36
widget, *see* controls
window layout, 10, 52, 185–192
  and design conflicts, 139
  and graphic design, 185
  density, 192
  position, 187
  size and shape, 186
  visual stability, 187
  see also detailed design; graphic design
window style, 142
windows, and modality, 144
word processor
  and closure, 93, 96, 99
  and guidance, 101
  and modes, 106, 107
  feedback in, 25, 26
work queues, 116
workflow, 53–54, 92
  and taskflow, 86–89
  common classes, 120
working styles, 37, 46–49, 57, 87, 91
  see also personality types
WYSIWYG, 26, 27, 79